365 Fun-to-Stitch QUILT BLOCKS™

Edited by Jeanne Stauffer & Sandra L. Hatch

HOUSE of
WHITE
BIRCHES
PUBLISHERS
SINCE 1947

365 Fun-to-Stitch Quilt Blocks

Copyright © 2002 House of White Birches, Berne, Indiana 46711

Editors: Jeanne Stauffer and Sandra L. Hatch
Design Manager: Vicki Blizzard
Associate Editors: Dianne Schmidt, Barb Sprunger
Editorial Assistant: Joanne Neuenschwander
Book and Cover Design: Jessi Butler
Copy Editors: Sue Harvey, Nicki Lehman, Mary Martin
Publications Coordinator: Tanya Turner

Photography: Jeff Chilcote, Tammy Christian, Kelly Heydinger, Justin P. Wiard
Photography Assistant: Linda Quinlan

Production Coordinator: Brenda Gallmeyer
Technical Artist: Connie Rand
Production Artist: Pam Gregory
Production Assistants: Janet Bowers, Marj Morgan
Traffic Coordinator: Sandra Beres

Publishers: Carl H. Muselman, Arthur K. Muselman
Chief Executive Officer: John Robinson
Marketing Director: Scott Moss
Book Marketing Manager: Craig Scott
Product Development Director: Vivian Rothe
Publishing Services Manager: Brenda R. Wendling

Printed in the United States of America
First Printing: 2002
Library of Congress Number: 00-112315
ISBN: 1-882138-78-3

Dear Quilter,

This book is for everyone who loves to quilt! We have included patterns for 365 different blocks, one for each day of the year. Chapter 1 contains blocks that can be rotary cut. The other seven chapters are divided into topics that we think will interest all quilters. Animal lovers will enjoy All God's Creatures, and nature lovers will especially have fun with Nature's Glory.

Each chapter starts with an outstanding sampler quilt featuring blocks related to that topic. Several projects that use only one block are also included in each chapter. You might be surprised at the wonderful gifts and home decorations you can make with just one 12-inch quilt block.

After the sampler and one-block projects, each chapter gives easy-to-follow written instructions as well as colorful illustrations to help you piece each block. All blocks are 12 inches square, so they can be interchanged.

Many blocks use common templates. These templates are numbered and begin on page 203. Other pieces that are used only in one block are given in the chapter for that block and are lettered. For example, the Alaska block on page 161 uses common templates 2, 5, 54, and pieces B7, BR7, C7, D7 and DR7. The number 7 after the letter means that these templates are from chapter 7; the R after a letter indicates that template is reversed when cut. Many blocks use all common templates, so once you've made these templates they can be used over and over again.

Whether you quilt 365 blocks in one year or use the blocks over your lifetime, you'll discover your quilting skills and your enjoyment of quilting growing with each block you create.

We wish you hours of happy quilting!

Jeanne Stauffer   Sandra L. Hatch

Contents

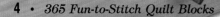

Nature's Glory

Beneath the Stars

Around the World

Blessed & Beloved

Strips and Pieces

The blocks from this chapter can all be rotary cut and strip pieced. Each one is quick and easy to prepare and fun to quilt— a winning combination!

You can make the 20 blocks in the sampler quilt with two templates, a triangle and a square. You may want to try this quick-cutting technique with other blocks.

Strips & Pieces Sampler

By Judith Sandstrom

Instead of using templates for piecing blocks, try using quick-cutting and -piecing methods.

PROJECT NOTE

Although we have given templates for every block pattern in this book, many of them may be made by cutting strips, squares or other units using a rotary cutter, ruler and mat. Cutting fabric-width strips for units in just one block isn't always productive, but when making multiple blocks, it saves lots of time and produces accurate results.

It is easy to cut most squares, rectangles or triangles from strips thus eliminating the need for templates. Because we have given templates for each pattern, it is easy to figure out the size strips you need for simple shapes. For example, if you need four 4 1/2" x 4 1/2" squares for your block and you are making 10 blocks, you will need 40 squares. You would cut your strips 4 1/2" by the width of the fabric. You can fit nine squares along the width of most fabrics, so you would need five 4 1/2" by fabric width strips to make 40 squares with some left over (fabric width divided by 9).

If you are making triangles, measure the square side of the triangle and cut fabric strips this width; then subcut the strip into squares this size. There is a simple formula to create this type of square—for a 3" finished square edge, add 7/8" to the size or cut a 3 7/8" x 3 7/8" square. Cut the square on the diagonal for a right-angle triangle as shown in Figure 1.

The sampler shown here uses quick-cutting methods to create each block. The designer divided the block patterns into 16 equal parts made up of triangles and squares to create the pieced design. All blocks use the common templates 12 triangle and 13 square. The coloration of the design remains the same, but the pieces change from our original drawings because most of our patterns are made with larger pieces wherever possible to cut down on the number of pieces and number of seams used in a block. Therefore, when being changed into 16 equal parts, a rectangle becomes two squares; a large right triangle becomes either two right triangles and a square or two right triangles as shown in Figure 2.

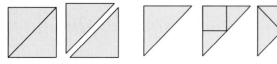

Figure 1	**Figure 2**
Cut the square on the diagonal for a right-angle triangle.	A large right triangle becomes either 2 right triangles and a square or 2 right triangles as shown.

The Pinwheel 2, X Quartet, Road to Oklahoma, Nelson's Victory and Broken Dishes blocks are pieced exactly the same as the drawings given in this chapter. The remaining blocks are pieced using pieces 12 and 13; refer to the block drawings given here for placement of pieces if you want to make the blocks using only these two pieces.

PROJECT SPECIFICATIONS

Quilt Size: 78" x 96"

Block Size: 12" x 12"

Number of Blocks: 20

FABRIC & BATTING

- 3/4 yard each rose, blue and green prints
- 3/4 yard yellow mottled
- 3/4 yard black print
- 2 1/2 yards gray print
- 5 1/2 yards cream-on-white print
- Backing 82" x 100"
- Batting 82" x 100"
- 10 1/8 yards self-made or purchased binding

SUPPLIES & TOOLS

- All-purpose thread to match fabrics
- Basic sewing tools and supplies and water-erasable marker or pencil

INSTRUCTIONS

1. Cut four strips cream-on-white print 12 1/2" by fabric width; subcut into twelve 12 1/2" square segments for fill-in squares. Set aside.

2. Cut two strips cream-on-white print 18 1/4" by fabric width; subcut into four 18 1/4" square segments. Cut each square in half on both diagonals to make the side fill-in triangles; set aside.

3. Cut two 9 3/8" x 9 3/8" squares cream-on-white print and cut each one on one diagonal to make four corner triangles; set aside.

4. The blocks used in the sampler quilt shown are listed in horizontal rows from left to right. Row 1: Crosses & Losses, Unknown Four-Patch, Pinwheel 2, Old Maid's Puzzle; Row 2: Simple Flower Basket, Mosaic 2, Road to Oklahoma, Windmill; Row 3: Nelson's Victory, Windblown Square, Flock of Geese, Broken Dishes; Row 4: Dutchman's Puzzle, Barbara Frietchie Star, Susannah, Next-Door Neighbor; Row 5: Ocean Wave, New Four-Patch, Mosaic 50, X Quartet. *Note: You may choose any 20 blocks from this chapter or from any other chapters in this book.*

5. If you choose a block which uses pieces other

than templates 12 and 13, divide the block into four equal parts in each direction to make 16 units. Divide each unit as necessary to create the design needed using Crosses & Losses as an example as shown in Figure 3.

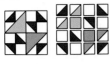

Figure 3
Divide the block into 16 units to create the design as shown with Crosses & Losses.

6. Once you have made these divisions, count the number of each color needed for pieces 12 and 13. For example, in Crosses & Losses you would need the following for piece 12: two each rose and green, six gray and 10 cream-on-white. For piece 13 you would need one each rose and green and four white.

7. Continue listing pieces needed for each block under each fabric color until you have listed all pieces needed for the blocks.

8. To determine the number of strips needed to piece 12 triangles, divide the number of triangles needed from one fabric by 2; divide this number by 11 (the number of 3 7/8" squares that can be cut from one fabric-width strip) to determine the number of strips to cut.

9. Cut the 3 7/8" by fabric width strips; subcut into 3 7/8" square segments as shown in Figure 4. Cut each square in half on one diagonal to make triangles as shown in Figure 1. Stack same-color triangles together.

3 7/8"

Figure 4
Cut the 3 7/8" by fabric width strips; subcut into 3 7/8" square segments.

10. To cut piece 13 squares, divide the number of squares needed from one fabric by 12 (the number of 3 1/2" squares that can be cut from one fabric-width strip) to determine the number of strips to cut. Cut strips 3 1/2" wide; subcut strips into 3 1/2" square segments.

11. To piece blocks, lay out triangles and squares in rows referring to the new block drawings shown in Figures 5–19. Sew the triangles together on the diagonal seams and join with the squares in rows. Join the rows to complete blocks.

12. Arrange the pieced blocks in diagonal rows with the fill-in squares and triangles as shown in Figure

Figure 5
Divide the Unknown Four-Patch block as shown.

Figure 6
Divide the Old Maid's Puzzle block as shown.

 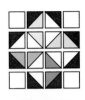

Figure 7
Divide the Simple Flower Basket block as shown.

Figure 8
Divide the New Four-Patch block as shown.

Figure 9
Divide the Mosaic 2 block as shown.

Figure 10
Divide the Windmill block as shown.

Figure 11
Divide the Windblown Square block as shown.

Figure 12
Divide the Flock of Geese block as shown.

Figure 13
Divide the Dutchman's Puzzle block as shown.

Figure 14
Divide the Susannah block as shown.

Figure 15
Divide the Next-Door Neighbor 1 block as shown.

Figure 16
Divide the Ocean Wave block as shown.

Figure 17
Divide the Barbara Frietchie Star block as shown.

Figure 18
Divide the Mosaic 50 block as shown.

Figure 19
Divide the Crosses & Losses block as shown.

20; join in diagonal rows. Join the diagonal rows; press seams in one direction. Add a corner triangle to each corner to complete pieced center.

13. Cut two strips each black print 3" x 68 1/2" and 2 1/2" x 90 1/2". Sew the shorter strips to the top and bottom and longer strips to opposite long sides; press seams toward strips.

14. Cut five strips cream-on-white print, three strips

gray print and one strip each rose, green and blue prints and yellow mottled 3 7/8" by fabric width. Subcut each strip into 3 7/8" square segments; cut each square on the diagonal to make triangles.

Figure 20
Arrange the pieced blocks in diagonal
rows with the fill-in squares and triangles.

15. Sew a colored triangle to a cream-on-white print triangle to make a square unit; repeat for 54 units. Sew a gray print triangle to a cream-on-white print triangle to make a square unit; repeat for 54 units. Join 24 units as shown in Figure 21; repeat to make top and bottom strips. Sew a pieced strip to the top and bottom of the pieced center.

Figure 21
Join 24 units as shown to
make a top and bottom strip.

16. Join 30 units for a side strip; repeat for two side strips. Cut four squares cream-on-white print 3 1/2" x 3 1/2". Sew a square to each end of each side strip. Sew a side strip to opposite long sides of the pieced center to complete the pieced top.

17. Mark the quilting design given in the fill-in squares and triangles using a water-erasable marker or pencil.

18. Sandwich batting between completed top and prepared backing piece; pin or baste layers together to hold flat.

Continued on page 16

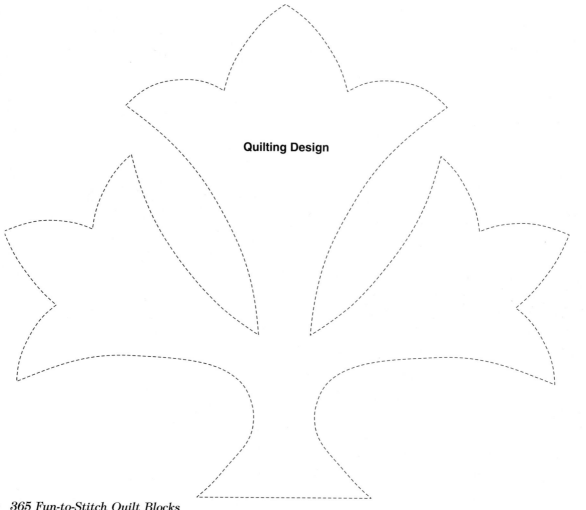

Quilting Design

2 1/2" x 68"

2" x 90"

Strips & Pieces Sampler
Placement Diagram
78" x 96"

Roman Square Pillow

By Julie Weaver

Using a juvenile print makes any pattern suitable for a child's pillow.

PROJECT SPECIFICATIONS

Project Size: 16" x 16"

Block Size: 12" x 12"

Number of Blocks: 1

FABRIC & BATTING

- 3 strips 1 7/8" x 42" contrasting prints or solids
- 1/4 yard juvenile print
- Muslin 20" x 20"
- Batting 20" x 20"
- 2 pieces backing 11 1/2" x 16 1/2"
- 2 yards self-made or purchased binding

SUPPLIES & TOOLS

- All-purpose thread to match fabrics
- 16" x 16" pillow form
- Basic sewing tools and supplies

INSTRUCTIONS

1. Prepare one Roman Square block referring to the Placement Diagram for placement of colors in the block.

2. Cut two strips each 2 1/2" x 12 1/2" and 2 1/2" x 16 1/2" juvenile print. Sew the shorter strips to two

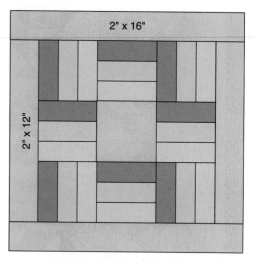

Roman Square Kid's Pillow
Placement Diagram
16" x 16"

opposite sides of the pieced block; sew the longer strips to the remaining sides. Press seam toward strips.

3. Sandwich batting between block and muslin square; pin or baste layers together to hold flat.

4. Machine-quilt in the ditch of seams and as desired.

5. Turn under one 16 1/2" edge on each of the backing pieces 1/4" and press. Turn under again 1/2"; press and stitch to form hems.

6. Lay backing pieces right side up on a flat surface, overlapping 5" as shown in Figure 1; baste in place.

7. Pin backing pieces wrong sides together with quilted front unit; stitch all around using 1/4" seam allowance.

8. Bind edges with self-made or purchased binding; insert pillow form to finish. ❖

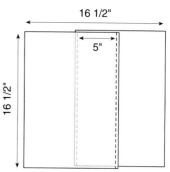

Figure 1
Lay backing pieces right sides up on a flat surface, overlapping 5".

Toad Puddle Candle Mat

By Connie Kauffman

Add a simple pieced border to one block to create a whole different look.

2. Using common templates 14 and 41, cut four burgundy mottled 41 pieces, reversing two for 41R; cut two green mottled 14 triangles.

3. Sew 41 and 41R to the short sides of 14 as shown in Figure 1; repeat.

Figure 1
Sew 41 and 41R to the short sides of 14.

4. Sew a 14-41 unit to two opposite sides of the pieced block referring to the Placement Diagram.

5. Lay the batting on a flat surface; place the backing piece on the batting right side up. Lay the pieced unit right sides together with the backing; pin layers together to hold.

6. Stitch around all sides, leaving a 4" opening on one side; clip points and trim batting and backing even with pieced top. Turn right side out and press. Hand-stitch opening closed to finish. ❖

PROJECT SPECIFICATIONS

Project Size: 18" x 12"
Block Size: 12" x 12"
Number of Blocks: 1

FABRIC & BATTING

- 1/8 yard each gold and brown mottleds
- 1/4 yard each green and burgundy mottleds
- Backing 19" x 13"
- Batting 19" x 13"

SUPPLIES & TOOLS

- All-purpose thread to match fabrics
- Basic sewing tools and supplies

INSTRUCTIONS

1. Prepare one Toad-in-a-Puddle block referring to the Placement Diagram for placement of colors in the block.

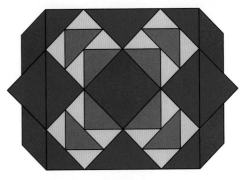

Toad-in-a-Puddle Candle Mat
Placement Diagram
18" x 12"

Sheepfold Place Mat

By Chris Malone

Adding border strips to opposite ends of a block creates the perfect-size place mat.

PROJECT SPECIFICATIONS
Project Size: 18" x 12"

Block Size: 12" x 12"

Number of Blocks: 1

FABRIC & BATTING
- 1/8 yard each dark blue and yellow florals
- 1/4 yard each light blue and red florals
- Backing 19" x 13"
- Batting 19" x 13"

SUPPLIES & TOOLS
- All-purpose thread to match fabrics
- 4 (7/8") yellow buttons
- Basic sewing tools and supplies

INSTRUCTIONS
1. Prepare one Sheepfold block referring to the Placement Diagram for placement of colors in the block.

2. Cut two 3 1/2" x 12 1/2" strips yellow floral. Sew a strip to two opposite sides of the block; press seams toward strips.

3. Place the batting piece on a flat surface; lay the prepared backing piece on top with right side up. Lay the pieced top right sides together with backing; pin layers together.

4. Stitch all around, leaving a 4" opening on one side; clip corners and trim backing and batting edges even with completed top. Turn right side out; press. Hand-stitch opening closed.

5. Machine-quilt in the ditch of seams and as desired.

6. Sew a yellow button in the corners of the block to complete the place mat. ❖

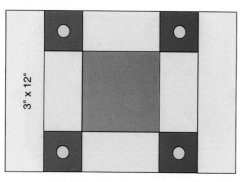

Sheepfold Place Mat
Placement Diagram
18" x 12"

3" x 12"

The Comfort Quilt Block Table Runner

By Chris Malone

Choose your favorite block for the center of this simple table runner.

PROJECT SPECIFICATIONS

Project Size: 38" x 12"

Block Size: 12" x 12"

Number of Blocks: 1

FABRIC & BATTING

- Scrap red solid
- 1/8 yard yellow floral
- 1/4 yard red and dark blue florals
- 1/2 yard light blue floral
- Backing 34" x 14" and 11" x 11"
- Batting 34" x 14" and 11" x 11"

SUPPLIES & TOOLS

- All-purpose thread to match fabrics

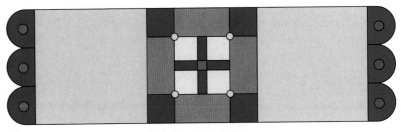

**The Comfort Quilt Block
Table Runner**
Placement Diagram
38" x 12"

- 4 (5/8") yellow buttons
- 6 (7/8") red buttons
- Basic sewing tools and supplies

INSTRUCTIONS

1. Prepare The Comfort Quilt block referring to the Placement Diagram for placement of colors in the block.

2. Cut two 10 1/2" x 12 1/2" rectangles light blue floral.

3. Sew a light blue floral rectangle to two opposite sides of the pieced block; press seams away from block.

4. Prepare template for A using pattern given; cut as directed on the piece.

5. Pin a dark blue floral A right sides together with a backing A; pin to a batting A. Sew all around curved edges, leaving straight edge open. Trim seam to 1/8", clip curve and turn right side out; press. Repeat for six A units.

6. Arrange three A units on each end of the pieced top, with dark blue floral right sides together with pieced top and aligning raw edges and leaving 1/4" at each end as shown in Figure 1; baste to hold.

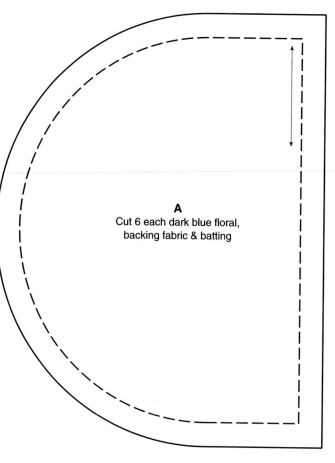

A
Cut 6 each dark blue floral,
backing fabric & batting

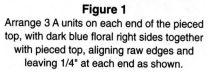

Figure 1
Arrange 3 A units on each end of the pieced top, with dark blue floral right sides together with pieced top, aligning raw edges and leaving 1/4" at each end as shown.

7. Place the 14" x 34" batting piece on a flat surface; lay the prepared backing piece on top with right side up. Lay the pieced top right sides together with backing with A pieces toward the inside; pin layers together.

8. Stitch all around, leaving a 6" opening on one side; clip corners and trim backing and batting edges even with completed top. Turn right side out; press. Hand-stitch opening closed.

9. Machine-quilt in the ditch of seams and as desired.

10. Sew a yellow button at block intersections and a red button in the center of each A piece to complete the table runner. ❖

Strips & Pieces Sampler
Continued from page 10

19. Quilt on marked lines and as desired by hand or machine. *Note: The quilt shown was hand-quilted using off-white quilting thread on marked lines, 1/4" inside seams on cream-on-white print pieces and in the ditch of border and block seams.*

20. When quilting is complete, trim edges even and remove pins or basting. Bind edges with self-made or purchased binding to finish. ❖

Air Castle

PIECING INSTRUCTIONS

1. Referring to the Piecing Diagram to piece one block, sew a light 2 to a dark 2 along the diagonal to complete one corner unit; repeat for four corner units.

2. Sew a colored 4 to a dark 4 and add a colored 2 to complete a side unit; repeat for four side units.

3. Sew a dark 5 to each side of a light 7 to complete a center unit.

4. Arrange the pieced units in rows referring to the Piecing Diagram. Join units in rows; join rows to complete one block.

Air Castle

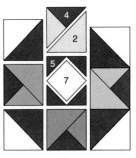

Templates needed:
2, 4, 5, & 7

Album 1

PIECING INSTRUCTIONS

1. Referring to the Piecing Diagram to piece one block, sew two light 5 triangles to two adjacent sides of a dark 3; add a dark 2 to complete one corner unit; repeat for four corner units.

2. Arrange the pieced corner units in rows with one light and four colored 1 squares referring to the Piecing Diagram. Join units in rows; join rows to complete one block.

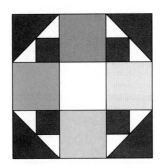

Album 1

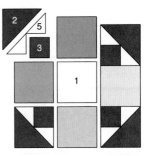

Templates needed:
1, 2, 3 & 5

At the Square

PIECING INSTRUCTIONS

1. Referring to the Piecing Diagram to piece one block, join two colored and two dark 4 triangles to complete one corner unit; repeat for four corner units.

2. Sew a colored 8 between two dark 8 pieces to complete a side unit; repeat for four side units.

3. Arrange the pieced units in rows with a light 1 square referring to the Piecing Diagram. Join units in rows; join rows to complete one block.

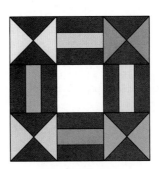

At the Square

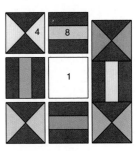

Templates needed:
1, 4 & 8

Attic Window

PIECING INSTRUCTIONS

1. Referring to the Piecing Diagram to piece one block, sew a light 2 to a colored 2 along the diagonal to complete one corner unit; repeat for four corner units.

2. Sew a dark 8 between two light 8 pieces to complete a side unit; repeat for four side units.

3. Arrange the pieced units in rows with the light 1 square referring to the Piecing Diagram. Join units in rows; join rows to complete one block.

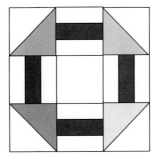

Attic Window

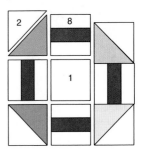

Templates needed:
1, 2 & 8

Barbara Frietchie Star

PIECING INSTRUCTIONS

1. Referring to the Piecing Diagram to piece one block, sew a light 12 to a dark 12 along the diagonal to complete a corner unit; repeat for four corner units.

2. Sew a colored 12 to a dark 12 along the diagonal; repeat for four units. Join four units to complete a pinwheel center.

3. Sew a dark 12 to two adjacent sides of a light 14 to complete one side unit; repeat for four side units.

4. Arrange the pieced units in rows referring to the Piecing Diagram. Join units in rows; join rows to complete one block.

Barbara Frietchie Star

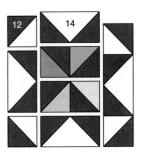

Templates needed:
12 & 14

Belle's Favorite

PIECING INSTRUCTIONS

1. Referring to the Piecing Diagram to piece one block, join two dark 19 squares with two light 14 triangles and four colored 12 triangles to make the center unit.

2. Sew a dark 13 to each end of a colored 57; repeat.

3. Sew the 13-57 units to opposite sides of the center unit to complete one block.

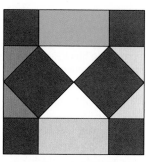

Belle's Favorite

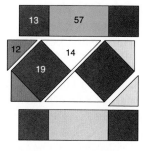

Templates needed:
12, 13, 14, 19 & 57

Birds in the Air

PIECING INSTRUCTIONS

1. Referring to the Piecing Diagram to piece one block, join six dark and three colored 5 triangles; sew a light 15 to the long side to complete a block quarter; repeat for four block quarters.

2. Join the block quarters to complete one block.

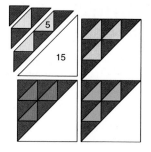

Birds in the Air

Templates needed:
5 & 15

Bright Hopes

PIECING INSTRUCTIONS

1. Referring to the Piecing Diagram to piece one block, sew two dark and two colored 6 rectangles to the sides of a light 3, finishing partial seam when all pieces have been added; repeat for four units.

2. Join the four units to complete one block.

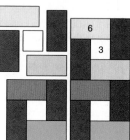

Bright Hopes

Templates needed:
3 & 6

Brock House

PIECING INSTRUCTIONS

1. Referring to the Piecing Diagram to piece one block, sew a dark 20 to a colored 20; sew to a light B1 square; repeat for two units.

2. Sew a light 20 to a dark 20; sew to a colored B1 square; repeat for two units.

3. Sew the units to a dark 20 square, finishing partial seam when all pieces have been added to complete one block.

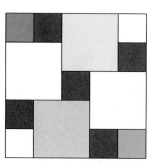

Brock House

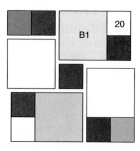

Templates needed:
20 & B1

Broken Dishes

PIECING INSTRUCTIONS

1. Referring to the Piecing Diagram to piece one block, sew a colored 12 to a dark 12 along the diagonal; repeat for 16 units.

2. Arrange four same-color units to make a block quarter; join units to complete one quarter. Repeat for four quarters. Join the quarters to complete one block.

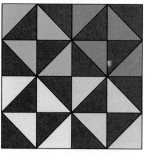

Broken Dishes

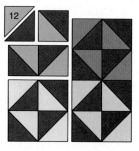

Template needed:
12

Calico Puzzle

PIECING INSTRUCTIONS

1. Referring to the Piecing Diagram to piece one block, sew a light 2 to a dark 2 along the diagonal to complete a corner unit; repeat for four corner units.

2. Arrange the corner units in rows with one dark and four colored 1 squares referring to the Piecing Diagram. Join units in rows; join rows to complete one block.

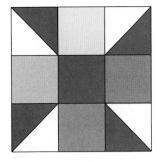

Calico Puzzle

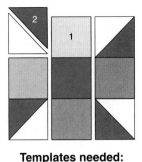

Templates needed:
1 & 2

Chain & Hourglass

PIECING INSTRUCTIONS

1. Referring to the Piecing Diagram to piece one block, join two dark and two light 4 triangles to complete a unit; repeat for four corner units. Join two colored and two light 4 triangles for one center unit.

2. Sew a colored 8 between two dark 8 pieces to complete a side unit; repeat for four side units.

3. Arrange the pieced units in rows referring to the Piecing Diagram. Join units in rows; join rows to complete one block.

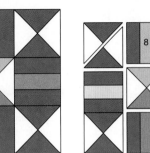

Chain & Hourglass

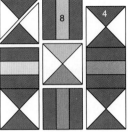

Templates needed:
4 & 8

Cheyenne

PIECING INSTRUCTIONS

1. Referring to the Piecing Diagram to piece one block, sew a light 12 to a colored 12 along the diagonal; repeat for two units for corners. Sew a light 12 to a dark 12 along the diagonal; repeat for two units for corners.

2. Sew two dark and two colored 12 triangles to each side of the light 19 square to complete the center unit.

3. Arrange pieced units in rows with four colored and four dark 13 squares referring to the Piecing Diagram. Join units in rows; join rows to complete one block.

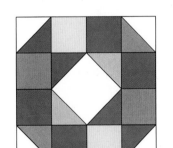

Cheyenne

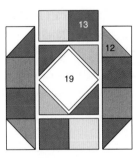

Templates needed:
12, 13 & 19

Churn Dash

PIECING INSTRUCTIONS

1. Referring to the Piecing Diagram to piece one block, sew a light 2 to a dark 2 along the diagonal to complete a corner unit; repeat for four corner units.

2. Sew a light 6 to a colored 6 to complete a side unit; repeat for four side units.

3. Arrange the pieced units in rows with the light 1 square referring to the Piecing Diagram. Join units in rows; join rows to complete one block.

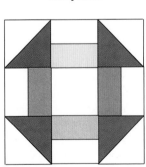

Churn Dash

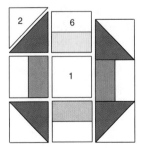

Templates needed:
1, 2 & 6

Colt's Corral

PIECING INSTRUCTIONS

1. Referring to the Piecing Diagram to piece one block, join two colored and two dark 53 pieces to complete one unit; repeat for eight units. Join two dark and two light 53 pieces for one center unit.

2. Arrange the pieced units in rows referring to the Piecing Diagram. Join units in rows; join rows to complete one block.

Colt's Corral

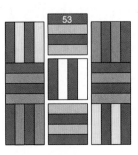

Template needed:
53

Coxey's Camp

PIECING INSTRUCTIONS

1. Referring to the Piecing Diagram to piece one block, join two light and two dark 59 squares to complete the center Four-Patch unit; sew a light 12 to each side.

2. Sew a light 82 to a dark 82 to complete a side unit; repeat for four side units.

3. Arrange the pieced units in rows with colored 13 squares referring to the Piecing Diagram. Join units in rows; join rows to complete one block.

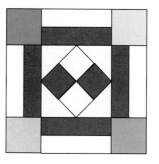

Coxey's Camp

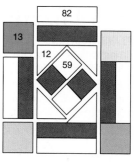

Templates needed:
12, 13, 59 & 82

Crosses & Losses

PIECING INSTRUCTIONS

1. Referring to the Piecing Diagram to piece one block, sew a light 12 to a dark 12 along the diagonal; repeat for six units.

2. Join two units with two light 13 squares to complete a quarter unit; repeat for two quarter units.

3. Join one dark and three light 12 triangles with a colored 15 to complete a quarter unit; repeat for two quarter units.

4. Join the quarter units to complete one block.

Crosses & Losses

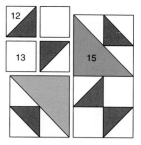

Templates needed:
12, 13 & 15

Double Anchor

PIECING INSTRUCTIONS

1. Referring to the Piecing Diagram to piece one block, sew a dark 86 between two light 86 pieces; sew a dark 14 triangle to each side to complete the block center.

2. Sew a colored 15 triangle to each side of the block center to complete one block.

Double Anchor

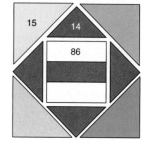

Templates needed:
14, 15 & 86

Double X

PIECING INSTRUCTIONS

1. Referring to the Piecing Diagram to piece one block, sew a light 2 to a dark 2 along the diagonal; repeat for four units. Join a light 2 to a colored 2; repeat for two units.

2. Arrange the pieced units in rows with one colored and two light 1 squares referring to the Piecing Diagram. Join units in rows; join rows to complete one block.

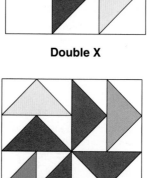

Double X

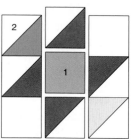

Templates needed:
1 & 2

Dutchman's Puzzle

PIECING INSTRUCTIONS

1. Referring to the Piecing Diagram to piece one block, sew a light 12 to two adjacent short sides of a colored 14; repeat for four units.

2. Sew a light 12 to two adjacent short sides of a dark 14; repeat for four units.

3. Join a colored and dark unit to complete a block quarter; repeat for four block quarters.

4. Join the block quarters to complete one block.

Dutchman's Puzzle

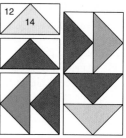

Templates needed:
12 & 14

Flock of Geese

PIECING INSTRUCTIONS

1. Referring to the Piecing Diagram to piece one block, sew a light 12 to a dark 12 along the diagonal; repeat for eight units.

2. Join four 12 units to complete a block quarter; repeat for two quarters.

3. Sew a colored 15 to a light 15 along the diagonal to complete a block quarter; repeat for two quarters.

4. Join the block quarters to complete one block.

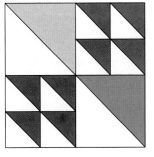

Flock of Geese

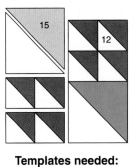

Templates needed:
12 & 15

Glorified Nine-Patch

PIECING INSTRUCTIONS

1. Referring to the Piecing Diagram to piece one block, join two light and one dark 68 squares to make a row; repeat for two rows. Join two dark and one light 68 squares to make a row. Join the rows to complete a Nine-Patch corner unit; repeat for four corner units.

2. Sew a colored 8 to a light 69 to complete a side unit; repeat for four side units.

3. Arrange the pieced units in rows with one light 1 square referring to the Piecing Diagram. Join units in rows; join rows to complete one block.

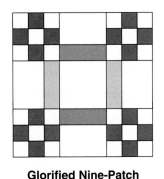

Glorified Nine-Patch

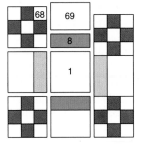

Templates needed:
1, 8, 68 & 69

Golden Gate

PIECING INSTRUCTIONS

1. Referring to the Piecing Diagram to piece one block, sew a light 2 to a colored 2 along the diagonal to complete a corner unit; repeat for four corner units.

2. Sew a light 8 between two dark 8 pieces to complete a side unit; repeat for four side units.

3. Arrange the pieced units in rows with one light 1 square referring to the Piecing Diagram. Join units in rows; join rows to complete one block.

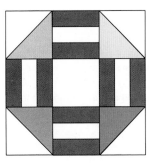

Golden Gate

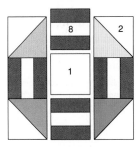

Templates needed:
1, 2 & 8

Hourglass

PIECING INSTRUCTIONS

1. Referring to the Piecing Diagram to piece one block, sew a dark 2 to a light 2 along the diagonal to complete one corner unit; repeat for two corner units.

2. Arrange the two pieced corner units with one light, two dark and four colored 1 squares in rows. Join units in rows; join rows to complete one block.

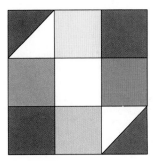

Hourglass

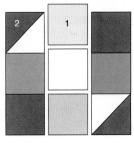

Templates needed:
1 & 2

Illinois

PIECING INSTRUCTIONS

1. Referring to the Piecing Diagram to piece one block, sew a colored 2 to a light 2 along the diagonal to complete a corner unit; repeat for four corner units.

2. Sew a colored 5 to two adjacent short sides of a light 4; repeat for eight units. Join two units to complete a side unit; repeat for four side units.

3. Sew a colored 5 to each side of the light 7 to complete the center unit.

4. Arrange the pieced units in rows referring to the Piecing Diagram. Join rows in rows; join rows to complete one block.

Illinois

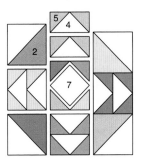

Templates needed:
2, 4, 5 & 7

Illinois Road

PIECING INSTRUCTIONS

1. Referring to the Piecing Diagram to piece one block, sew a colored 32 to a light 32; repeat. Sew a dark 32 to a light 32; repeat. Join the four pieced units to complete one corner unit; repeat for one center and four corner units.

2. Arrange the pieced units in rows with four light 1 squares referring to the Piecing Diagram. Join units in rows; join rows to complete one block.

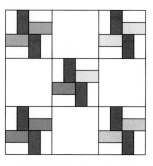

Illinois Road

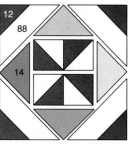

Templates needed:
1 & 32

Mosaic 2

PIECING INSTRUCTIONS

1. Referring to the Piecing Diagram to piece one block, sew a light 12 to a dark 12 along the diagonal; repeat for four units. Join the units to complete a pinwheel center unit.

2. Sew a colored 14 to each side of the pieced center unit.

3. Sew a light 88 to each side of the pieced unit; sew a dark 12 to each corner to complete one block.

Mosaic 2

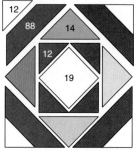

Templates needed:
12, 14 & 88

Mosaic 50

PIECING INSTRUCTIONS

1. Referring to the Piecing Diagram to piece one block, sew a dark 12 to each side of the light 19; sew a colored 14 to each side of this pieced unit.

2. Sew a dark 88 to each side of the pieced unit and a light 12 to each corner to complete one block.

Mosaic 50

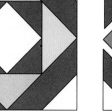

Templates needed:
12, 14, 19 & 88

Nelson's Victory

PIECING INSTRUCTIONS

1. Referring to the Piecing Diagram to piece one block, sew a light 12 to a colored 12 along the diagonal; repeat for four units. Join the units to complete the pinwheel center unit.

2. Arrange four dark, four colored and four light 13 squares in rows with the center unit referring to the Piecing Diagram. Join the units in rows; join rows to complete one block.

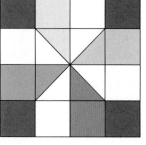

Nelson's Victory

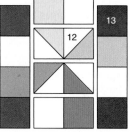

Templates needed:
12 & 13

New Album

PIECING INSTRUCTIONS

1. Referring to the Piecing Diagram to piece one block, sew a light 5 to two adjacent sides of a dark 3 square; add a dark 2 to complete one corner unit. Repeat for four corner units.

2. Sew a dark 5 to each side of a colored 7 to complete the center unit.

3. Arrange units in rows with four colored 1 squares referring to the Piecing Diagram. Join the units in rows; join rows to complete one block.

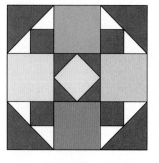

New Album

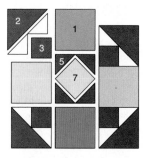

Templates needed:
1, 2, 3, 5 & 7

New Four-Patch

PIECING INSTRUCTIONS

1. Referring to the Piecing Diagram to piece one block, sew a colored 15 to a dark 15 along the diagonal to complete a quarter block; repeat for two quarter blocks.

2. Join two colored and two dark 13 squares to make a Four-Patch unit; repeat for two units.

3. Arrange units in rows and join referring to the Piecing Diagram to complete one block.

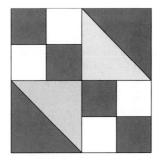

New Four-Patch

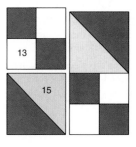

Templates needed:
13 & 15

Next-Door Neighbor 1

PIECING INSTRUCTIONS

1. Referring to the Piecing Diagram to piece one block, sew a light 12 to two adjacent short sides of a dark 14; repeat for two units.

2. Sew a dark 12 to the angled end of a light 111; repeat for two units. Join this unit with a 12-14 unit to complete a quarter block; repeat for two quarter blocks.

3. Sew a light 12 to two adjacent short sides of a colored 14; repeat for two units.

4. Sew a colored 12 to the angled end of a light 111; repeat for two units. Join this unit with a 12-14 unit to complete a quarter block; repeat for two quarter blocks.

5. Join the four quarter blocks to complete one block.

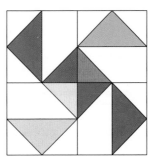

Next-Door Neighbor 1

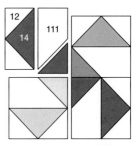

Templates needed:
12, 14 & 111

Ocean Wave

PIECING INSTRUCTIONS

1. Referring to the Piecing Diagram to piece one block, sew a colored 12 to a dark 12 along the diagonal; repeat for 10 units.

2. Join four units to make a block quarter; repeat for two block quarters.

3. Sew two colored 12 triangles to the dark side of a 12 unit; add a light 15 to complete a block quarter. Repeat with two dark 12 triangles.

4. Join the four quarters to complete one block.

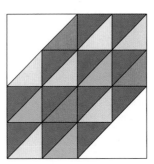

Ocean Wave

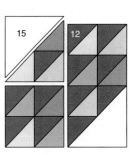

Templates needed:
12 & 15

Old Maid's Puzzle

PIECING INSTRUCTIONS

1. Referring to the Piecing Diagram to piece one block, sew a light 12 to a dark 12 along the diagonal; repeat for four units.

2. Join two pieced units with two colored 13 squares to complete one corner unit; repeat for two quarter units.

3. Sew a light 15 to a dark 15 quarter along the diagonal; repeat for two units.

4. Join the 12-13 quarter units with the 15 quarter units to complete one block.

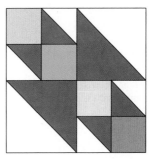

Old Maid's Puzzle

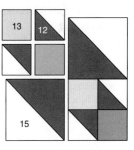

Templates needed:
12, 13 & 15

Pinwheel 1

PIECING INSTRUCTIONS

1. Referring to the Piecing Diagram to piece one block, sew a colored 2 to a light 2 along the diagonal to complete a side unit; repeat for four side units.

2. Arrange the pieced units in rows with one dark and four light 1 squares referring to the Piecing Diagram. Join units in rows; join rows to complete one block.

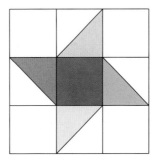

Pinwheel 1

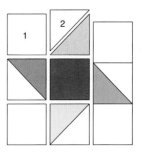

Templates needed:
1 & 2

Pinwheel 2

PIECING INSTRUCTIONS

1. Referring to the Piecing Diagram to piece one block, sew a light 12 to a dark 12 along the diagonal; repeat for four units.

2. Arrange the pieced units in quarters with one each dark, light and colored 13 squares referring to the Piecing Diagram. Join quarter units to complete one block.

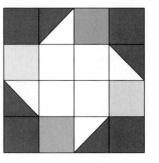

Pinwheel 2

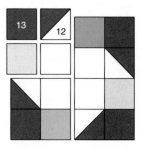

Templates needed:
12 & 13

Prairie Queen

PIECING INSTRUCTIONS

1. Referring to the Piecing Diagram to piece one block, sew a light 2 to a dark 2 along the diagonal to complete one corner unit; repeat for four corner units.

2. Join two light and two colored 3 squares to make a Four-Patch side unit; repeat for four side units.

3. Arrange the pieced units in rows with a light 1 square referring to the Piecing Diagram. Join the units in rows; join the rows to complete one block.

Prairie Queen

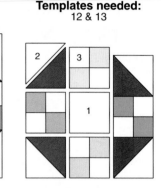

Templates needed:
1, 2 & 3

Road to Oklahoma

PIECING INSTRUCTIONS

1. Referring to the Piecing Diagram to piece one block, sew a light 12 to a colored 12 along the diagonal; repeat for four units. Sew a 12 unit to a light and colored 13 square. Join the 12-13 units to make a block quarter; repeat for two quarters.

2. Join two light and two dark 13 squares to complete a Four-Patch block quarter; repeat for two quarters.

3. Join the block quarters to complete one block.

Road To Oklahoma

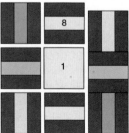

Templates needed:
12 & 13

Roman Square

PIECING INSTRUCTIONS

1. Referring to the Piecing Diagram to piece one block, sew a colored 8 between two dark 8 pieces; repeat for eight units.

2. Arrange the pieced units in rows with the colored 1 square referring to the Piecing Diagram. Join the units in rows; join the rows to complete one block.

Roman Square

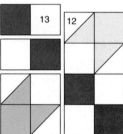
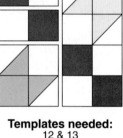

Templates needed:
1 & 8

Sheepfold Quilt

PIECING INSTRUCTIONS

1. Referring to the Piecing Diagram to piece one block, sew a light 57 to opposite sides of a dark 34.

2. Sew a colored 13 to each end of two light 57 pieces; sew these units to the sides of the 34 unit to complete one block.

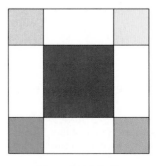

Sheepfold Quilt

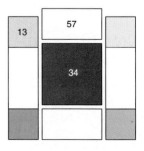

Templates needed:
13, 34 & 57

Simple Flower Basket

PIECING INSTRUCTIONS

1. Referring to the Piecing Diagram to piece one block, sew a light 12 to a dark 12 along the diagonal; repeat for five units. Sew a colored 12 to a dark 12.

2. Join the pieced units with two colored 12 triangles to complete the basket top; add a dark 15.

3. Sew a dark 12 to one end of a light 57; repeat and sew to the sides of the pieced unit.

4. Sew a light 15 to the corner to complete one block.

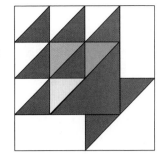

Simple Flower Basket

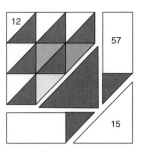

Templates needed:
12, 15 & 57

Susannah

PIECING INSTRUCTIONS

1. Referring to the Piecing Diagram to piece one block, sew a colored 13 to a light 13. Sew a light 12 to the angled end of a dark 111. Join the two pieced units to complete one block quarter; repeat for four block quarters.

2. Join the block quarters to complete one block.

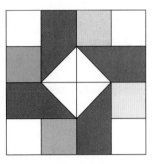

Susannah

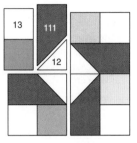

Templates needed:
12, 13 & 111

The Comfort Quilt

PIECING INSTRUCTIONS

1. Referring to the Piecing Diagram to piece one block, join two light 106 squares with a dark A1; repeat.

2. Join two dark A1 pieces with a light 24; sew between two previously pieced units to complete the block center.

3. Sew a colored 57 to two opposite sides of the block center; sew a light 13 to each end of two colored 57 pieces.

4. Sew the 13-57 units to the remaining sides of the pieced center to complete one block.

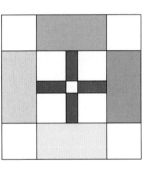

The Comfort Quilt

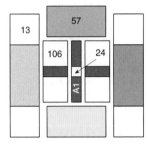

Templates needed:
13, 24, 57, 106 & A1

Thrifty

PIECING INSTRUCTIONS

1. Referring to the Piecing Diagram to piece one block, join two light and two dark 3 squares to complete a Four-Patch corner unit; repeat for four corner units.

2. Arrange the corner units in rows with a one dark and four colored 1 squares referring to the Piecing Diagram. Join the units in rows; join the rows to complete one block.

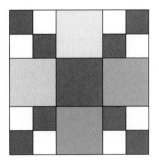

Thrifty

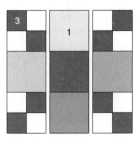

Templates needed:
1 & 3

Toad in a Puddle

PIECING INSTRUCTIONS

1. Referring to the Piecing Diagram to piece one block, sew a light 16 to two adjacent sides of a colored 12; repeat for eight units.

2. Join two pieced units with a light 12 and two light 14 triangles to complete a large corner unit; repeat for two large corner units.

3. Join two 12-16 units and add a light 12; repeat. Sew these units to opposite sides of the light 19 to complete the center unit.

4. Sew a large corner unit to each side of the center unit to complete one block.

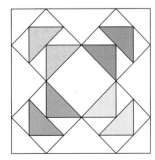

Toad in a Puddle

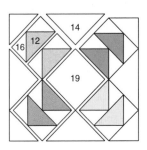

Templates needed:
12, 14, 16 & 19

Triangle Squares

PIECING INSTRUCTIONS

1. Referring to the Piecing Diagram to piece one block, sew a light 12 to a colored 12 on the diagonal; repeat for four units.

2. Sew a light 12 to a dark 12 on the diagonal; repeat for four units. Join one of these units with a light/colored unit to complete a side unit; repeat for four side units.

3. Sew a light 12 to each side of a colored 19 to complete the center unit.

4. Arrange the pieced units in rows with four colored 13 squares referring to the Piecing Diagram. Join the units in rows; join rows to complete one block.

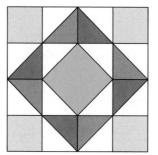

Triangle Squares

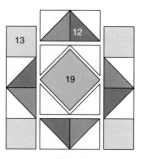

Templates needed:
12, 13 & 19

Unknown Four-Patch

PIECING INSTRUCTIONS

1. Referring to the Piecing Diagram to piece one block, join two colored and two dark 12 triangles to make square units; join four square units to create the pinwheel center.

2. Sew a light 14 to a dark 14 on the short sides to complete a corner unit; repeat for four corner units.

3. Sew a corner unit to each side of the center unit to complete one block.

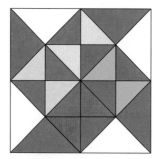

Unknown Four-Patch

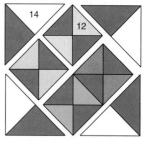

Templates needed:
12 & 14

Virginia Worm Fence

PIECING INSTRUCTIONS

1. Referring to the Piecing Diagram to piece one block, sew a colored 6 to a dark 6; repeat for nine units.

2. Arrange the pieced units in rows referring to the Piecing Diagram. Join the units in rows; join rows to complete one block.

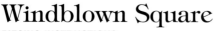

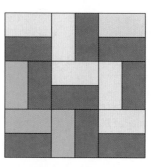

Virginia Worm Fence

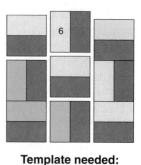

Template needed:
6

Windblown Square

PIECING INSTRUCTIONS

1. Referring to the Piecing Diagram to piece one block, sew two colored and two dark 12 triangles to the sides of the light 19 square to complete the block center.

2. Sew a dark 12 to a light 12 on the short sides; repeat for two units. Sew to opposite sides of the block center.

3. Sew a colored 12 to a light 12 on the short side; repeat for two units. Sew to the remaining sides of the block center.

4. Sew a light 14 to a dark 14 on the short side to complete a corner unit; repeat for two light/dark and two light/colored corner units.

5. Sew a corner unit to each side of the pieced center to complete one block.

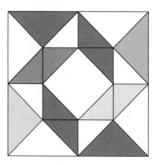

Windblown Square

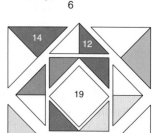

Templates needed:
12, 14 & 19

Windmill

PIECING INSTRUCTIONS

1. Referring to the Piecing Diagram to piece one block, sew a light 14 to a colored 14 along the diagonal; repeat for four units. Join the units to complete the pinwheel center unit.

2. Sew a dark 12 to two adjacent sides of a light 13 to complete a corner unit; repeat for four corner units.

3. Sew a corner unit to each side of the center unit to complete one block.

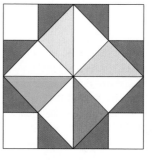

Windmill

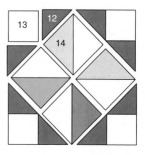

Templates needed:
12, 13 & 14

X Quartet

PIECING INSTRUCTIONS

1. Referring to the Piecing Diagram to piece one block, sew a light 12 to a dark 12 along the diagonal; repeat for four units.

2. Sew a colored 12 to a dark 12 along the diagonal; repeat for four units. Join the units to make the pinwheel center unit.

3. Arrange the pieced units in rows with four each colored and dark 13 squares referring to the Piecing Diagram. Join units in rows; join rows to complete one block.

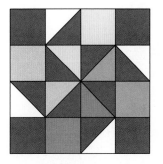

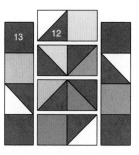

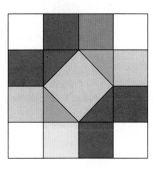

X Quartet

Templates needed:
12 & 13

Y-Bridge

PIECING INSTRUCTIONS

1. Referring to the Piecing Diagram to piece one block, sew two colored and two dark 12 triangles to the sides of a colored 19.

2. Arrange four each light, dark and colored 13 squares in rows with the pieced unit referring to the Piecing Diagram. Join units in rows; join rows to complete one block.

Y-Bridge

Templates needed:
12, 13 & 19

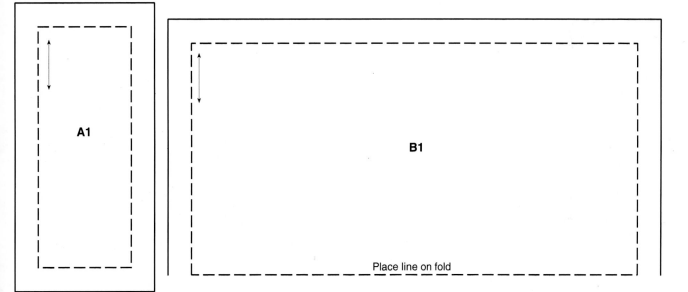

A1

B1

Place line on fold

The Good Old Days

Add a touch of nostalgia to a quilt using blocks from this chapter. Each block is named after a person, an event or an object that will take you on a trip down memory lane.

The setting on this sampler quilt is simple, but very effective for highlighting each block of this beautiful quilt.

The Good Old Days Sampler

By Ruth Swasey

Remember the good old days with old-fashioned blocks in a beautiful sampler quilt.

PROJECT SPECIFICATIONS

Quilt Size: 96" x 96"

Block Size: 12" x 12"

Number of Blocks: 25

FABRIC & BATTING

- 1/2 yard each dark green and cream prints
- 1 1/4 yards each rose and burgundy prints
- 2 3/4 yards green print
- 4 1/4 yards green-on-cream print
- Backing 100" x 100"
- Batting 100" x 100"
- 11 1/8 yards self-made or purchased binding

SUPPLIES & TOOLS

- All-purpose thread to match fabrics
- Cream quilting thread
- Basic sewing tools and supplies

INSTRUCTIONS

1. Cut 16 strips green-on-cream print and eight strips green print 2 1/2" x 92" along length of fabrics. Cut four green-on-cream print strips and two green print strips 2 1/2" by fabric width. Set aside.

2. The blocks used in the sampler quilt shown are listed in vertical rows from top to bottom. Row 1: Silver Lane, Secret Drawer, Dinah's Choice, Emma, Aunt Vinah's Favorite; Row 2: Fort Sumter, Treasure Chest, Contrary Wife, President Carter, Wheel of Fortune; Row 3: President's Choice, Indian Puzzle, Beggar Block, New Barrister Block, Follow the Leader; Row 4: Album 2, Aunt Dinah, Century of Progress, Single Wedding Ring, Twin Darts; Row 5: Country Village, Arrowheads, Hull's Victory, Hobson's Kiss, Road to the White House. *Note: You may choose any 25 blocks from this chapter or from other chapters in this book.*

3. Cut pieces for blocks using fabrics listed above, referring to the Placement Diagram and piecing diagrams given with each block for positioning of colors. Piece blocks referring to the instructions and colored piecing diagrams given with each block.

4. Square up blocks to 12 1/2" x 12 1/2".

5. Sew a green print strip between two green-on-cream print strips with right sides together along length; press seams toward dark strip. Repeat for eight 92"-long strip sets and two 42"-long strip sets.

6. Cut two strip sets of each length into 12 1/2" sashing segments as shown in Figure 1; you will need 20 sashing segments. Set aside strip sets and segments.

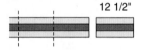

Figure 1
Cut 3 strip sets into 12 1/2"
sashing segments.

7. Arrange the blocks in five rows of five blocks each referring to the Placement Diagram or in a pleasing arrangement.

8. Join five blocks with four sashing segments to make one vertical row as shown in Figure 2; repeat for five vertical rows. Press seams toward sashing segments.

Figure 2
Join 5 blocks with 4 sashing segments to make 1 vertical row.

9. Join the five vertical rows with six strip sets as shown in Figure 3; press seams toward strip sets. Trim strip sets even with blocks. *Note: The pieced top should now measure 96" x 84".*

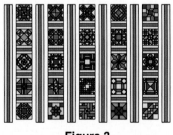

Figure 3
Join the 5 vertical rows with
6 strip sets as shown.

10. Cut two strips each rose and burgundy prints and four strips green-on-cream print 7 1/4" by fabric width. Subcut strips into 7 1/4" square segments.

Good Old Days Sampler
Placement Diagram
96" x 96"

You will need eight each rose and burgundy squares and 16 green-on-cream print squares.

11. Cut each square in half on both diagonals to make triangles.

12. Join 16 burgundy print and 15 green-on-cream print triangles to make a strip as shown in Figure 4; repeat for two strips. Repeat with 16 green-on-cream print and 15 rose print triangles to make a strip; repeat for two strips. Press seams toward dark triangles.

Figure 4
Join 16 burgundy print and 15 green-on-cream print triangles to make a strip as shown.

13. Cut two squares each green-on-cream and rose prints 3 7/8" x 3 7/8". Cut each square on one diagonal to make triangles. Sew a green-on-cream print triangle to each end of the burgundy/cream strips and a rose print triangle to each end of the rose/cream strips.
Continued on page 46

Album Block Cushion

By Connie Kauffman

Make a seat cushion for a favorite chair using colors to match your home.

sides of the pieced block; sew the longer strips to the remaining sides. Press seam toward strips.

4. Sandwich batting between the completed top and lining piece; pin or baste to hold.

5. Machine-quilt in the ditch of seams and as desired; trim edges even. Remove pins or basting.

6. Cut four strips each dark blue print 2" x 14 1/2" for ties; fold strips along length with right sides together. Sew along long side and across one short end with an angled seam as shown in Figure 1; trim excess seam at angle. Turn right side out; press.

7. Pin two tie strips to two adjacent corners of the completed top unit as shown in Figure 2; baste in place and remove pins.

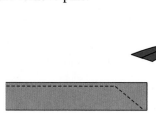 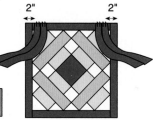

Figure 1
Sew along long side and across
1 short end with an angled seam.

Figure 2
Pin 2 tie strips to 2
adjacent corners of the
completed top unit.

8. Cut a 14 1/2" x 14 1/2" square dark blue print for cushion backing. Lay right sides together with completed top unit; sew all around, making a gentle curve at the corners and leaving a 6" opening on one side. Trim excess at corners; turn right side out and press.

9. Insert foam pad through the opening; hand-stitch opening closed to finish. ❖

PROJECT SPECIFICATIONS
Project Size: 13" x 13"

Block Size: 12" x 12"

Number of Blocks: 1

FABRIC & BATTING
- Fat eighth each yellow and light blue prints
- 1/4 yard white-on-white print
- 5/8 yard dark blue print
- Batting 15" x 15"
- Lining 15" x 15"

SUPPLIES & TOOLS
- All-purpose thread to match fabrics
- 13" x 13" x 1" foam seat pad
- Basic sewing tools and supplies

INSTRUCTIONS
1. Prepare one Album block referring to the Placement Diagram for placement of colors in the block.

2. Cut the corners of the 13" x 13" x 1" foam seat pad to make a gentle curve.

3. Cut two strips each dark blue print 1 1/2" x 12 1/2" and 1 1/2" x 14 1/2". Sew the shorter strips to opposite

Album Block Seat Cushion
Placement Diagram
13" x 13"

Melon Patch Runner

By Kathy Brown

Appliqué the melon shapes to a background and make a difficult block in no time at all.

PROJECT SPECIFICATIONS
Project Size: 44" x 44"

Block Size: 12" x 12"

Number of Blocks: 1

FABRIC & BATTING
- Fat quarter red print
- 1/4 yard green print
- 1 yard red stripe
- 1 1/3 yards quilted muslin

SUPPLIES & TOOLS
- All-purpose thread to match fabrics and black
- 1/4 yard fusible transfer web
- 3/8 yard fabric stabilizer
- 2 packages black wide bias tape
- Basic sewing tools and supplies

INSTRUCTIONS
1. Prepare the E2 template for the Melon Patch block; remove seam allowance. Cut four 6 1/2" x 6 1/2" squares green print.

2. Bond the fusible transfer web to the wrong side of the red print. Trace four E2 pieces onto the paper side of the fused layers. Cut out shapes on traced lines; remove paper backing.

3. Fuse an E2 piece to each green print square referring to Figure 1; repeat for four units.

Melon Patch Table Runner
Placement Diagram
44" x 44"

4. Cut four 6 1/2" x 6 1/2" squares fabric stabilizer; pin a square to the wrong side of each fused unit.

5. Using black all-purpose thread and a machine buttonhole stitch, machine-appliqué each E2 shape in place. When stitching is complete, remove fabric stabilizer.

6. Join the four fused units to complete one Melon Patch block referring to the Placement Diagram.

7. Cut four 12 1/2" x 16 1/2" runner pieces from red stripe. ***Note: The runners can be made longer or***

Continued on page 46

Figure 1
Fuse an E2 piece to each green print square.

Flower Basket Pillow

By Marian Shenk

*Add some appliquéd flowers, lace and a ruffle to the
Flower Basket block to create a beautiful pillow.*

PROJECT SPECIFICATIONS
Pillow Size: 16" x 16" (not including ruffle)
Block Size: 12" x 12"
Number of Blocks: 1

FABRIC & BATTING
- 12 1/2" x 12 1/2" cream tone-on-tone
- Scraps green and purple prints and purple solid
- 14" x 14" scrap beige print
- 1/3 yard multicolored mottled
- 1 yard lavender print
- Batting 20" x 20"

SUPPLIES & TOOLS
- All-purpose thread to match fabrics
- White quilting thread
- 3 yards 2 1/2" gathered lace
- 1 package 1/2"-wide single-fold purple bias tape
- 16" square pillow form
- 5 (1/2") yellow buttons
- Basic sewing tools and supplies

INSTRUCTIONS
1. Prepare one Flower Basket block referring to the Placement Diagram for placement of colors in the block.

2. Cut two 9 3/8" x 9 3/8" squares multicolored mottled; cut each square on one diagonal to make four triangles.

3. Sew a triangle to each side of the Flower Basket block; press seams toward triangles.

4. Prepare templates for V2, W2 and X2 appliqué shapes using patterns given; cut as follows, adding a 1/8"–1/4" seam allowance for hand appliqué: V2—five purple print, W2—five purple solid and X2—22 green print.

5. Position a flower with four leaves on each triangle referring to the Placement Diagram; hand-appliqué in place using all-purpose thread to match fabrics and beginning with the leaves and ending with the flower center.

Flower Basket Pillow
Placement Diagram
16" x 16"
(not including ruffle)

6. Position a flower with six leaves on the appliquéd basket referring to the Placement Diagram; hand-appliqué in place using all-purpose thread to match fabrics and beginning with leaves and ending with the flower center.

7. Cut four 13" pieces purple bias tape; center over seam between block and triangles. Hand-stitch in place with matching all-purpose thread; trim even with edges of top.

8. Pin batting to the wrong side of the pieced and appliquéd pillow top; quilt as desired by hand or machine. *Note: The sample was hand-quilted around each appliqué shape with white quilting thread.*

9. Sew a button to the center of each appliquéd flower motif.

10. Cut three strips lavender print 6" by fabric width; join strips on short ends to make a tube. Fold in half with wrong sides together; press.

11. Sew two lines of machine gathering stitches

close to raw edges; divide tube into four equal parts. Pin each part to one side of the quilted pillow top; pull gathering stitches to make fit. Unpin and pin gathered lace to gathered ruffle; pin to the pillow top and stitch all around using a 1/8" seam allowance.

12. Cut a 16 1/2" x 16 1/2" backing piece from lavender print; pin to pillow top with right sides together and ruffle to the inside. Stitch all around, leaving an 8" opening on one side; clip corners and turn right side out.

13. Insert pillow form through opening. Hand-stitch the opening closed to finish. ❖

Tall Ships Wall Quilt

By Julie Weaver

Make a wall quilt with a nautical theme using the Tall Ships block.

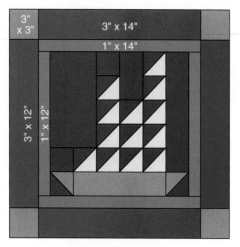

Tall Ships Wall Quilt
Placement Diagram
20" x 20"

PROJECT SPECIFICATIONS

Project Size: 20" x 20"

Block Size: 12" x 12"

Number of Blocks: 1

FABRIC & BATTING

- 1/8 yard each cream mottled, red print and red/blue print
- 1/4 yard dark blue print
- 1/4 yard blue stripe
- Backing 23" x 23"
- Batting 23" x 23"
- 2 1/2 yards self-made or purchased binding

SUPPLIES & TOOLS

- All-purpose thread to match fabrics
- Basic sewing tools and supplies

INSTRUCTIONS

1. Prepare one Tall Ships block referring to the Placement Diagram for placement of colors in the block.

2. Cut two 1 1/2" by fabric width strips red/blue print; subcut into two 12 1/2" and two 14 1/2" strips. Sew the shorter strips to opposite sides of the pieced blocks; sew the longer strips to the remaining sides. Press seams toward strips.

3. Cut two 3 1/2" by fabric width strips blue stripe; subcut into four 14 1/2" strips. Sew a strip to opposite sides of the pieced center.

4. Cut four squares red print 3 1/2" x 3 1/2"; sew a square to each end of the remaining blue stripe strips and sew these strips to the remaining sides of the pieced center to complete the pieced top.

5. Sandwich batting between completed top and prepared backing piece; pin or baste to hold.

6. Quilt as desired by hand or machine. *Note: The quilt shown was machine-quilted in the ditch of seams and in 1/4" echoing designs on patchwork using thread to match fabrics.*

7. When quilting is complete, trim edges even; remove pins or basting.

8. Bind edges with self-made or purchased binding to finish. ❖

Album 2

PIECING INSTRUCTIONS

1. Referring to the Piecing Diagram to piece one block, sew medium M2 to opposite sides of the dark 117; sew a medium 27 to each end of two M2 pieces and sew to the remaining sides of the 117 unit to complete the center unit.

2. Sew a light 28 to each end of a dark M2; sew to a dark L2 and add a light 21 to the M2 side to complete a corner unit; repeat for two corner units.

3. Sew a corner unit to opposite sides of the center unit.

4. Sew a light 28 to each end of a dark L2 and to each end of a dark M2; join the units and add a light 21 to the M2 side to complete a large corner unit; repeat for two large corner units.

5. Sew a large corner unit to the remaining sides of the center unit to complete one block.

Arrowheads

PIECING INSTRUCTIONS

1. Referring to the Piecing Diagram to piece one block, join four light and five dark 17 squares to make a Nine-Patch corner unit; repeat for four corner units.

2. Sew a light 16 to a darkest 16 on the short sides; sew to a medium 93 and add a darkest 18 to the remaining corners to complete one side unit; repeat for four side units.

3. Join two dark and two light 17 squares to make a Four-Patch center unit.

4. Arrange the pieced units in rows referring to the Piecing Diagram. Join units in rows; join rows to complete one block.

Aunt Dinah

PIECING INSTRUCTIONS

1. Referring to the Piecing Diagram to piece one block, sew two lightest 5 triangles to adjacent sides of a dark 3; add a dark 2 to make a corner unit. Repeat for four corner units.

2. Join two dark and two light 4 triangles to make a side unit; repeat for four side units.

3. Arrange the pieced units in rows with the medium 1 square referring to the Piecing Diagram. Join units in rows; join rows to complete one block.

Aunt Vinah's Favorite

PIECING INSTRUCTIONS

1. Referring to the Piecing Diagram to piece one block, sew a lightest 2 to a darkest 2 along the diagonal to complete one corner unit; repeat for four corner units.

2. Join two medium and two dark 64 squares to complete a Four-Patch unit; sew two light and two lightest 5 triangles to each side to complete a side unit. Repeat for four side units.

3. Arrange the pieced units in rows with a darkest 1 square referring to the Piecing Diagram. Join units in rows; join rows to complete one block.

Beggar Block

PIECING INSTRUCTIONS

1. Referring to the Piecing Diagram to piece one block, sew a light 61 to each angled side of a dark 67; repeat for 16 units.

2. Join two units with a medium 8 to complete one unit; repeat for eight units.

3. Arrange the pieced units in rows with a lightest 1 square referring to the Piecing Diagram. Join units in rows; join rows to complete one block.

Album 2

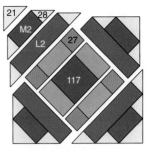

Templates needed:
21, 27, 28, 117, L2 & M2

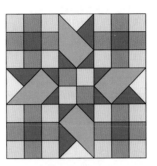

Arrowheads

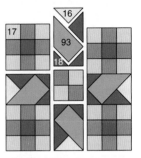

Templates needed:
16, 17, 18 & 93

Aunt Dinah

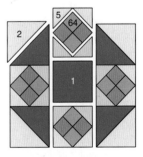

Templates needed:
1, 2, 3, 4 & 5

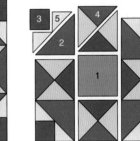
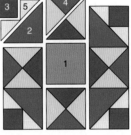

Aunt Vinah's Favorite

Templates needed:
1, 2, 5 & 64

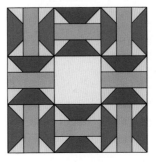

Beggar Block

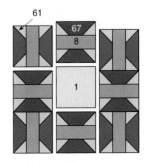

Templates needed:
1, 8, 61 & 67

Bridal Path

PIECING INSTRUCTIONS

1. Referring to the Piecing Diagram to piece one block, join five medium and four light 24 squares to make a Nine-Patch corner unit; repeat for four corner units.

2. Sew two dark 12 triangles to two adjacent sides of a lightest 14 to complete one side unit; repeat for four side units.

3. Sew a medium 32 to opposite sides of the dark 3. Sew a dark 24 to opposite ends of the remaining 32 pieces; sew to the dark 3.

4. Sew two each lightest 53 and lightest 65 pieces to the 3 unit to complete the center unit.

5. Arrange the pieced units in rows referring to the Piecing Diagram. Join units in rows; join rows to complete one block.

Bridal Path

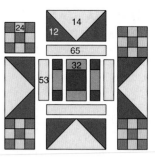
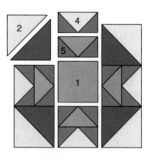

Templates needed:
3, 12, 14, 24, 32, 53 & 65

Capital T

PIECING INSTRUCTIONS

1. Referring to the Piecing Diagram to piece one block, sew a light 2 to a darkest 2 along the diagonal to complete one corner unit; repeat for four corner units.

2. Sew a dark 5 to two adjacent sides of a light 4; repeat for four units. Sew a dark 5 to two adjacent sides of a medium 4; repeat for four units. Join two units to complete a side unit; repeat for four side units.

3. Arrange the pieced units in rows with a medium 1 square referring to the Piecing Diagram. Join units in rows; join rows to complete one block.

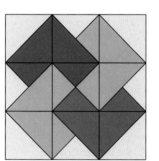

Capital T

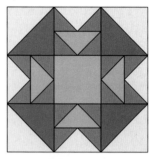

Templates needed:
1, 2, 4 & 5

Card Trick

PIECING INSTRUCTIONS

1. Referring to the Piecing Diagram to piece one block, sew a light 2 to a dark 2 along the diagonal to complete one corner unit; repeat for two corner units. Repeat with a light 2 and a medium 2 to complete two more corner units.

2. Sew a light 4 to a medium 4 on the short sides; add a dark 2 to the long side of the pieced unit to complete a side unit. Repeat for two side units. Repeat with light and dark 4 triangles and a medium 2 to complete two more side units.

3. Join two medium and two dark 4 triangles to complete the center unit.

4. Arrange the pieced units in rows referring to the Piecing Diagram. Join units in rows; join rows to complete one block.

Card Trick

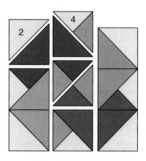

Templates needed:
2 & 4

Carpenter's Wheel

PIECING INSTRUCTIONS

1. Referring to the Piecing Diagram to piece one block, join four medium 40R and four dark 40 pieces to make a star shape; set in four light 59 squares to complete the center star unit.

2. Join three dark and three medium 40 and 40R pieces; set in three light and one dark 17 squares and two light 16 triangles to complete a corner unit; repeat for four corner units.

3. Sew the corner units into the star center to complete one block.

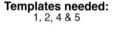

Carpenter's Wheel

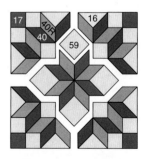

Templates needed:
16, 17, 40, 40R & 59

Carrie Nation

PIECING INSTRUCTIONS

1. Referring to the Piecing Diagram to piece one block, join two lightest and two dark 24 squares to make a Four-Patch unit; repeat for 10 units.

2. Join two Four-Patch units with two light 3 squares to make a corner unit; repeat for four corner units and one center unit.

3. Join two light and two medium 3 squares to make a side unit; repeat for four side units.

4. Arrange the pieced units in rows referring to the Piecing Diagram. Join units in rows; join rows to complete one block.

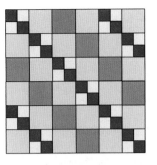

Carrie Nation

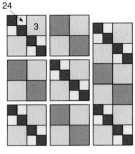

Templates needed:
3 & 24

Century of Progress

PIECING INSTRUCTIONS

1. Referring to the Piecing Diagram to piece one block, sew a light 95R to a medium 95; repeat for two units. Repeat with a medium 95R and a light 95 for two units.

2. Sew one of each unit to the sides of a dark O2 to complete block quarter; repeat for two quarters.

3. Repeat with light and darkest 95 and 95R pieces to make two more quarters.

4. Join the quarters to complete one block.

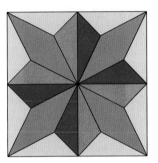

Century of Progress

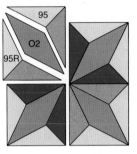

Templates needed:
95, 95R & O2

Contrary Wife

PIECING INSTRUCTIONS

1. Referring to the Piecing Diagram to piece one block, sew a light 5 to a dark 5 along the diagonal; repeat for 16 units.

2. Join two 5 units with a light and dark 3 square to make a corner unit; repeat for four corner units.

3. Sew a medium 5 to two adjacent sides of a light 4. Join two 5 units and sew to the 4-5 unit to complete a side unit; repeat for four side units.

4. Arrange the pieced units in rows with a dark 1 square referring to the Piecing Diagram. Join units in rows; join rows to complete one block.

Contrary Wife

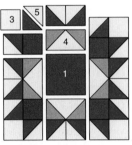

Templates needed:
1, 3, 4 & 5

Country Village

PIECING INSTRUCTIONS

1. Referring to the Piecing Diagram to piece one block, sew a dark P2 to a light 13; set in a medium 41 to complete a side unit; repeat for four side units.

2. Join the side units with five darkest 13 squares using partial and set-in seams to complete one block.

Country Village

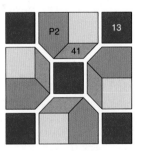

Templates needed:
13, 41 & P2

Dinah's Choice

PIECING INSTRUCTIONS

1. Referring to the Piecing Diagram to piece one block, sew a lightest C2 to a dark C2 along the diagonal; repeat for four units. Join the four units to make a pinwheel center.

2. Sew a medium Z2 to each side of the pinwheel center. Sew a light 89 to each side of this pieced unit to complete the center unit.

3. Sew a dark B2 and BR2 to a lightest A2; repeat for eight units.

4. Join two A-B units on the A ends with a darkest 59; sew a light 26 to one side to make a corner unit; repeat for four corner units. Sew one of these corner units to opposite sides of the center unit.

5. Sew a darkest 16 triangle to the B ends of the remaining corner units to make large corner units; sew these units to the pieced center to complete one block.

Dinah's Choice

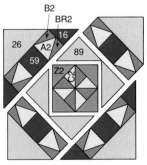

Templates needed:
16, 26, 59, 89, A2,
B2, BR2, C2 & Z2

Dolly Madison Star

PIECING INSTRUCTIONS

1. Referring to the Piecing Diagram to piece one block, sew a light 54 to a medium 54 along the diagonal; repeat for 12 units.

2. Sew a light 54 to two adjacent medium sides of four 54 units to make light units. Sew a medium 54 to two adjacent light sides of eight 54 units to make medium units.

3. Join two medium units with one light unit and a lightest 4 to complete one side unit; repeat for four side units.

4. Join four light and five dark 68 squares to complete a Nine-Patch center unit.

5. Arrange the pieced units in rows with four lightest 1 squares referring to the Piecing Diagram. Join units in rows; join rows to complete one block.

Dolly Madison Star

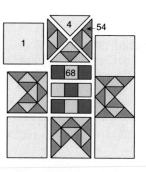

Templates needed:
1, 4, 54 & 68

Emma C

PIECING INSTRUCTIONS

1. Referring to the Piecing Diagram to piece one block, sew a dark S2 to opposite sides of a dark 63. Sew a dark T2 to opposite straight sides of a dark S2; repeat for two units. Sew these units to the remaining sides of the 63 square to complete the center unit.

2. Sew a dark 8 between two medium 8 pieces to complete a side unit; repeat for four side units.

3. Sew a medium 2 to a light 2 along the diagonal to complete a corner unit; repeat for four corner units.

4. Arrange the pieced units in rows referring to the Piecing Diagram. Join units in rows; join rows to complete one block.

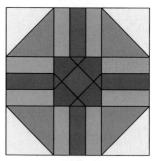

Emma C

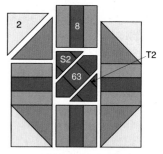

Templates needed:
2, 8, 63, S2 & T2

Eva's Delight

PIECING INSTRUCTIONS

1. Referring to the Piecing Diagram to piece one block, sew a dark 64 to one end of a medium 115; repeat for two units. Join the two units with a medium 113 and add a light 12 to complete a corner unit. Repeat for four corner units.

2. Join five light and four dark 64 squares to make a Nine-Patch center unit.

3. Join two corner units with the center unit.

4. Sew a light 14 triangle to two opposite sides of each remaining corner unit; sew these units to the remaining sides of the pieced center unit to complete one block.

Eva's Delight

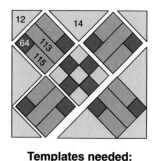

Templates needed:
12, 14, 64, 113 & 115

Flower Basket

PIECING INSTRUCTIONS

1. Referring to the block drawing to piece one block, cut a 12 1/2" x 12 1/2" lightest square; fold and crease to mark center.

2. Prepare U2, V2, W2, X2 and Y2 pieces for appliqué, adding a seam allowance when cutting for hand appliqué.

3. Position pieces on creased background and appliqué in place to complete one block.

Flower Basket

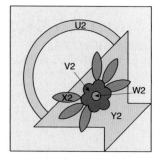

Templates needed:
U2, V2, W2, X2 & Y2

Follow the Leader

PIECING INSTRUCTIONS

1. Referring to the Piecing Diagram to piece one block, sew a medium 5 to a dark 5 along the diagonal; sew between a medium and light 3.

2. Sew a medium 5 to a light 5 along the diagonal; sew to the end of a medium 6.

3. Join the two pieced units with a dark 86 to make a quarter block; repeat for four quarter blocks.

4. Join the quarter blocks to complete one block.

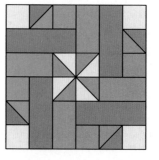

Follow the Leader

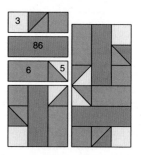

Templates needed:
3, 5, 6 & 86

Fort Sumter

PIECING INSTRUCTIONS

1. Referring to the Piecing Diagram to piece one block, join four medium 2 triangles to complete the block center.

2. Sew a dark Q2 to opposite sides of the center; sew a medium 64 square to each end of the remaining Q2 pieces. Sew these pieces to the remaining sides of the center.

3. Sew a dark 119 between two light 4 triangles to complete one corner unit; repeat for four corner units.

4. Sew a corner unit to each side of the pieced center unit to complete one block.

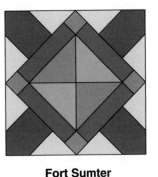

Fort Sumter

Templates needed:
2, 4, 64, 119 & Q2

Four Crowns

PIECING INSTRUCTIONS

1. Referring to the Piecing Diagram to piece one block, sew a lightest 5 to a medium 5 along the diagonal; repeat for 5 units. Join two units to make a row; join three units to make a row.

2. Sew a light 2 to a dark 2 along the diagonal.

3. Sew the two- and three-unit 5 rows with the 2 unit to complete one quarter unit; repeat for four quarter units.

4. Join the quarter units to complete one block.

Four Crowns

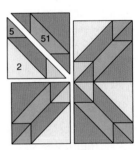

Templates needed:
2 & 5

Gretchen

PIECING INSTRUCTIONS

1. Referring to the Piecing Diagram to piece one block, sew a medium and light 5 to the angled ends of a dark 51; sew a lightest 2 to the pieced unit. Repeat for four units.

2. Sew a dark 5 triangle to each angled end of a medium 51; sew a dark 2 to the pieced unit. Repeat for four units.

3. Join two opposite-color units to complete one quarter block; repeat for four quarters.

4. Join the four quarters to complete one block.

Gretchen

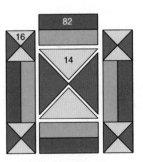

Templates needed:
2, 5, & 51

Hobson's Kiss

PIECING INSTRUCTIONS

1. Referring to the Piecing Diagram to piece one block, join two light and two dark 16 triangles to make a corner unit; repeat for four corner units.

2. Sew a medium 82 to a dark 82 to make a side unit; repeat for four side units.

3. Join two light and two dark 14 triangles to make a center unit.

4. Arrange the pieced units in rows referring to the Piecing Diagram. Join units in rows; join rows to complete one block.

Hobson's Kiss

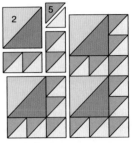

Templates needed:
14, 16 & 82

Hull's Victory

PIECING INSTRUCTIONS

1. Referring to the Piecing Diagram to piece one block, sew a medium 16 to two adjacent sides of a medium 59; sew a lightest 12 to the remaining two sides of the 59 unit to complete one side unit. Repeat for four side units.

2. Sew a light 18 to two adjacent sides of a medium 16; repeat for four units. Sew one unit to two opposite sides of the medium 13. Sew a dark 17 to each end of the remaining two units; sew to the remaining sides of the center square to complete the center unit.

3. Arrange the pieced units in rows with the dark 13 corner squares referring to the Piecing Diagram. Join units in rows; join rows to complete one block.

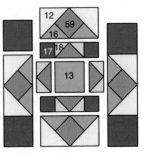

Hull's Victory

Templates needed:
12, 13, 16, 17, 18 & 59

Indian Puzzle

PIECING INSTRUCTIONS

1. Referring to the Piecing Diagram to piece one block, sew a lightest 5 to a medium 5 along the diagonal; repeat for eight units. Join two units with a light and medium 3 squares to complete one corner unit; repeat for four corner units.

2. Sew a light 5 to two adjacent sides of a dark 4; repeat with dark 5 and lightest 4 triangles. Join the two pieced units to complete a side unit; repeat for four side units.

3. Sew a dark 5 to each side of the medium 7 to complete the block center.

4. Arrange the pieced units in rows referring to the Piecing Diagram. Join units in rows; join rows to complete one block.

Ladies Aid Album

PIECING INSTRUCTIONS

1. Referring to the Piecing Diagram to piece one block, sew a dark 5 to adjacent short sides of a medium 4; sew a light 6 to the unit to complete one side unit. Repeat for four side units.

2. Arrange the pieced units in rows with four medium and one light 1 square referring to the Piecing Diagram. Join units in rows; join rows to complete one block.

Melon Patch

PIECING INSTRUCTIONS

1. Referring to the Piecing Diagram to piece one block, sew a medium D2 to each side of a dark E2, centering D2 on E2 and clipping inside curves on D2 pieces to fit; repeat for two units. Repeat with dark D2 and medium E2 pieces.

2. Join the four units to complete one block.

Mother's Dream

PIECING INSTRUCTIONS

1. Referring to the Piecing Diagram to piece one block, sew a light 61 to a medium 61 along the diagonal; repeat for 24 units.

2. Join three 61 units to make a row; repeat for eight rows. Join two rows with a medium 8 to make a side unit; repeat for four side units.

3. Sew a light 5 to each side of a dark 7 to make a unit; repeat for one center and four corner units.

4. Arrange the pieced units in rows referring to the Piecing Diagram. Join units in rows; join rows to complete one block.

New Barrister Block

PIECING INSTRUCTIONS

1. Referring to the Piecing Diagram to piece one block, sew a light 18 to a dark 18 along the diagonal; repeat for eight units.

2. Sew a pieced unit together with one medium, two light and four dark 17 squares to make a corner unit; repeat for two corner units.

3. Sew a light 18 to a medium 18 along the diagonal; repeat for 24 units.

4. Join four pieced units with four dark and one medium 17 squares to make a corner unit; repeat for two corner units.

5. Join four pieced units with one dark/light unit and one light 17 to make a side unit; repeat for four side units.

6. Arrange the pieced units in rows with the light 13 square referring to the Piecing Diagram. Join units in rows; join rows to complete one block.

Indian Puzzle

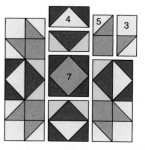

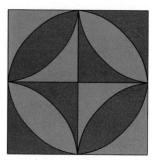

Templates needed:
3, 4, 5 & 7

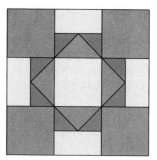

Ladies Aid Album

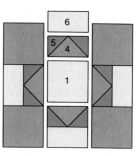

Templates needed:
1, 4, 5 & 6

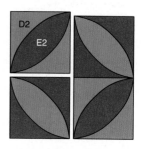

Melon Patch

Templates needed:
D2 & E2

Mother's Dream

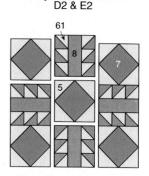

Templates needed:
5, 7, 8 & 61

New Barrister Block

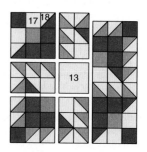

Templates needed:
13, 17 & 18

Next-Door Neighbor 2

PIECING INSTRUCTIONS

1. Referring to the Piecing Diagram to piece one block, sew a lightest 12 to one angled end and medium 12 to the opposite angled end of a darkest 112 to make an outside unit; repeat for four outside units.

2. Sew a lightest 12 to a dark 12 along the diagonal; repeat for two units. Sew a light 12 to a lightest 12; repeat for two units. Join the units to complete the center unit.

3. Sew an outside unit to each side of the center unit, sewing the remainder of the first seam last to complete one block.

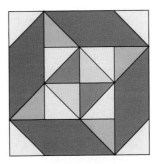

Next-Door Neighbor 2

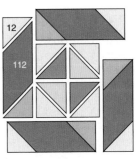

Templates needed:
12 & 112

President Carter

PIECING INSTRUCTIONS

1. Referring to the Piecing Diagram to piece one block, sew a light 10 to a dark 10; repeat for four units. Sew a light 10R to a medium 10R; repeat for four units.

2. Join one of each unit combination to complete one side unit; repeat for four side units.

3. Join two light and two dark 4 triangles to complete the center unit.

4. Arrange the side units with the center unit and four dark 1 squares in rows referring to the Piecing Diagram. Join units in rows; join rows to complete one block.

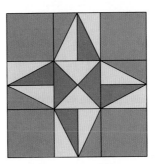

President Carter

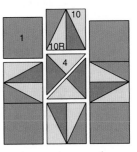

Templates needed:
1, 4, 10 & 10R

President's Choice

PIECING INSTRUCTIONS

1. Referring to the Piecing Diagram to piece one block, sew a medium 18 to a medium 102 to a light 12; repeat for four corner units.

2. Sew a dark 18 to a medium 102; repeat. Sew a unit to each angled side of a lightest 14; repeat for four side units.

3. Sew a medium 18 to a medium 102; repeat for four units.

4. Sew a dark 16 to a light 16 along the diagonal; repeat. Join these units with two light 59 squares; add an 18-102 unit to each side to complete the center unit.

5. Arrange the pieced units in rows referring to the Piecing Diagram. Join units in rows; join rows to complete one block.

President's Choice

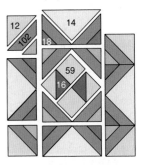

Templates needed:
12, 14, 16, 18, 59 & 102

Road to the White House

PIECING INSTRUCTIONS

1. Referring to the Piecing Diagram to piece one block, join two light and two dark 3 squares to make a Four-Patch unit; repeat for three units.

2. Sew a medium 2 to a darkest 2 along the diagonal to make a side unit; repeat for four side units.

3. Arrange the pieced units in rows with two lightest 1 squares referring to the Piecing Diagram. Join units in rows; join rows to complete one block.

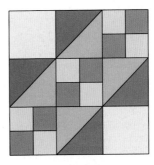

Road to the White House

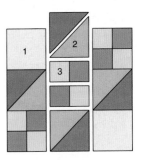

Templates needed:
1, 2 & 3

Secret Drawer

PIECING INSTRUCTIONS

1. Referring to the Piecing Diagram to piece one block, sew one light, one lightest and two dark R2 pieces to a dark 64; repeat for four units.

2. Sew a medium 12 to the light side of each unit.

3. Sew two units to opposite sides of the medium 19 square.

4. Sew a light 14 to the dark sides of each remaining two R2-64-12 units; sew these units to the remaining sides of 19 to complete one block.

Secret Drawer

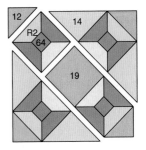

Templates needed:
12, 14, 19, 64 & R2

Silver Lane

PIECING INSTRUCTIONS

1. Referring to the Piecing Diagram to piece one block, sew a light 5 to a dark 5 along the diagonal; repeat for four units. Join the four units to complete a pinwheel center.

2. Sew a darkest 6 to opposite sides of the center unit; sew a medium 3 to each end of the remaining two 6 pieces. Sew one of these units to the remaining sides of the center unit.

3. Sew a dark 38 and 38R to two adjacent sides of a medium 4; sew a medium 5 to the remaining sides of the 38 pieces to complete one side unit; repeat for four side units.

4. Arrange the pieced units in rows with the lightest 3 squares referring to the Piecing Diagram. Join units in rows; join rows to complete one block.

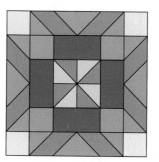

Silver Lane

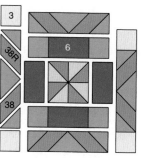

Templates needed:
3, 4, 5, 6, 38 & 38R

Single Wedding Ring

PIECING INSTRUCTIONS

1. Referring to the Piecing Diagram to piece one block, sew one medium and three dark 5 triangles to a lightest 7 to complete a corner unit; repeat for four corner units.

2. Sew a medium 6 to a light 6 to complete a side unit; repeat for four side units.

3. Arrange the pieced units in rows with one lightest 1 square referring to the Piecing Diagram. Join units in rows; join rows to complete one block.

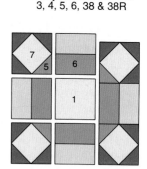

Single Wedding Ring

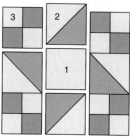

Templates needed:
1, 5, 6, & 7

Square & Half-Square

PIECING INSTRUCTIONS

1. Referring to the Piecing Diagram to piece one block, join two dark and two light 3 squares to make a Four-Patch corner unit; repeat for four corner units.

2. Sew a light 2 to a medium 2 along the diagonal to make one side unit; repeat for four side units.

3. Arrange the pieced units in rows with one light 1 square referring to the Piecing Diagram. Join units in rows; join rows to complete one block.

Square & Half-Square

Templates needed:
1, 2 & 3

Swing in the Center

PIECING INSTRUCTIONS

1. Referring to the Piecing Diagram to piece one block, sew a light 5 to two adjacent sides of a medium 4; sew a medium 5 to each end and a light 4 to the 5 side to complete one side unit; repeat for four side units.

2. Sew a medium 7 to a dark 119 to make a side row; repeat for four side rows.

3. Sew a side unit to each side of a side row to make one large corner unit; repeat for two large corner units.

4. Sew a side row to each side of a darkest 7 to complete the center row.

5. Join the two large corner units with the center row to complete one block.

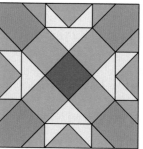

Swing in the Center

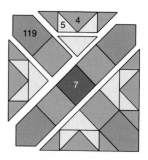

Templates needed:
4, 5, 7 & 119

Tall Ship

PIECING INSTRUCTIONS

1. Referring to the Piecing Diagram to piece one block, sew a light 5 to a medium 5 along the diagonal; repeat for 13 units.

2. Join three units to make the center row; join four units to make a side row and join five units to make the opposite side row.

3. Sew a medium 3 to the four-unit row and a medium 6 to the three-unit row. Join the pieced rows to complete the center sail section of the ship.

Continued on page 46

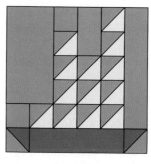

Tall Ship

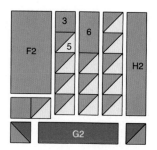

Templates needed:
3, 5, 6, F2, G2 & H2

Treasure Chest

PIECING INSTRUCTIONS

1. Referring to the Piecing Diagram to piece one block, sew a lightest 5 to a dark 51; repeat for four units.

2. Sew a light 5 to a dark 51; repeat for four units.

3. Join one of each color version of the 5-51 units to complete one corner unit; repeat for four corner units.

4. Join one light and three medium 4 triangles to make a side unit; repeat for four side units.

5. Arrange the pieced units in rows with one medium 1 square referring to the Piecing Diagram. Join units in rows; join rows to complete one block.

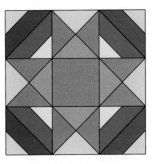

Treasure Chest

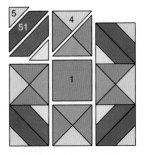

Templates needed:
1, 4, 5 & 51

Twin Darts

PIECING INSTRUCTIONS

1. Referring to the Piecing Diagram to piece one block, sew a dark 70 between the medium N2 and NR2 pieces; add a dark 14 to complete a side unit. Repeat for two side units. Repeat with medium N2 and N2R pieces and dark 70 and 14 pieces to complete two more side units.

2. Join the side units to complete one block.

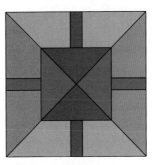

Twin Darts

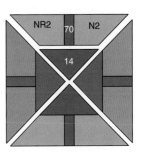

Templates needed:
14, 70, N2 & NR2

Weathervane Variation

PIECING INSTRUCTIONS

1. Referring to the Piecing Diagram to piece one block, join one light and three dark 54 triangles to make a square unit; repeat for eight square units.

2. Join two square units with one dark and one light 3 square to make a corner unit; repeat for four corner units.

3. Sew a light 5 to two adjacent sides of a medium 4; sew a medium 6 to the 4 side of the pieced unit to complete a side unit. Repeat for four side units.

4. Arrange the pieced units in rows with one lightest 1 square referring to the Piecing Diagram. Join units in rows; join rows to complete one block.

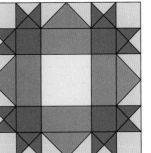

Weathervane Variation

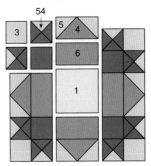

Templates needed:
1, 3, 4, 5, 6 & 54

Wheel of Fortune

PIECING INSTRUCTIONS

1. Referring to the Piecing Diagram to piece one block, sew a light 57 to opposite sides of the dark 34 to make the center row.

2. Sew a dark 13 to opposite ends of a light 57 to make a side row; repeat.

3. Sew a side row to opposite sides of the center row. Prepare J2 and K2 pieces; appliqué in place to complete one block.

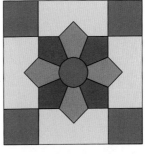

Wheel of Fortune

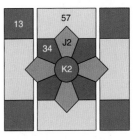

Templates needed:
13, 34, 57, J2 & K2

Yankee Puzzle

PIECING INSTRUCTIONS

1. Referring to the Piecing Diagram to piece one block, sew a light 12 to a dark 12 along the diagonal; repeat for four units. Sew a medium 12 to a dark 12 along the diagonal; repeat for four units.

2. Sew a dark 12 to two adjacent sides of a medium 14; repeat for four units.

3. Join two 12 units with a 12-14 unit to complete one quarter block; repeat for four quarter blocks.

4. Join the quarter blocks to complete one block.

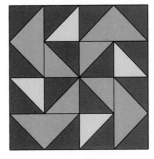

Yankee Puzzle

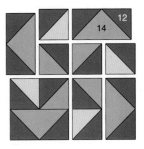

Templates needed:
12 & 14

The Good Old Days Sampler
Continued from page 31

14. Join a burgundy/cream and rose/cream strip as shown in Figure 5; repeat for two strips. Press seams in one direction.

Figure 5
Join a burgundy/cream and
rose/cream strip as shown.

15. Mark the center of each strip; mark the center of the top and bottom of the pieced top. Center and pin a pieced strip to the pieced top with the rose/cream strip on the inside; stitch in place. Press seam toward strips; trim excess strip even with pieced top on ends to complete the quilt top.

16. Sandwich batting between completed top and prepared backing piece; pin or baste layers together to hold flat.

17. Quilt as desired by hand or machine. ***Note:*** *The quilt shown was machine-quilted in an overall clamshell design using cream quilting thread.*

18. When quilting is complete, trim edges even and remove pins or basting. Bind edges with self-made or purchased binding to finish. ❖

Melon Patch Runner
Continued from page 33

shorter to fit different size tables. To determine the size you need, measure your table, subtract 12" and divide the remainder in half to get the length needed for your runner. If you want the runner to hang over the edge of the table, add at least 6" to each side.

8. Sew a runner piece to each side of the pieced block.

Prepare a backing piece from the quilted muslin using the pieced top as a pattern; pin the layers together.

9. Place a large dinner plate at each end and trace shape to make rounded corners; trim excess.

10. Machine-quilt straight lines along stripes of runner fabric and around the melon shapes on the center block.

11. Bind edges with black wide bias tape to finish. ❖

Tall Ship
Continued from page 44

4. Sew a medium 3 to a pieced 5 unit; sew this to one short edge of the medium F2. Sew this to the four-unit side of the sail section and the medium H2 to the five-unit side to complete the top section of the ship.

5. Sew a medium 5 to a dark 5; repeat. Sew a unit to the ends of the dark G2. Sew to the bottom of the ship section to complete one block.

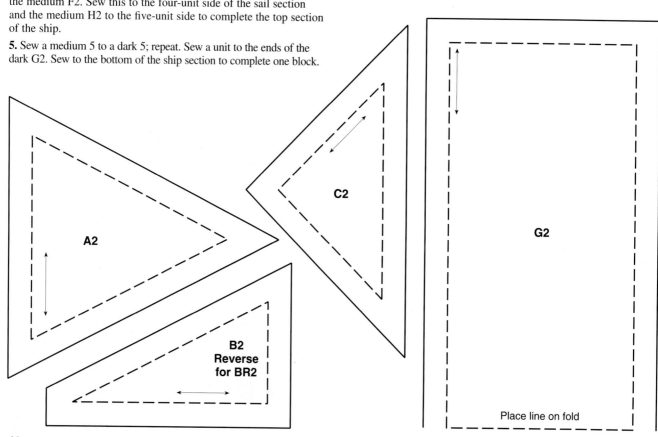

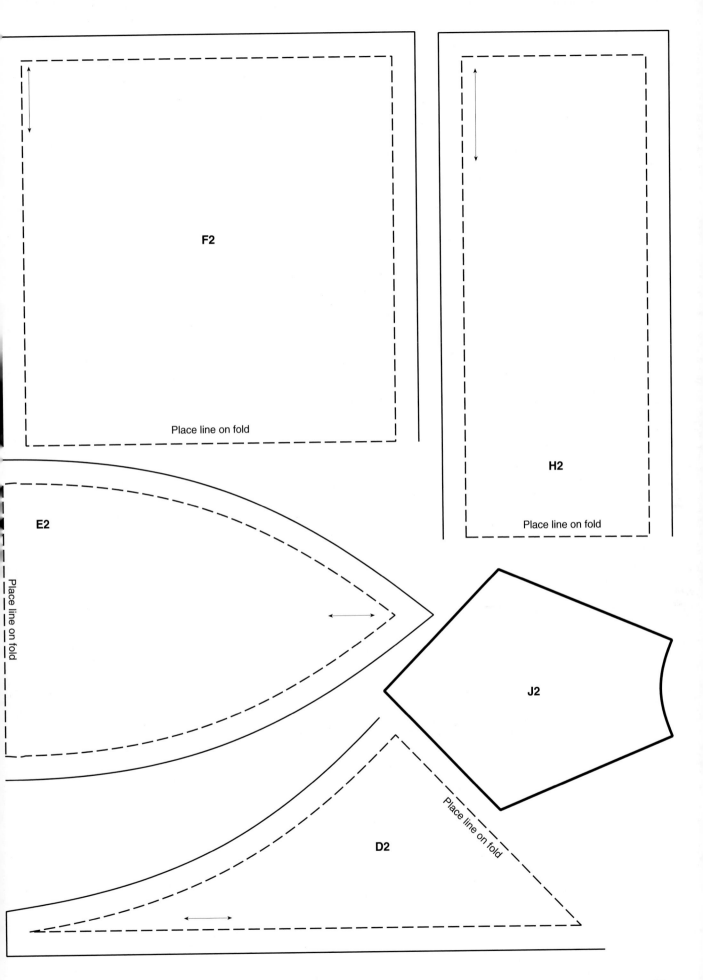

F2

Place line on fold

H2

Place line on fold

E2

Place line on fold

J2

D2

Place line on fold

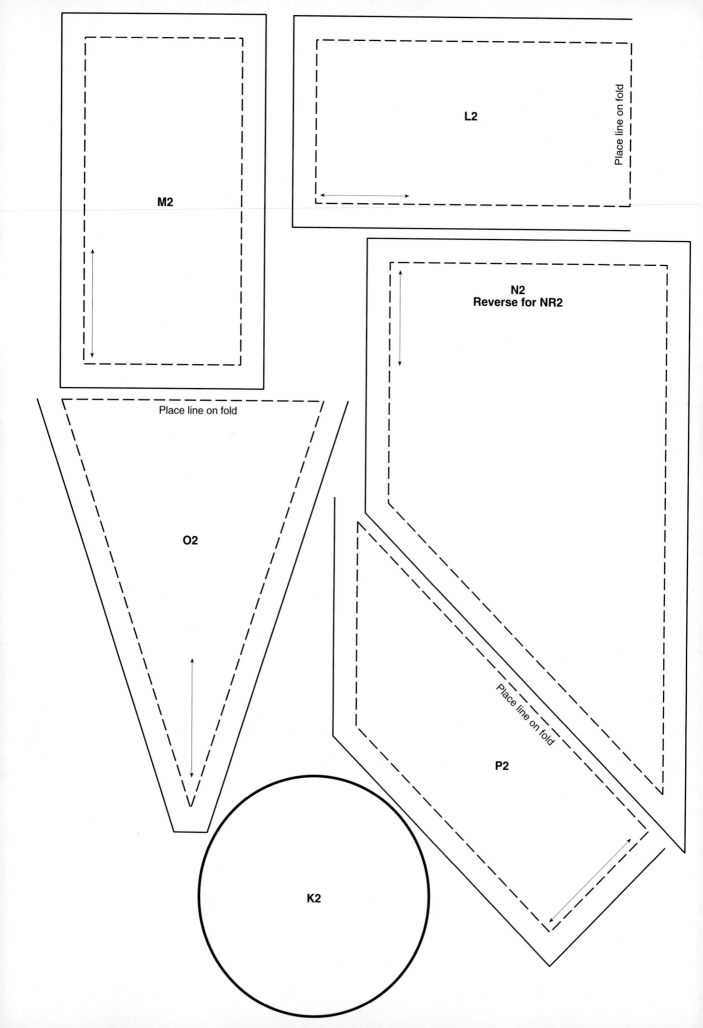

U2

Place line on fold

Q2

Place line on fold

S2

R2

Place line on fold

X2

V2

W2

Place line on fold

Z2

T2

Y2

In the Garden

*You're sure to
create a lovely garden
quilt with the blocks
in this chapter.
Whether it has been
named for a flower
or just looks like a flower,
every block design
is fun to stitch.
Not everyone has
a green thumb, but we
can all add life and
beauty to our homes
with lovely, vibrant
quilt blocks.*

In the Garden Sampler

Design by Sue Harvey

Take a walk through a quilt garden using flower theme blocks in a variety of colors and setting blocks that resemble stepping stones in a grassy path.

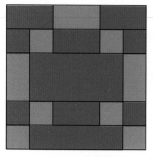

Edge Setting
12" x 12" Block

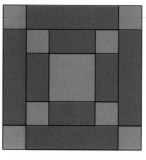

Inside Setting
12" x 12" Block

PROJECT SPECIFICATIONS
Quilt Size: 76" x 76"
Block Size: 12" x 12"
Number of Blocks: 25

FABRIC & BATTING
- Scraps light, medium and dark pink, peach, yellow, rose and mauve prints
- Scraps light and dark red, purple and periwinkle prints
- 1/4 yard each light and dark green prints
- 1 yard tan print
- 1 3/4 yards cream print
- 2 yards floral print
- 3 yards medium green print
- Backing 80" x 80"
- Batting 80" x 80"

SUPPLIES & TOOLS
- All-purpose thread to match fabrics
- Basic sewing tools and supplies, rotary cutter, mat and ruler

INSTRUCTIONS
1. The following blocks and fabric colors are used in the sample quilt shown. Row 1: Sue's Delight—mauve, Mystery Flower Garden—rose, Prairie Flower—peach; Row 2: Wedding Bouquet—red, Triple Link Chain—periwinkle; Row 3: Flowering Star—purple, Squash Blossom—yellow, Dogtooth Violet—purple; Row 4: Wildflower—pink, Diamond Star—red; Row 5: Whirling Square—peach, Double Aster—rose, Bouquet—mauve.

Note: You may choose any 13 blocks from this chapter or from any other chapters in this book.

2. Cut pieces for blocks using fabrics listed above, referring to the Placement Diagram and piecing diagrams given with each block for positioning of colors. Piece blocks referring to the instructions and colored piecing diagrams given with each block. *Note: The 43–48 units in the Bouquet block were inadvertantly positioned differently in the sampler than in the colored piecing diagram.*

3. Square up blocks to 12 1/2" x 12 1/2".

4. Cut the following fabric-width strips: tan print—eight 2 1/2" and two 4 1/2"; cream print—two 1 1/4", ten 1 1/2", one 2 7/8" and four 6 1/2"; floral print—one 1 1/4", nine 1 1/2" and five 2 1/2"; and medium green print—one 1 1/4", five 1 1/2", four 2 1/2", four 4 1/2" and three 8 1/2".

5. Combine the fabric-width strips in the order specified to make strip sets and segments as follows and as shown in Figure 1:

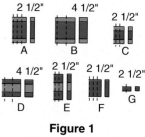

Figure 1
Make strip sets and segments as shown.

A—2 1/2" tan—8 1/2" green—2 1/2" tan. Cut into 2 1/2" segments. You will need 16 A segments.

B—2 1/2" tan—8 1/2" green—2 1/2" tan. Cut into 4 1/2" segments. You will need eight B segments.

C—2 1/2" tan—4 1/2" green—2 1/2" tan; make two strip sets. Cut into 2 1/2" segments. You will need 24 C segments.

D—2 1/2" green—4 1/2" tan—2 1/2" green. Cut into 4 1/2" segments. You will need four D segments.

E—4 1/2" green—4 1/2" tan—4 1/2" green. Cut into 2 1/2" segments. You will need eight E segments.

F—Cut the remaining 8 1/2" green strip into 2 1/2" segments. You will need eight F segments.

G—Cut the remaining 2 1/2" green strips into

In the Garden Sampler
Placement Diagram
76" x 76"

2 1/2" square segments. You will need 32 G squares.

6. To piece one Inside Setting block, sew a C segment to opposite sides of a D segment as shown in Figure 2. Sew an F segment to opposite sides of the C-D unit; add an A segment to the remaining sides of the C-D unit to complete one block again referring to Figure 2. Repeat for four blocks.

7. To piece one Edge Setting block, sew a G square to each end of two C segments as shown in Figure 3. Sew a C-G segment to opposite sides of a B segment; add an A segment to one side of the

B-C-G unit and an E segment to the opposite side to complete one block, again referring to Figure 3. Repeat for eight blocks.

Figure 2
Join segments to
complete 1 Inside
Setting block as shown.

Figure 3
Join segments to
complete 1 Edge Setting
block as shown.

8. Arrange Edge and Inside Setting blocks with pieced blocks in rows as shown in Figure 4; join blocks in rows. Join rows to complete the pieced center.

Figure 4
Arrange Edge and Inside Setting blocks with pieced blocks in rows.

9. Cut and piece two strips each 2 1/2" x 60 1/2" and 2 1/2" x 64 1/2" green print. Sew the shorter strips to opposite sides and longer strips to the remaining sides of the pieced center; press seams toward strips.

10. Join fabric-width strips cut in step 4 to make a strip set as follows and as shown in Figure 5: 2 1/2" floral—1 1/2" cream—1 1/2" floral—1 1/2" cream—1 1/2" green. Repeat for five strip sets.

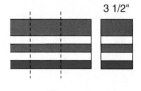

3 1/2"

Figure 5
Make a strip set as shown.

11. Cut the strips sets into 40 segments 3 1/2"-wide and eight segments 4 1/2" wide to make rail segments.

12. Cut the 6 1/2" fabric-width cream print strips into 2 1/2" segments. You will need 52 cream segments.

13. Cut the remaining 1 1/2" fabric-width floral print strips into 1 1/2" square segments. You will need 112 floral H squares.

14. Draw a diagonal line on the wrong side of each floral H square. Place an H square on one corner of a cream segment as shown in Figure 6; stitch on the marked line. Trim seam allowance to 1/4" and press open as shown in Figure 7.

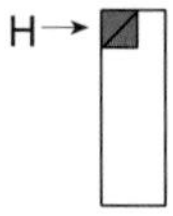

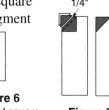

H→

1/4"

Figure 6
Place an H square on 1 corner of a cream segment.

Figure 7
Trim seam allowance and press open.

15. Repeat on adjacent corner to complete one fence post unit as shown in Figure 8. Repeat to

make 52 fence post units. Set aside remaining floral H squares.

16. Join five 3 1/2"-wide rail units with six fence post units to make an I strip as shown in Figure 9; repeat to make eight I strips.

Figure 8
Complete 1 fence post unit as shown.

Figure 9
Join units to make an I strip as shown.

17. Join two 4 1/2"-wide rail units with one fence post unit to make a J strip as shown in Figure 10; repeat to make four J strips.

J

Figure 10
Join units to make a J strip as shown.

18. Join two I strips with one J strip to make a border strip as shown in Figure 11; repeat to make four border strips.

I J I

Figure 11
Join 2 I strips with 1 J strip to make a border strip.

19. Sew a strip to opposite sides of the pieced and bordered center referring to the Placement Diagram for positioning of strips.

20. Cut 2 7/8" fabric-width cream print strip cut in step 2 into four 2 7/8" x 2 7/8" squares. Cut each square on one diagonal to make K triangles.

21. Place a floral H square on corner of K as shown in Figure 12; stitch, trim and press open as in step 14. Repeat to make eight H-K units.

22. Join fabric-width strips cut in step 2 to make a strip set as follows and as shown in Figure 13: 1 1/4" cream—1 1/4" floral—1 1/4" cream—1 1/4" green.

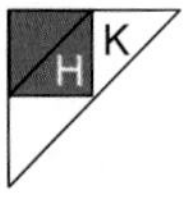

H K

Figure 12
Place an H square on K as shown.

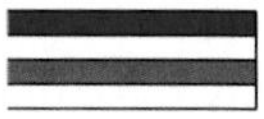

Figure 13
Make a strip set as shown.

23. Prepare templates for pattern pieces given transferring lines on A piece to template; cut B, C and D pieces as directed on each piece.

24. Place A template on strip set aligning lines on template with seam lines as shown in Figure 14; cut four A pieces.

25. To piece one corner square, sew C to B and add

D as shown in Figure 15. Sew an H-K unit to opposite sides of the pieced unit, again referring to Figure 15. Sew A to the remaining B side of the pieced unit to complete one corner square; repeat to make four corner squares.

Figure 14
Place A template on strip set aligning lines on template with seam lines.

Figure 15
Join pieces to complete 1 corner square as shown.

26. Sew a corner square to opposite ends of the remaining pieced border strip as shown in Figure 16; sew a strip to the remaining sides of the pieced center to complete the top.

Figure 16
Sew a corner square to opposite ends of a pieced border strip.

27. Sandwich batting between the completed top and prepared backing piece; pin or baste to hold.

28. Hand- or machine-quilt as desired. *Note: The sample shown was professionally machine-quilted using thread to match fabrics and in a variety of quilting designs.*

29. Trim edges even with top. Cut eight strips 2 1/2" by fabric width floral print. Join strips on short ends to make a long strip. Fold strip in half with wrong sides together; press to make binding strip. Bind edges of quilt to finish. ❖

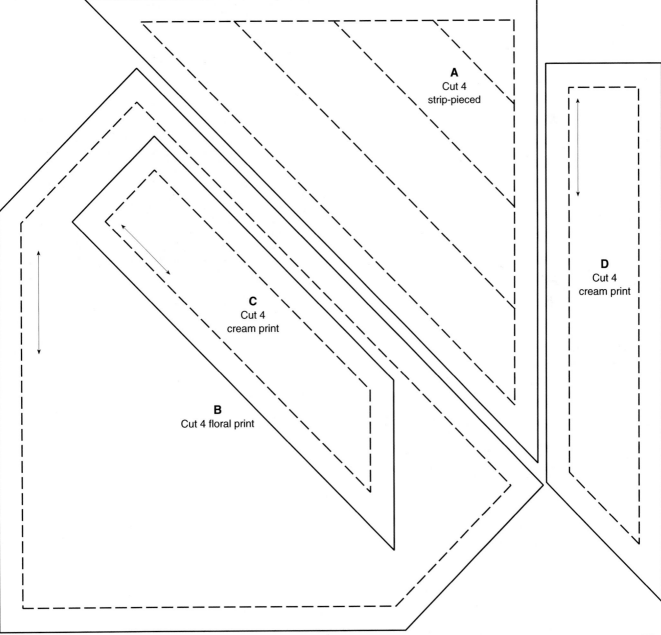

A
Cut 4
strip-pieced

D
Cut 4
cream print

C
Cut 4
cream print

B
Cut 4 floral print

In the Garden Pillow Sham

Design by Sue Harvey

Us any block in a pillow sham to match your quilt.

PROJECT NOTE
One sham was made as a sample project with the Tulips pattern given on page 60. Materials listed below are for one sham only. To make two, double the yardage given for each fabric and prepare two each lining and batting pieces.

PROJECT SPECIFICATIONS
Sham Size: 20" x 28" (without flange)

Block Size: 12" x 12"

Number of Blocks: 1

FABRIC & BATTING
- Scraps light, medium and dark pinks, light and dark greens and yellow prints for block piecing
- 1/4 yard cream print
- 3/8 yard medium green print
- 1 5/8 yards floral print
- Lining 24" x 32"
- Batting 24" x 32"

SUPPLIES & TOOLS
- All-purpose thread to match fabrics
- Dark green and cream machine-quilting thread
- Basting spray
- Basic sewing tools and supplies, rotary cutter, mat and ruler

INSTRUCTIONS
1. Complete one 12" block of your choice.

In the Garden Pillow Sham
Placement Diagram
20" x 28"
(without flange)

2. Cut four squares green print and five squares floral print 5 1/4" x 5 1/4"; subcut each square on both diagonals to make A triangles. You will need 16 green and 18 floral A triangles.

3. Cut two squares floral print and four squares green print 2 7/8" x 2 7/8"; subcut each square on one diagonal to make B triangles. You will need four floral and eight green B triangles.

4. Cut four squares floral print 2 1/2" x 2 1/2" for C.

5. Cut two strips cream print each 2 1/2" x 16 1/2" for D, 2 1/2" x 24 1/2" for E and 2 1/2" x 20 1/2" for F.

6. Join three floral A triangles with two green A triangles to make a strip as shown in Figure 1; repeat for four strips.

Figure 1
Join 3 floral and 2 green A
triangles to make a strip; sew a
green B triangle to each end.

7. Sew a green B triangle to each end of each pieced strip, again referring to Figure 1.

8. Sew a strip to opposite sides of the pieced block as shown in Figure 2. Sew a C square to opposite ends of the remaining pieced strips; sew to the remaining sides of the pieced block.

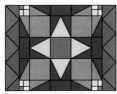

Figure 2
Sew a strip to opposite
sides of the pieced block.

9. Join three floral A triangles with four green A triangles to make a strip as shown Figure 3; repeat for two strips.

Figure 3
Join 3 floral and 4 green A
triangles to make a strip; sew a
floral B triangle to each end.

10. Sew a floral B triangle to each end of each pieced strip, again referring to Figure 3.

11. Sew D to the green side of each pieced strip as shown in Figure 4. Sew a resulting strip to opposite short sides of the bordered block referring to the Placement Diagram for positioning of strips.

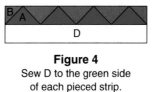

Figure 4
Sew D to the green side
of each pieced strip.

12. Sew E to opposite long sides of the bordered block; press seams toward E. Sew F to the remaining sides of the bordered block to complete the pieced top.

13. Spray one side of batting with basting spray; place on prepared lining piece and smooth. Spray remaining side of batting; place pieced top on batting and smooth.

14. Hand- or machine-quilt as desired. *Note: The sample shown was machine-quilted in the ditch of seams using dark green machine-quilting thread and 1/4" from seams in the cream strips using cream machine-quilting thread.*

15. When quilting is complete, trim edges even with top.

16. Cut two strips each green print 1" x 26" and 1" x 34 1/2". Cut two strips each floral print 3 1/2" x 26 1/2" and 3 1/2" x 34 1/2".

17. Fold each green print strip in half along length with wrong sides together; press. Place a folded strip on a same-length floral print strip with raw edges aligned as shown in Figure 5; baste in place 1/8" from raw edge. Repeat with all strips.

Figure 5
Place a folded strip on a
floral print strip with raw
edges aligned.

18. Sew the longer layered strips to opposite long sides of the pieced center and the shorter layered strips to the remaining sides; miter corners. Press.

19. Cut two pieces floral print 17 1/2" x 20 1/2". Turn under one 20 1/2" edge of each piece 1/4"; press. Turn under again 1/2"; topstitch to hem.

20. Overlap pieces 5" to make a 20 1/2" x 28 1/2" backing piece as shown in Figure 6; baste together along overlapped edges.

Continued on page 74

Nez Pearce Purse

Design by Carla Schwab

Make a purse to coordinate with your latest quilted garment using one pieced block.

PROJECT SPECIFICATIONS

Project Size: 12" x 12"

Block Size: 12" x 12"

Number of Blocks: 1

FABRIC & BATTING

- 1/8 yard each green and brown plaids
- 1/4 yard mustard plaid
- 1 yard Osnaburg

SUPPLIES & TOOLS

- All-purpose thread to match fabrics
- 2 yards 5/8" natural rope cord
- 2 gold tassels
- 12" square lightweight fusible interfacing
- Basic sewing tools and supplies

INSTRUCTIONS

1. Prepare one Nez Pearce block referring to the Placement Diagram for placement of colors in the block.

2. Fuse the lightweight fusible interfacing square to the wrong side of the completed block to stabilize.

3. Cut three squares Osnaburg 12 1/2" x 12 1/2" for backing and lining.

4. Place one Osnaburg square right sides together with the pieced block; sew along one end as shown in Figure 1.

5. Place the remaining two Osnaburg squares right sides together; sew along one end, leaving a 6" opening in the center.

Figure 1
Place 1 Osnaburg square right sides together with the pieced block; sew along 1 end as shown.

6. Pin ends of rope cord at corner seams on the right side of the pieced block piece, knotting rope cord at top edge of block before pinning to the second corner; pin gold tassels to bottom corners. Place the lining piece right sides together with the pieced block piece; stitch all around, catching tassels and rope cord in seam. Turn right side out through opening left in bottom of lining; press seams flat. Press bag flat.

7. Hand-stitch rope cord to side seams, starting at bottom corner in which cord was caught in the seam. ❖

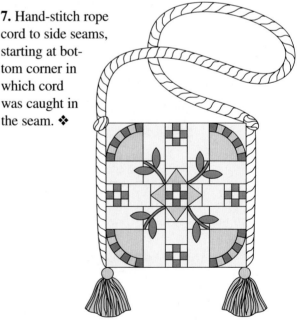

Nez Pearce Purse
Placement Diagram
12" x 12"

Maple Leaf Trivet

Design by Julie Weaver

Add to your kitchen's tasty aroma with this quilted trivet stuffed with scented rice.

PROJECT SPECIFICATIONS

Project Size: Approximately 9" x 12"

Block Size: 12" x 12"

Number of Blocks: 1

FABRIC & BATTING

- 1/8 yard fall print
- 1/4 yard each tan and rust prints
- Backing 12 1/2" x 12 1/2"
- 2 pieces flannel 12 1/2" x 12 1/2" for lining

SUPPLIES & TOOLS

- All-purpose thread to match fabrics
- 6 cups scented rice
- Cinnamon potpourri oil
- Basic sewing tools and supplies

INSTRUCTIONS

1. Prepare one Maple Leaf 1 block referring to the Placement Diagram for placement of colors in the block.

2. Place one flannel square wrong sides together with the pieced block; quilt along seam lines or as desired by hand or machine to hold layers together.

3. Layer the remaining flannel square with the 12 1/2" x 12 1/2" backing piece wrong sides together; quilt as desired to hold layers together for backing.

4. Place the block and backing layers right sides together; stitch around three sides, leaving one side open as shown in Figure 1.

5. Turn right side out; press seams flat. Turn under open ends 1/4". press.

Figure 1
Stitch around 3 sides, leaving 1 side open.

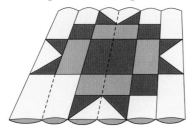

Maple Leaf Trivet
Placement Diagram
Approximately 9" x 12"

6. Stitch through all thicknesses every 2" using the block seams as guides to make six tubes as shown in Figure 2.

7. Scent six cups raw rice with several drops cinnamon potpourri oil to desired strength. Fill each stitched tube with rice to within 1/2" of opening. Pin opening closed. Fill all six tubes and pin. Adjust amount of rice in each tube to be as equal as possible.

8. Hand-stitch openings closed to finish. ❖

Figure 2
Stitch through all thicknesses every 2" using the block seams as guides to make 6 tubes.

Double Tulip Pillow

Design by Barbara Clayton

Lots of accent quilting makes this pillow an attractive decorative accent for any room.

PROJECT SPECIFICATIONS

Project Size: 18" x 18" without ruffle

Block Size: 12" x 12"

Number of Blocks: 1

FABRIC & BATTING

- 1/8 yard each 2 different rose prints and medium green print
- 1/4 yard dark green print
- 2 1/8 yards white solid
- Batting 24" x 24"

SUPPLIES & TOOLS

- All-purpose thread to match fabrics and black
- White and dark green quilting thread
- 3 1/4 yards dark green piping
- 18" pillow form
- Basic sewing tools and supplies and water-erasable marker or pencil

INSTRUCTIONS

1. Prepare one Double Tulip block referring to the Placement Diagram for placement of colors in the block.

2. Cut one strip each white solid and dark green print 2 3/8" by fabric width; subcut each strip into 2 3/8" square segments.

3. Cut each square in half on one diagonal to make triangles. Sew a white solid triangle to a dark green print triangle on the diagonal edge; press open to complete a triangle unit as shown in Figure 1. Repeat for 36 units.

Double Tulip Pillow
Placement Diagram
18" x 18"
(without ruffle)

Figure 1
Press open to complete a triangle unit.

4. Join eight units to make a strip as shown in Figure 2; repeat for four strips. Press seams in one direction. Sew a unit to each end of two strips as shown in Figure 3.

Figure 2
Join 8 units to make a strip.

Figure 3
Sew a unit to each end of 2 strips.

5. Sew an eight-unit strip to opposite sides of the pieced block; sew a 10-unit strip to the remaining sides. Press seams toward pieced strips.

6. Cut two strips each 4 1/2" x 15 1/2" and 4 1/2" x 23 1/2". Sew the shorter strips to two opposite sides of the pieced unit; sew the longer strips to the remaining sides. Press seams toward strips.

7. Using a water-erasable marker or pencil, mark the rope quilting design given onto the white solid strips 1/4" from seam as shown in Figure 4. Draw a line 1/4" on the opposite side of the quilting design.

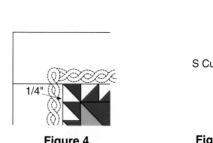

Figure 4
Mark the rope quilting design given onto the white solid strips 1/4" from seam.

Figure 5
Fold the pillow top in half and cut an S curve on each side using the S curve pattern given.

8. Round corners using pattern given. Fold the pillow top in half and cut an S curve on each side using the S curve pattern given as shown in Figure 5. Mark two side quilting designs on each side and a corner quilting design in each corner referring to the Placement Diagram for positioning.

9. Cut a white solid lining piece 24" x 24". Sandwich batting between the pieced top and the lining piece; pin or baste layers together to hold flat.

10. Quilt 1/4" inside seams on pieced block using dark green quilting thread in the white solid areas and white quilting thread in the dark areas. Quilt on marked lines on borders using dark green quilting thread.

11. When quilting is complete, trim batting and lining even with quilted top piece; remove pins or basting.

12. Pin and stitch the dark green piping along the curved edges of the pillow top, catching the lining and batting in the stitching. To finish the beginning and ends of piping, unpick the piping stitching about 2" on each end. Find where the ends will meet and stitch the fabric layers together. Trim the seam and cord to meet the seam. Fold the bias fabric back over the cord and stitch to pillow top.

13. Cut two rectangles white solid 18 1/4" x 22". Fold each rectangle in half and press to make two

18 1/4" x 11" rectangles. Lay one folded edge over the other folded edge as shown in Figure 6 to make an 18 1/4" square.

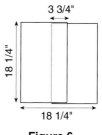

Figure 6
Lay 1 folded edge over the
other folded edge as shown
to make an 18 1/4" square.

14. Cut two strips each white solid 3 1/4" x 18 1/4" and 3 1/4" x 24"; sew the shorter strips to opposite sides and the longer strips to the remaining sides of the 18 1/4" backing square. Press seams toward strips.

15. Pin the bordered backing right sides together with the quilted top; trim backing to fit quilted top shape. Stitch all around sides; turn right side out through opening in backing square.

16. Topstitch on the line marked 1/4" beyond the rope quilting design to create a flat ruffle.

17. Insert pillow form through opening in pillow backing to finish. ❖

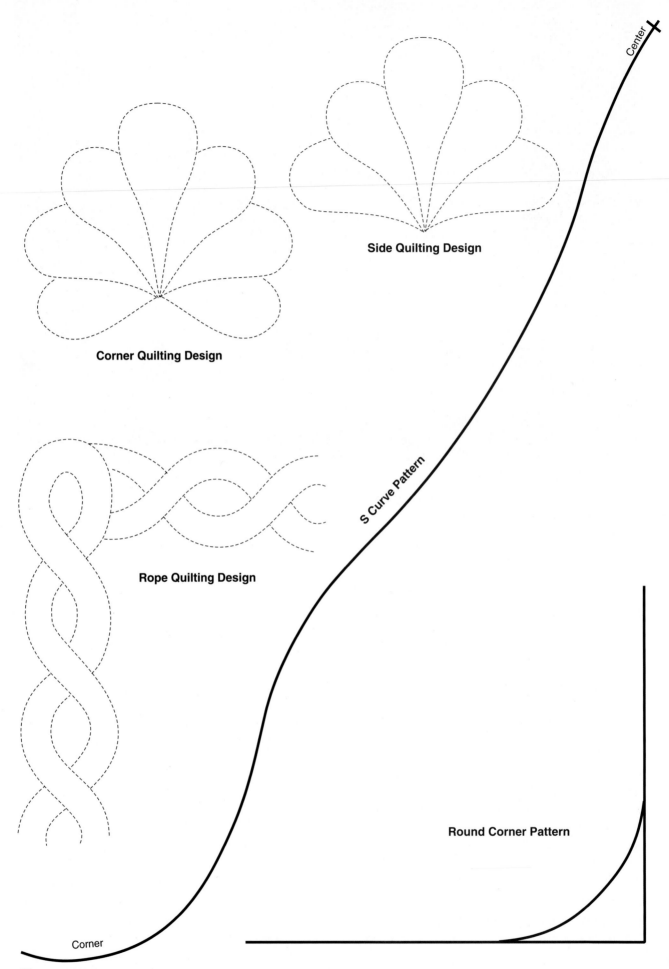

Side Quilting Design

Corner Quilting Design

Rope Quilting Design

S Curve Pattern

Center

Round Corner Pattern

Corner

Rosebud Table Mat

Design by Julie Weaver

Add a checkerboard border to the sides of a bordered block to create an eye-opening table mat.

PROJECT SPECIFICATIONS
Project Size: 20" x 20"
Block Size: 12" x 12"
Number of Blocks: 1

FABRIC & BATTING
- 1/8 yard each red dot and green print
- 1/3 yard red print
- 1/2 yard beige print
- Backing 24" x 24"
- Batting 24" x 24"
- 2 1/2 yards self-made or purchased binding

SUPPLIES & TOOLS
- All-purpose thread to match fabrics
- Basic sewing tools and supplies

INSTRUCTIONS

1. Prepare one Rosebud block referring to the Placement Diagram for placement of colors in the block.

2. Cut two strips each green print 1 1/2" x 12 1/2" and 1 1/2" x 14 1/2". Sew the shorter strips to opposite sides of the pieced block; sew the longer strips to the remaining sides. Press seams toward strips.

3. Cut three strips each red and beige prints 1 1/2" by fabric width. Sew a red print strip between two beige print strips with right sides together along length; press seams toward darker fabric.

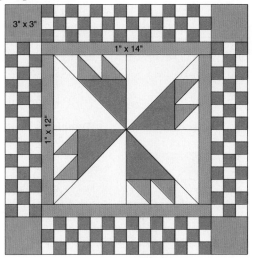

Rosebud Table Mat
Placement Diagram
20" x 20"

4. Sew a beige print strip between two red print strips with right sides together along length; press seams toward darker fabric.

5. Subcut each strip set into 1 1/2" A and B segments as shown in Figure 1.

6. Join seven each A and B segments to make a strip as shown in Figure 2; repeat for four strips.

7. Sew a pieced strip to opposite sides of the bordered block; press seams toward strips.

8. Cut four squares red dot 3 1/2" x 3 1/2". Sew a square to each end of the remaining two pieced strips. Sew these strips to the remaining sides of the bordered block; press seams toward strips.

9. Sandwich batting between completed top and prepared backing piece; pin or baste layers together. Quilt as desired by hand or machine. When quilting is complete, trim edges even. Bind with self-made or purchased binding to finish. ❖

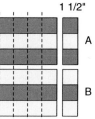

Figure 1
Subcut each strip set into 1 1/2" A and B segments as shown.

Figure 2
Join 7 each A and B segments to make a strip as shown.

April Tulips

PIECING INSTRUCTIONS

1. Referring to the Piecing Diagram to piece one block, sew a light 23 to two opposite sides of a medium 13. Sew a medium 17 to each end of the remaining light 23 pieces and sew to the remaining sides of the pieced unit to complete the center unit.

2. Sew a medium 78 and 78R to the angled ends of a light 55; set in two dark 17 squares to complete one side unit. Repeat for four side units.

3. Sew a medium 78 to a medium 78R; set in a dark 17 to complete one corner unit. Repeat for four corner units.

4. Arrange the pieced units in rows referring to the Piecing Diagram. Join units in rows; join rows to complete one block.

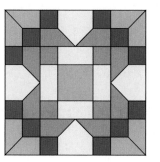

April Tulips

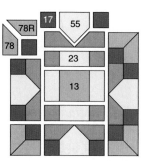

Templates needed:
13, 17, 23, 55, 78 & 78R

Arrowhead

PIECING INSTRUCTIONS

1. Referring to the Piecing Diagram to piece one block, sew a dark 116 to each side of a light 7 to complete a center unit.

2. Sew a light 10 and 10R to a dark 3 to complete a corner unit; repeat for four corner units.

3. Set the medium U3 pieces into the pieced center unit; sew a corner unit to each side to complete one block.

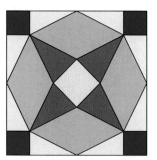

Arrowhead

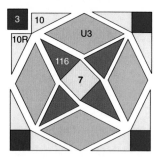

Templates needed:
3, 7, 10, 10R, 116 & U3

Bird of Paradise

PIECING INSTRUCTIONS

1. Referring to the Piecing Diagram to piece one block, join two light and two medium 3 squares to make a Four-Patch corner unit; repeat for two corner units.

2. Join two light and two dark 3 squares to make a Four-Patch corner unit; repeat for two corner units and one center unit.

3. Sew a medium 10 and a dark 10R to the sides of a light 9 to complete one side unit; repeat for two side units.

4. Sew a dark 10 and a medium 10R to the sides of a light 9 to complete one side unit; repeat for two side units.

5. Arrange the pieced units in rows referring to the Piecing Diagram. Join units in rows; join rows to complete one block.

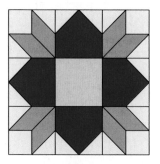

Bird of Paradise

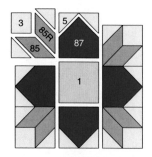

Templates needed:
3, 9, 10 & 10R

Blossom

PIECING INSTRUCTIONS

1. Referring to the Piecing Diagram to piece one block, sew a medium 85 to a medium 85R; set in a light 3 and sew a light 5 to sides to complete one corner unit. Repeat for four corner units.

2. Sew a light 5 to the angled sides of a dark 87 to complete a side unit; repeat for four side units.

3. Arrange the pieced units in rows with a light 1 square referring to the Piecing Diagram. Join units in rows; join rows to complete one block.

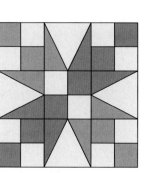

Blossom

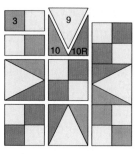

Templates needed:
1, 3, 5, 85, 85R & 87

Boston Belle

PIECING INSTRUCTIONS

1. Referring to the Piecing Diagram to piece one block, sew a dark 89 to a light V3; repeat for four units.

2. Sew a pieced unit to opposite sides of the light 17 square. Sew a dark 96 to each side of the remaining 89-V3 units and set onto the remaining sides of the 17 square to complete the block center.

3. Sew a medium 89 to each long side of a light 103; sew a dark 18 to one end to complete a corner unit. Repeat for four corner units.

4. Sew a corner unit to each side of the block center to complete one block.

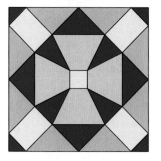

Boston Belle

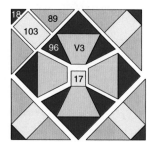

Templates needed:
17, 18, 89, 96, 103 & V3

Bouquet

PIECING INSTRUCTIONS

1. Referring to the Piecing Diagram to piece one block, sew a darkest 48 and 48R to a light 43; repeat for four units.

2. Sew a darkest 28 to a dark 28 along the diagonal; repeat for eight units.

3. Join one light and two medium 27 squares with two 28 units and a 43-48 unit to complete one corner unit; repeat for four corner units.

4. Join two corner units with a light 44; repeat.

5. Sew a dark 27 between two light 44 pieces; sew this unit between the two previously pieced units to complete one block.

Bouquet

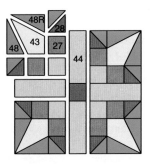

Templates needed:
27, 28, 43, 44, 48 & 48R

Butterfly Block

PIECING INSTRUCTIONS

1. Referring to the Piecing Diagram to piece one block, sew a light 2 to a medium 2 along the diagonal; repeat for four units.

2. Sew a light 10 and 10R to the medium sides of a 2 unit to complete one corner unit; repeat for four corner units.

3. Sew a dark LL3 to each side of the medium MM3. Set a medium KK3 between the LL3 points.

4. Sew a corner unit to each side of the pieced unit to complete one block.

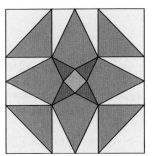

Butterfly Block

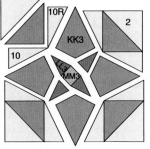

Templates needed:
2, 10, 10R, KK3, LL3 & MM3

Climbing Roses

PIECING INSTRUCTIONS

1. Referring to the Piecing Diagram to piece one block, join three light and four dark 20 squares to make the center unit.

2. Sew a medium 76 and a dark 76R to a light 25 to complete a side unit; repeat for two side units.

3. Sew a dark 76 and 76R to a light 25 to complete one side unit; repeat for two side units.

4. Sew a medium 76 to a medium 76R; set in a light 20 to complete a corner unit. Repeat for two corner units.

5. Sew a side unit to each edge of the center unit; set in the corner units to complete one block.

Climbing Roses

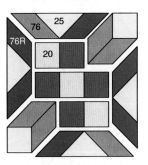

Templates needed:
20, 25, 76 & 76R

Diamond Star

PIECING INSTRUCTIONS

1. Referring to the Piecing Diagram to piece one block, sew a dark 108 to two adjacent sides of a darkest 124; repeat for four units.

2. Sew a medium A3 and AR3 to each pieced unit.

3. Sew a pieced unit to each side of a dark 13, joining seams between units to finish unit piecing.

4. Set in a light 13 at the corners to complete one block.

Diamond Star

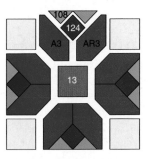

Templates needed:
13, 108, 124, A3 & AR3

Dogtooth Violet

PIECING INSTRUCTIONS

1. Referring to the Piecing Diagram to piece one block, sew a dark 95 and 95R to opposite sides of a medium 116 to complete a corner unit; repeat for four corner units.

2. Sew a light 91 and 91R to opposite sides of a dark 92; repeat for four units.

3. Join one dark and four light 7 squares with the 91-92 units to complete the block center.

4. Sew a corner unit to each side of the block center to complete one block.

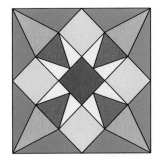

Dogtooth Violet

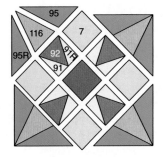

Templates needed:
7, 91, 91R, 92, 95, 95R & 116

Double Aster

PIECING INSTRUCTIONS

1. Referring to the Piecing Diagram to piece one block, sew a dark 18 to a darkest 18 along the short sides; add a darkest 16. Add a light 12 to complete a triangle unit; repeat for four triangle units.

2. Sew a medium 14 to each triangle unit.

3. Join two darkest and one dark 16 triangles; repeat for four units. Sew a unit to each previously pieced unit.

4. Sew the pieced units to each side of the dark 59, finishing end of first seam after all pieces have been added.

5. Sew a medium 26 to each side of the pieced unit to complete one block.

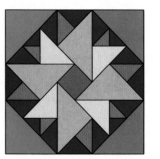

Double Aster

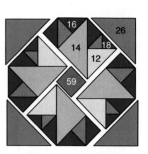

Templates needed:
12, 14, 16, 18, 26 & 59

Double Basket

PIECING INSTRUCTIONS

1. Referring to the Piecing Diagram to piece one block, sew a light 22 to a dark 22 along the diagonal to make a corner unit; repeat for two corner units.

2. Sew a dark 21 to two adjacent sides of a light 25; repeat for four units.

3. Sew a light 21 to a dark 21 along the diagonal; repeat for two units.

4. Sew a dark 73 to a light 22; repeat for two units.

5. Join two 21-25 units with one 22-73 unit and one 21 unit to complete a pieced unit; repeat for two pieced units.

6. Join the two pieced units on the 73 sides and set in the 22 corner units to complete one block.

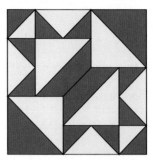

Double Basket

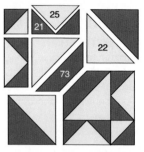

Templates needed:
21, 22, 25 & 73

Double Tulip

PIECING INSTRUCTIONS

1. Referring to the Piecing Diagram to piece one block, sew a dark 10 and 10R to a dark 11; repeat for two units.

2. Sew a dark 5 to one angled end of a light B3; repeat for four units.

3. Sew two 5-B3 units to the dark 10-11 unit to complete one quarter block. Repeat for two dark units.

4. Repeat steps 1–3 with medium and light pieces to complete two medium units.

5. Join the four units to complete one block.

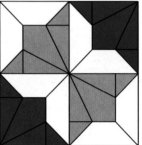

Double Tulip

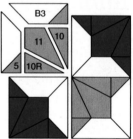

Templates needed:
5, 10, 10R, 11 & B3

Flower Garden Path

PIECING INSTRUCTIONS

1. Referring to the Piecing Diagram to piece one block, sew a dark 81 to each side of a light 109 to complete the center unit.

2. Sew a dark 5 to a light 5 along the diagonal; repeat for eight units.

3. Join two pieced 5 units with three light 5 triangles and a medium 3 to complete one corner unit; repeat for four corner units.

4. Sew a corner unit to each side of the center unit to complete one block.

Flower Garden Path

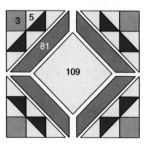

Templates needed:
3, 5, 81 & 109

Flowering Star

PIECING INSTRUCTIONS

1. Referring to the Piecing Diagram to piece one block, sew a dark D3 and DR3 to a medium C3 to complete a corner unit; repeat for four corner units.

2. Sew a dark E3 and ER3 to the light F3 piece and to each light G3 piece.

3. Join two corner units with an E3-G3 unit; repeat for two units. Sew a unit to each side of the E3-F3 unit to complete block piecing.

4. Prepare appliqué shapes H3 and I3 and circle J3. Appliqué shapes in place on the pieced block referring to the Piecing Diagram to complete one block.

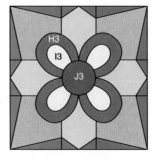

Flowering Star

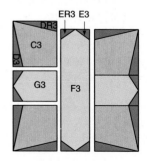

Templates needed:
C3, D3, DR3, E3, ER3, F3,
G3, H3, I3 & J3

Flower Pot

PIECING INSTRUCTIONS

1. Referring to the Piecing Diagram to piece one block, join three medium and one light 22 triangles to complete a triangle unit.

2. Sew a dark 21 to each light 75; sew to the short sides of the triangle unit; sew a light 22 triangle to the corner to complete the base of the block.

3. Sew a light 21 to a dark 21 along the diagonal; repeat for two units. Sew a dark 21 to one short side of a light 25; repeat for two units.

4. Sew a 21 unit to a 21-25 unit; sew to a short side of a light 22. Sew a 21 unit to a 21-25 unit to a light 20 square; sew this unit to the remaining short side of the light 22 to complete the top corner of the block.

5. Join the top corner and the base unit to complete one block.

Flower Pot

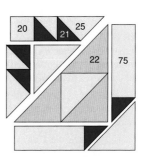

Templates needed:
20, 21, 22, 25 & 75

Full-Blown Tulip

PIECING INSTRUCTIONS

1. Referring to the Piecing Diagram to piece one block, sew a light HH3 and HHR3 to a dark GG3; set in a darkest 16.

2. Sew a medium JJ3 and JJR3 to the pieced units to complete a large quarter-block triangle; repeat for four quarter-block triangles.

3. Join the quarter-block triangles to complete one block.

Full-Blown Tulip

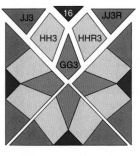

Templates needed:
16, GG3, HH3, HHR3, JJ3 & JJR3

Hazy Daisy

PIECING INSTRUCTIONS

1. Referring to the Piecing Diagram to piece one block, sew a dark 16 to two adjacent sides of a medium 59 square; repeat for eight units.

2. Join two units with two light 14 triangles to complete a quarter block; repeat for four quarters.

3. Join the quarters to complete one block.

Hazy Daisy

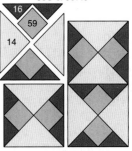

Templates needed:
14, 16 & 59

Jackknife Variation

PIECING INSTRUCTIONS

1. Referring to the Piecing Diagram to piece one block, sew a light 2 to a dark 51 to a light 5 to complete one corner unit; repeat for four corner units.

2. Join two light and two dark 4 triangles to complete one side unit; repeat for four side units.

3. Arrange the pieced units in rows with a medium 1 square referring to the Piecing Diagram. Join units in rows; join rows to complete one block.

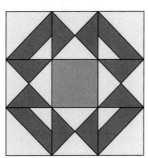

Jackknife Variation

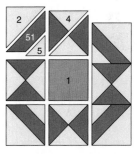

Templates needed:
1, 2, 4, 5 & 51

Magnolia Bud

PIECING INSTRUCTIONS

1. Referring to the Piecing Diagram to piece one block, sew a light 79 to a lightest L3; sew a dark K3 to a lightest L3. Join these two units to make an uneven Four-Patch unit; repeat for four units.

2. Sew a medium 58R to a darkest 58R; repeat for four units. Sew a medium 58 to a darkest 58; repeat for four units.

3. Sew a Four-Patch unit to one end of a 58 unit; sew a 58R unit to one side of a medium 43. Join these two units to complete a corner unit; repeat for four corner units.

4. Sew a darkest 58 and 58R to a light 29; sew a darkest 23 to the pieced unit to complete one side unit; repeat for four side units.

5. Arrange the pieced units in rows with a dark 43 referring to the Piecing Diagram. Join units in rows; join rows to complete one block.

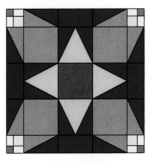

Magnolia Bud

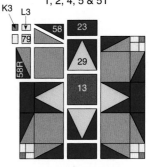

Templates needed:
23, 29, 43, 58, 58R, 79, K3 & L3

Maple Leaf 1

PIECING INSTRUCTIONS

1. Referring to the Piecing Diagram to piece one block, sew a dark 5 to two adjacent sides of a light 4; add a medium 6 to complete one side unit. Repeat for four side units.

2. Sew a light 3 to a dark 3; add a light 6 to complete a corner unit. Repeat for three corner units referring to Piecing Diagram for color placement.

3. Cut a 1" x 7" strip dark bias; turn under 7" edges 1/4". Appliqué in a curving shape onto a light 1 square.

4. Arrange the pieced units in rows with the appliquéd square and one dark 1 square referring to the Piecing Diagram. Join units in rows; join rows to complete one block.

Maple Leaf 1

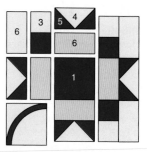

Templates needed:
1, 3, 4, 5 & 6

Mayor's Garden

PIECING INSTRUCTIONS

1. Referring to the Piecing Diagram to piece one block, sew a darkest 7 between two medium 7 squares to make a row; repeat for two rows. Sew a medium 7 between two darkest 7 squares to make a row; join the rows to complete the Nine-Patch center unit.

2. Sew a light 81 to a dark 2; repeat for four units. Sew a unit to each side of the center unit to complete one block.

Mayor's Garden

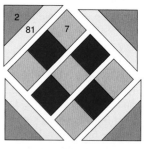

Templates needed:
2, 7 & 81

Midsummer Garden

PIECING INSTRUCTIONS

1. Referring to the Piecing Diagram to piece one block, sew a medium X3 and XR3 to the short angled sides of a dark Y3; set in a light 16. Repeat for four units.

2. Join the four units with light W3 pieces.

3. Join a light 78 and 78R with a dark 17 to make a corner unit; repeat for four corner units.

4. Set a corner unit onto each W3 point of the previously pieced unit to complete one block.

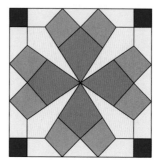

Midsummer Garden

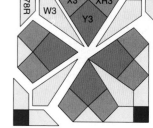

Templates needed:
16, 17, 78, 78R, W3, X3, XR3 & Y3

Mosaic Rose

PIECING INSTRUCTIONS

1. Referring to the Piecing Diagram to piece one block, arrange dark, medium and light 27 squares in seven rows; join the pieces in rows. Join the rows to complete one block.

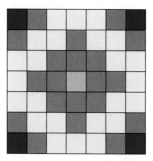

Mosaic Rose

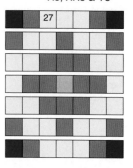

Template needed:
27

Mystery Flower Garden

PIECING INSTRUCTIONS

1. Referring to the Piecing Diagram to piece one block, join one dark, one light and two medium 4 triangles to complete one side unit; repeat for four side units.

2. Join one light and one dark 4 with a darkest 2 to complete one corner unit; repeat for four corner units.

3. Arrange the pieced units in rows with the dark 1 square referring to the Piecing Diagram. Join units in rows; join rows to complete one block.

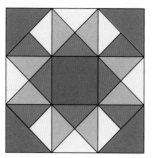

Mystery Flower Garden

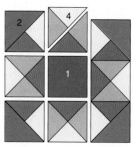

Templates needed:
1, 2 & 4

Nez Pearce

PIECING INSTRUCTIONS

1. Referring to the Piecing Diagram to piece one block, join four dark and three medium BB3 pieces to make a curved unit; sew this unit between a light OO3 and a medium PP3 to complete one pieced unit. Repeat for four pieced units.

2. Cut four 3/4" x 4" strips dark for stems; turn under 4" edges 1/4". Center and curve a piece on a light 63 square to make a stem unit; repeat for four stem units.

3. Sew a light QQ3 to one side of the pieced unit; sew a stem unit to one end of a light QQ3 and sew to the adjacent side of the pieced unit to complete one corner unit. Repeat for four corner units.

4. Sew a dark NN3 between two lightest NN3 squares; repeat for two units. Sew a lightest NN3 between two dark NN3 squares. Join the pieced units to complete a side Nine-Patch unit; repeat for four Nine-Patch side units.

5. Sew a darkest NN3 between two lightest NN3 squares; repeat. Sew a lightest NN3 between two darkest NN3 squares. Join the pieced units to complete a Nine-Patch center unit.

6. Sew a medium SS3 and SSR3 to two adjacent sides of a darkest RR3; repeat for four units. Sew a unit to a light 63; sew this unit to a Nine-Patch side unit to complete one side unit. Repeat for four side units.

7. Arrange the pieced units in rows referring to the Piecing Diagram. Join units in rows; join rows to complete block piecing.

8. Appliqué TT3 leaf shapes onto the pieced block referring to the Piecing Diagram to complete one block.

Nosegay

PIECING INSTRUCTIONS

1. Referring to the Piecing Diagram to piece one block, sew a light 17 between two dark 17 squares; repeat for two units. Sew a dark 17 between two light 17 squares. Join the units to complete a Nine-Patch corner unit; repeat for four corner units.

2. Sew a light AA3 and AAR3 to the sides of a medium Z3 to complete a side unit; repeat for four side units.

3. Arrange the pieced units in rows with a lightest 13 square referring to the Piecing Diagram. Join units in rows; join rows to complete one block.

Paducah Peony

PIECING INSTRUCTIONS

1. Referring to the Piecing Diagram to piece one block, sew a lightest 18 to a dark 18 along the diagonal; repeat for four units.

2. Join two lightest 18 triangles with one lightest 12, a pieced 18 unit and two light 17 squares and add a medium 12 triangle to complete one corner unit; repeat for four corner units.

3. Sew a lightest 16 to a dark 16 on the short sides. Sew a lightest 18 to a light 17; sew this unit to the pieced 16 unit. Add a medium 14 to the pieced unit to create a side unit; repeat for four side units.

4. Sew a side unit to a corner unit; repeat for four pieced units.

5. Sew the pieced units onto a light 59 square, finishing beginning seam after sewing other seams to complete one block.

Practical Orchard

PIECING INSTRUCTIONS

1. Referring to the Piecing Diagram to piece one block, join two light and two dark 4 triangles to complete the center unit.

2. Arrange the center unit in rows with four dark and four medium 1 squares referring to the Piecing Diagram. Join units in rows; join rows to complete one block.

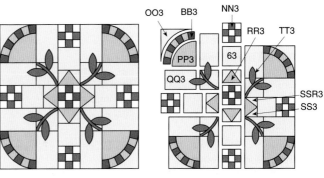

Nez Pearce

Templates needed:
63, BB3, NN3, OO3, PP3,
QQ3, RR3, SS3, SSR3 & TT3

Nosegay

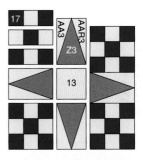

Templates needed:
13, 17, Z3, AA3 & AAR3

Paducah Peony

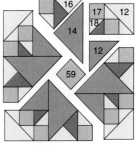

Templates needed:
12, 14, 16, 17, 18 & 59

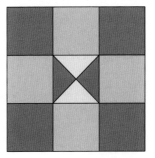

Practical Orchard

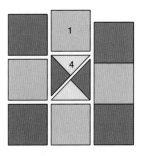

Templates needed:
1 & 4

Prairie Flower

PIECING INSTRUCTIONS

1. Referring to the Piecing Diagram to piece one block, sew a medium 5 to two adjacent sides of a lightest 4; add a medium 6 to complete one side unit; repeat for four side units.

2. Sew a darkest 5 to a medium 5 along the diagonal; repeat for eight units.

3. Join two 5 units with two light 3 squares to complete one corner unit; repeat for four corner units.

4. Arrange the pieced units in rows with a dark 1 square referring to the Piecing Diagram. Join units in rows; join rows to complete one block.

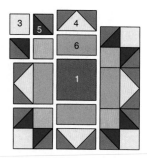
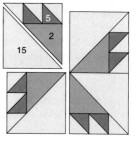

Prairie Flower

Templates needed:
1, 3, 4, 5 & 6

Rosebud

PIECING INSTRUCTIONS

1. Referring to the Piecing Diagram to piece one block, sew a dark 5 to a light 5 along the diagonal; repeat for eight units.

2. Join two pieced units; add a light 5 to one end and a medium 2 to one side. Sew the pieced unit to a light 15 to complete one block quarter; repeat for four quarters.

3. Join the block quarters to complete one block.

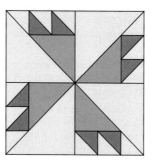
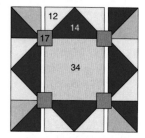

Rosebud

Templates needed:
2, 5 & 15

Rose Garden

PIECING INSTRUCTIONS

1. Referring to the Piecing Diagram to piece one block, sew a light 12 to two adjacent sides of a dark 14 to complete one side unit; repeat for four side units.

2. Sew a dark 12 to a medium 12 to complete one corner unit; repeat for four corner units.

3. Arrange the pieced units in rows with the lightest 34 square referring to the Piecing Diagram. Join units in rows; join rows to complete piecing.

4. Turn under seam allowance on each dark 17 square; appliqué in place at seam intersections referring to the Piecing Diagram to complete one block.

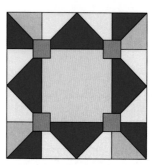

Rose Garden

Templates needed:
12, 14, 17 & 34

Rose Trellis

PIECING INSTRUCTIONS

1. Referring to the Piecing Diagram to piece one block, join four light 12 triangles to complete the center unit.

2. Sew a light 12 to one angled end of a medium 112; sew a dark 14 to one long side of the pieced unit. Repeat for four units.

3. Sew a pieced unit to each side of the pieced center unit, finishing beginning seam after all units have been added to complete one block.

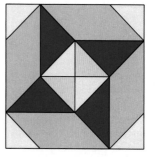
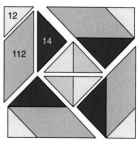

Rose Trellis

Templates needed:
12, 14 & 112

St. John's Pavement

PIECING INSTRUCTIONS

1. Referring to the Piecing Diagram to piece one block, sew a medium 120 to a dark N3; sew to opposite dark N3 to opposite sides of a medium M3 square.

2. Sew a light 54 to each end of the remaining N3 strips; add a medium 120.

3. Sew to remaining corners of the pieced unit to complete one block.

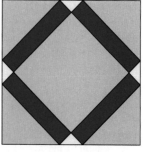
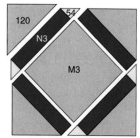

Saint John's Pavement

Templates needed:
54, 120, M3 & N3

Squash Blossom

PIECING INSTRUCTIONS

1. Referring to the Piecing Diagram to piece one block sew a lightest 5 to two adjacent sides of a darkest 4; sew a medium 6 to the pieced unit to complete one side unit. Repeat for four side units.

2. Sew a darkest 5 to a lightest 5; add a dark 3 to the dark side. Sew a light 6 to the pieced unit to complete one corner unit; repeat for four corner units.

3. Join two medium and two darker 4 triangles to complete the center unit.

4. Arrange the pieced units in rows referring to the Piecing Diagram. Join units in rows; join rows to complete one block.

Squash Blossom

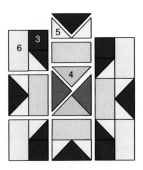

Templates needed:
3, 4, 5 & 6

Sue's Delight

PIECING INSTRUCTIONS

1. Referring to the Piecing Diagram to piece one block, sew a dark VV3 to opposite sides of a dark 63. Sew a dark UU3 to each end of the remaining VV3 pieces; sew these to the remaining sides of 63 to complete the center unit.

2. Sew a medium P3 to a medium PR3; set in a darkest R3; repeat for four units.

3. Sew the P3-R3 units to the center unit, joining seams between units as you stitch; set in dark Q3 pieces.

4. Join two light 94 squares with one light O3; sew to one end of a dark 78. Sew a light 18 to the short side of a dark 78R; join with the O3-78-94 unit to complete one corner unit. Repeat for four corner units.

5. Sew a corner unit to each side of the pieced unit to complete one block.

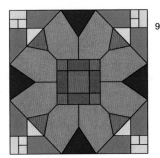

Sue's Delight

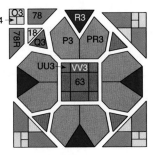

Templates needed:
18, 63, 78, 78R, 94, O3, P3, PR3, Q3, R3, UU3 & VV3

Swing on the Outside

PIECING INSTRUCTIONS

1. Referring to the Piecing Diagram to piece one block, sew a dark 38 and 38R to two adjacent sides of a light 4; sew a light 5 to each short 38 and 38R side to complete one side unit; repeat for four side units.

2. Sew a light 7 to a darkest 7 to a light 5 to complete one corner unit; repeat for four corner units.

3. Join two darkest and two medium 5 triangles to complete the center unit.

4. Sew a corner unit to two opposite sides of the center unit.

5. Sew a side unit to each side of the remaining two corner units; sew one of these units to each side of the center unit to complete one block.

Swing on the Outside

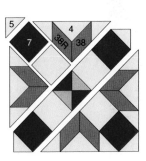

Templates needed:
4, 5, 7, 38 & 38R

Tennessee Tulip

PIECING INSTRUCTIONS

1. Referring to the Piecing Diagram to piece one block, sew a darkest 16 to a dark 16 along the diagonal; repeat for two units. Sew a light and dark 16 to opposite sides.

2. Sew a light 78 to a medium 18 and sew to the pieced unit. Sew a light 16 to a lightest 16 and sew to the pieced unit to complete one tulip unit; repeat for two tulip units.

3. Sew a lightest 57 to each tulip unit; join the units to complete the top half of the block.

4. Sew a medium 18 to a light 102 to a darkest 88 to a lightest 15 to complete one bottom unit; repeat for two bottom units. Join the two units to complete the bottom half of the block.

5. Join the top half of the block with the bottom half to complete one block.

Tennessee Tulip

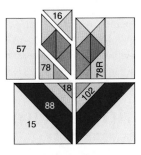

Templates needed:
15, 16, 18, 57, 78, 78R, 88 & 102

The Arrowhead

PIECING INSTRUCTIONS

1. Referring to the Piecing Diagram to piece one block, sew a light 64 to a dark 64; repeat. Join the 64 units to complete the Four-Patch center unit.

2. Sew a dark CC3 to a light CCR3; repeat. Sew a light CC3 to a dark CCR3; repeat.

3. Sew a CC unit to opposite sides of the Four-Patch center unit to complete the center row.

4. Sew a light and dark 90 to opposite sides of the remaining CC units. Sew a unit to opposite sides of the center row to complete one block.

The Arrowhead

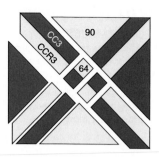

Templates needed:
64, 90, CC3 & CCR3

Triple Link Chain

PIECING INSTRUCTIONS

1. Referring to the Piecing Diagram to piece one block, sew a medium 16 to a light S3; repeat for four units.

2. Sew a light 49 to the dark 50 with a partial seam; sew a 16-S3 unit to the pieced unit. Sew a light 49 to the 16-S3 side. Continue adding pieces and units around piece 50 to complete the center unit.

3. Sew a darkest 41 and 41R to two adjacent sides of a medium 12; sew a lightest 12 to the pieced unit to complete one corner unit. Repeat for four corner units.

4. Sew a corner unit to each side of the center unit to complete one block.

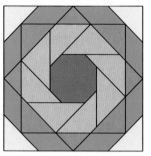

Triple Link Chain

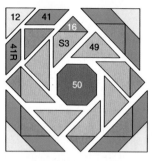

Templates needed:
12, 16, 41, 41R, 49, 50 & S3

Tulip

PIECING INSTRUCTIONS

1. Referring to the Piecing Diagram to piece one block, sew a dark 36 to a dark 36R; sew a light 12 to sides and set in a light 13 to complete the small corner unit.

2. Sew a light 12 to one side of a dark 36 and 36R; sew to adjacent sides of the small corner unit. Sew 15 to the 36 side of the pieced unit.

3. Sew a light 12 to a dark 12; repeat. Sew a 12 unit to one end of a dark 57; sew to one 15 side of the pieced unit.

4. Sew a dark 13 and a 12 unit to opposite ends of the remaining dark 57; sew to the remaining 15 side of the pieced unit to complete one block.

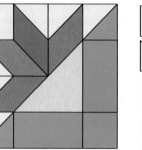

Tulip

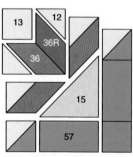

Templates needed:
12, 13, 15, 36, 36R & 57

Tulip Basket

PIECING INSTRUCTIONS

1. Referring to the Piecing Diagram to piece one block, join one each lightest and medium and two dark EE3 pieces to make a diamond unit; repeat for four diamond units.

2. Join the four diamond units and add a medium 62 to the straight side.

3. Set in two light DD3 triangles and one light 72 between diamond points.

4. Sew a medium 12 to one end of a light 57; repeat for two units. Sew a unit to adjacent 62 sides of the pieced unit.

5. Sew a light 15 to the 12-triangle end of the pieced unit to complete one block.

Tulip Basket

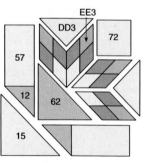

Templates needed:
12, 15, 57, 62, 72, DD3 & EE3

Tulip Ladyfingers

PIECING INSTRUCTIONS

1. Referring to the Piecing Diagram to piece one block, sew a lightest 5 to a medium 5 along the diagonal; repeat for eight units.

2. Join two units with one lightest and one dark 3 to complete one corner unit; repeat for four corner units.

3. Arrange the pieced units in rows with one dark and four light 1 squares referring to the Piecing Diagram. Join units in rows; join rows to complete one block.

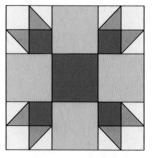

Tulip Ladyfingers

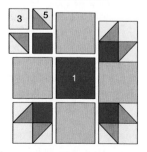

Templates needed:
1, 3 & 5

Tulips

PIECING INSTRUCTIONS

1. Referring to the Piecing Diagram to piece one block, sew a light 18 to each side of a dark 59 to complete the center unit.

2. Sew a light 18 to two adjacent sides of a dark 16; sew a light and a darkest 23 to opposite sides to complete one side unit. Repeat for four side units.

3. Sew a light 18 to a darkest 18 along the diagonal; repeat for 16 units. Sew a medium 18 to a dark 18 along the diagonal; repeat for eight units. Sew a medium 18 to a light 18 along the diagonal; repeat for four units.

4. Cut four 3/4" x 3" strips dark for stems; turn under 3" edges 1/4". Appliqué a stem piece to each light 17 square.

5. Join the pieced 18 units with a 17 stem square and a darkest 17 to complete one corner unit; repeat for four corner units.

6. Arrange the pieced units in rows referring to the Piecing Diagram. Join units in rows; join rows to complete one block.

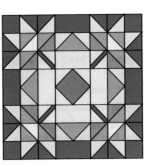

Tulips

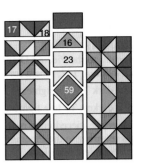

Templates needed:
16, 17, 18, 23 & 59

Wedding Bouquet

PIECING INSTRUCTIONS

1. Referring to the Piecing Diagram to piece one block, sew a light 5 to a medium 5 along the diagonal; repeat for four units. Sew a dark 5 to a medium 5 along the diagonal; repeat for eight units.

2. Sew three medium and one darker 5 to a darkest 7 square; repeat for four units.

3. Join two dark/medium and one light/medium 5 units with the 5-7 unit and two medium 3 squares to make a quarter block; repeat for four quarter units.

4. Join the quarter units to complete one block.

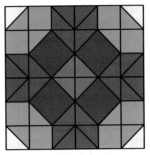

Wedding Bouquet

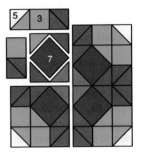

Templates needed:
3, 5 & 7

Whirling Square

PIECING INSTRUCTIONS

1. Referring to the Piecing Diagram to piece one block, sew a light 48 to a darkest 48; repeat for eight units. Sew a medium 48 to a dark 48; repeat for eight units.

2. Sew a light/darkest unit to a medium 27 with a partial seam; add a second light/darkest unit and two medium/dark units around the 27 square; sew a lightest 44 to one side to complete one unit. Repeat for four units.

3. Sew the units to the center dark 27 square using partial seams and finishing beginning seam when all pieced units have been added to complete one block.

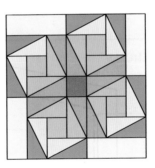

Whirling Square

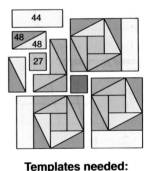

Templates needed:
27, 44 & 48

Windblown Lily

PIECING INSTRUCTIONS

1. Referring to the Piecing Diagram to piece one block, sew a medium 5 to a light 5 along the diagonal; repeat for three units.

2. Join these units with one medium and two light 5 triangles to make a triangle unit; sew a medium 15 to the long side to complete one corner unit.

3. Sew a dark 5 to a light 5 along the diagonal; repeat for four units. Join two units; repeat.

4. Sew a light 2 to a dark 2 along the diagonal; repeat for two units.

5. Sew a 5 unit to a 2 unit; add a light 86 to complete a corner unit. Repeat for two corner units.

6. Cut a 1" x 7" piece dark for stem; turn under 7" edges 1/4". Appliqué in a curved shape onto a light 34 square for stem square.

7. Arrange the three corner units and the stem square referring to the Piecing Diagram; join units to complete one block.

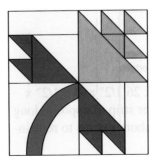

Windblown Lily

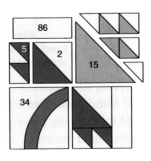

Templates needed:
2, 5, 15, 34 & 86

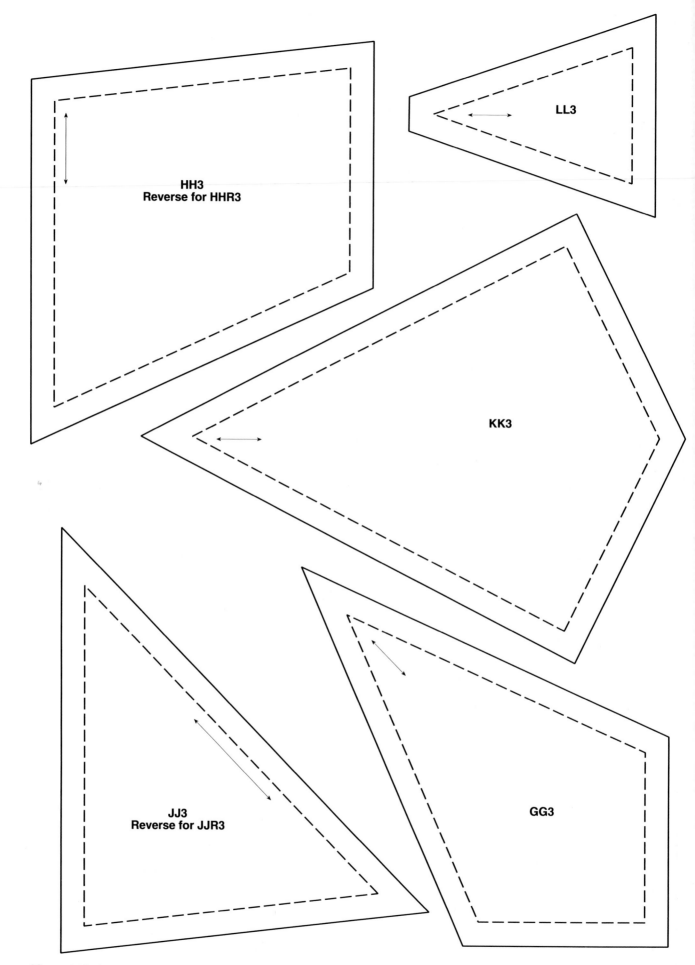

HH3
Reverse for HHR3

LL3

KK3

JJ3
Reverse for JJR3

GG3

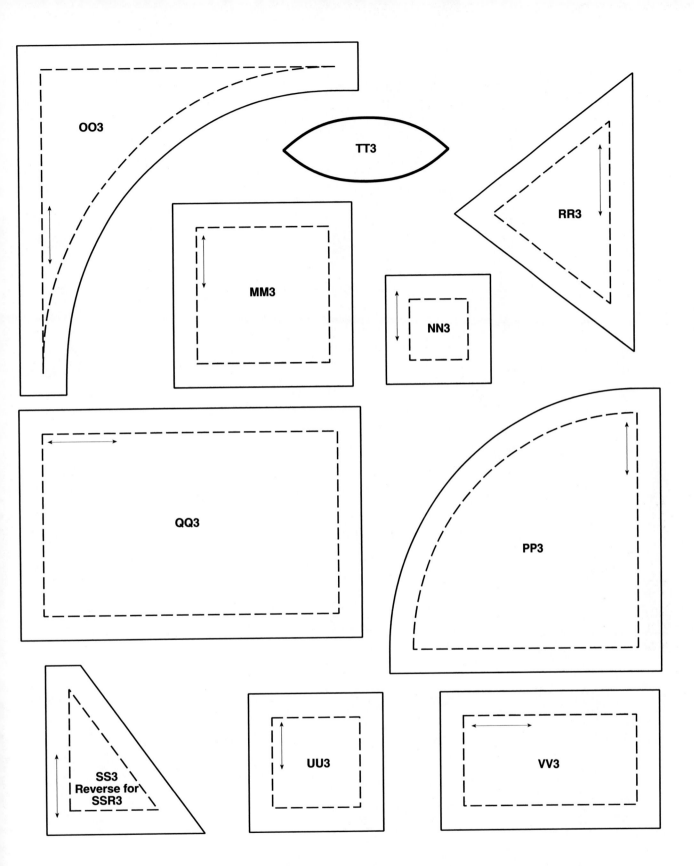

OO3

TT3

RR3

MM3

NN3

QQ3

PP3

SS3
Reverse for
SSR3

UU3

VV3

All God's Creatures

*Animals, bugs, fish
and even creepy
crawly things are
part of a quilter's world.
We've included lots
of critters for you to
quilt in this chapter.*

*Kid's love animals so
much, and there are so
many animal and bug fabrics
available today that it is
easy to find fabric that will
delight a child. Match the
fabric to the block for
a winning combination!*

All God's Creatures Sampler

Design by Connie Rand

Combine 12 blocks in a sampler quilt using blocks dedicated to earth's creatures great and small.

PROJECT SPECIFICATIONS

Quilt Size: 64" x 80"
Block Size: 12" x 12"
Number of Blocks: 12

FABRIC & BATTING

- 1/2 yard each rust and light green prints
- 5/8 yard green shell print
- 3/4 yard dark brown print
- 1 yard each blue and rust mottleds
- 1 yard each blue, orange and green prints and light beige solid
- 1 1/2 yards multicolored print
- Backing 68" x 84"
- Batting 68" x 84
- 8 1/2 yards self-made or purchased binding

SUPPLIES & TOOLS

- All-purpose thread to match fabrics
- Basic sewing tools and supplies, rotary cutter, mat and ruler

INSTRUCTIONS

1. Complete 12 blocks as desired using orange, blue, green and multicolored prints and light beige solid for piecing and referring to the Placement Diagram for positioning of colors within blocks. The following blocks are used in the sample. Row 1: Claws, The Owl Quilt, Flying Bats; Row 2: Flying Fish 2, The Hen & Her Chicks, Bird's Nest; Row 3: The Crab, Fly Away Feathers, Cats & Mice; Row 4: Kitty Corner, Turkey Tracks 1, Crow's Foot 2. *Note: You may choose any 12 blocks from this chapter or from other chapters in this book.*

2. Square up blocks to 12 1/2" x 12 1/2".

3. Prepare templates for pieces A and B and common templates 2 and 7 using patterns given; cut as directed on A and B pieces. Cut four dark brown print 2 triangles and 40 each light green print and rust print 7 squares.

4. Join four 7 squares referring to Figure 1 to make a Four-Patch unit; repeat for 20 units.

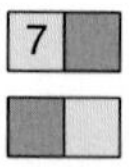

Figure 1
Join four 7 squares to make a Four-Patch unit.

5. Sew four rust mottled A pieces to one block referring to Figure 2; repeat for six blocks. Repeat with blue mottled A pieces for six blocks.

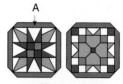

Figure 2
Sew 4 rust mottled A pieces to 1 block; repeat with blue mottled A pieces.

6. Join three blocks to make a row as shown in Figure 3; repeat for four rows referring to the Placement Diagram for positioning of blocks.

Figure 3
Join 3 blocks to make a row.

7. Join two rows setting in Four-Patch units at inside corners as shown in Figure 4; repeat with all rows to complete inner center of pieced top.

Figure 4
Join 2 rows setting in Four-Patch units at inside corners as shown.

8. Sew a green shell print A to B as shown in Figure 5. Repeat for 14 A-B units.

Make 14

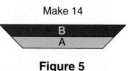

Figure 5
Sew a green shell print A to B as shown.

9. Set in A-B units and remaining Four-Patch units as shown in Figure 6; sew 2 triangles to corners. Press seams toward A-B units.

All God's Creatures Sampler
Placement Diagram
64" x 80"

Figure 6
Set in A-B units and add
2 triangles as shown.

10. Cut and piece two strips each 4 1/2" x 56 1/2" and 4 1/2" x 80 1/2" multicolored print. Sew shorter strips to top and bottom, and longer strips to opposite long sides to complete quilt top; press seams toward strips.

11. Sandwich batting between the completed top and prepared backing piece; pin or baste layers together to hold.

12. Quilt as desired by hand or machine. *Note: The sample shown was machine-quilted in the ditch of seams using thread to match fabrics.*

13. When quilting is complete, trim edges even; remove pins or basting.

14. Bind edges with self-made or purchased binding to finish. ❖

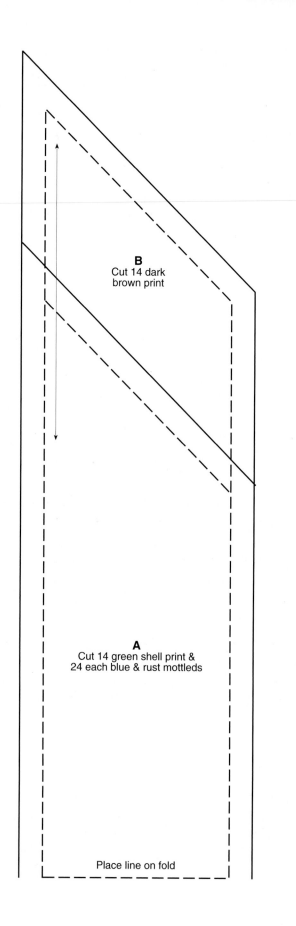

B
Cut 14 dark
brown print

A
Cut 14 green shell print &
24 each blue & rust mottleds

Place line on fold

Cats & Mice Vest

Design by Patsy S. Moreland

Use one block to create an interesting design on the back of a denim vest.

PROJECT NOTE

An adult size 10 is the smallest-size vest pattern that will accommodate a 12" x 12" block on the back. Construct or purchase a denim vest of your choice for use in this project.

PROJECT SPECIFICATIONS

Project Size: Size varies

Block Size: 12" x 12"

Number of Blocks: 1

FABRIC & BATTING

- 1/8 yard cat print
- 1/8 yard blue print
- 1/3 yard denim
- Denim vest

Mouse Shape

SUPPLIES & TOOLS

- All-purpose thread to match fabrics
- Black and gold metallic permanent markers
- Basic sewing tools and supplies

INSTRUCTIONS

1. Prepare one Cats & Mice 1 block using common templates 3, 5, 7 and 90 referring to Figure 1 for placement of pieces. *Note: Center cat faces in the 3 squares. The sample shown uses the wrong side of the cat print for the 7 square in the block center.*

2. Transfer four mouse shapes to the center 7 square with black permanent marker using pattern given. Fill in heart and bow loops with gold metallic permanent marker.

3. Fold under the edges of the completed block 1/4" all around; press. Center the

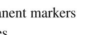

Figure 1
Complete the block using piece 3 as shown.

block on the top backside of the vest; pin in place. Hand-stitch the block in place to hold.

4. To make pieced sections for the vest fronts, cut two common template 2 triangles from denim, eight 5 triangles blue print and four denim, one 3 square cat print and one 3 square from the wrong side of the cat print.

5. Join pieces as shown in Figure 2 to make one pieced front unit; repeat for two units. Transfer one mouse to the wrong side of the cat print 3 square as in step 2.

6. Fold under edges of each pieced unit 1/4" all around; pin one pieced unit to each vest front referring to the Placement Diagram for positioning. Hand-stitch in place to finish. ❖

Figure 2
Join pieces as shown to make 1 pieced front unit.

Cats & Mice Vest Front
Placement Diagram
Size Varies

Cats & Mice Vest Back
Placement Diagram
Size Varies

Snail's Trail Picnic Cloth

Design by Marian Shenk

Serve a picnic for two on this one-block quilted picnic cloth.

PROJECT SPECIFICATIONS

Project Size: Approximately 23" x 23"

Block Size: 12" x 12"

Number of Blocks: 1

FABRIC & BATTING

- 1/4 yard each medium and dark teal prints
- 1/3 yard cream print
- 3/4 yard teal stripe
- Backing 27" x 27"
- Batting 27" x 27"
- 3 yards self-made or purchased binding

SUPPLIES & TOOLS

- All-purpose thread to match fabrics
- Cream quilting thread
- Basic sewing tools and supplies

INSTRUCTIONS

1. Prepare one Snail's Trail block referring to the Placement Diagram for placement of colors in the block.

Snail's Trail Picnic Cloth
Placement Diagram
Approximately 23" x 23"

2. Cut four strips teal stripe 1 1/4" x 14". Sew a strip to each side of the pieced block, mitering corners. Press seams toward strips.

3. Cut two squares cream print 10 1/2" x 10 1/2". Cut each square on one diagonal to make triangles. Sew a triangle to each side of the bordered square; press seams toward triangles.

4. Cut four identical strips teal stripe 2 1/2" x 24 1/2"; center and sew a strip to each side of the bordered block, mitering corners. Press seams toward strips; trim excess seams at corners. ***Note:*** *The strips are cut just a bit longer than needed for the mitered seam to make stitching easier.*

5. Sandwich batting between completed top and prepared backing piece; pin or baste layers together to hold flat for quilting.

6. Quilt as desired by hand or machine. ***Note:*** *The quilt shown was hand-quilted in the ditch of block and border seams and with a purchased quilting design in the large triangles using cream quilting thread.*

7. When quilting is complete, trim edges even; remove pins or basting. Bind edges with self-made or purchased binding to finish. ❖

Dad's Flannel Pillow

Design by Julie Weaver

Look for a camp-theme flannel print to create a masculine pillow using one block with borders.

PROJECT SPECIFICATIONS

Project Size: 20" x 20"

Block Size: 12" x 12"

Number of Blocks: 1

FABRIC & BATTING

- 7 different flannel fabric strips 2 1/2" x 22"
- 1/4 yard each rust solid and camping print flannel
- 2 pieces backing fabric 13 1/2" x 20 1/2"
- Muslin 24" x 24"
- Batting 24" x 24"
- 2 3/4 yards self-made or purchased binding

SUPPLIES & TOOLS

- All-purpose thread to match fabrics
- 20" pillow form
- Basic sewing tools and supplies

INSTRUCTIONS

1. Prepare one Puss in the Corner 2 block referring to the Placement Diagram for placement of colors in the block.

2. Cut two strips each 1 1/2" x 12 1/2" and 1 1/2" x 14 1/2" rust solid. Sew the shorter

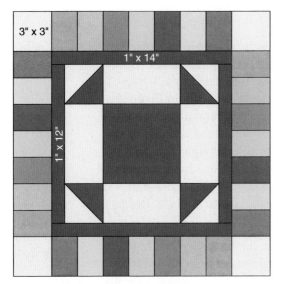

Dad's Flannel Pillow
Placement Diagram
20" x 20"

strips to opposite sides and the longer strips to the remaining sides of the pieced block; press seams toward strips.

3. Join the seven different 2 1/2" x 22" flannel strips with right sides together along length; press seams in one direction.

4. Subcut the strip set into 3 1/2" segments as shown in Figure 1; you will need four segments.

3 1/2"

Figure 1
Subcut the strip set into 3 1/2" segments.

5. Sew a pieced segment to two opposite sides of the pieced center. Cut four 3 1/2" x 3 1/2" squares camping print. Sew a square to each end of the remaining two strips; sew these strips to the remaining sides of the pieced center. Press seams toward strips.

6. Sandwich batting between completed top and

Continued on page 102

Pigeon Toes Place Mat

Design by Barbara Clayton

Add borders and prairie points to a block to make the perfect-size place mat.

PROJECT SPECIFICATIONS
Project Size: 16 1/2" x 13 1/2" without prairie points

Block Size: 12" x 12"

Number of Blocks: 1

FABRIC & BATTING
- 1/8 yard each rust/brown solid and white-on-white print
- 1/8 yard each black and dark brown prints
- 1/4 yard each black solid and tan print
- Backing 14" x 18"
- Batting 14" x 18"

SUPPLIES & TOOLS
- All-purpose thread to match fabrics
- Black quilting thread
- Basic sewing tools and supplies

INSTRUCTIONS
1. Prepare one Pigeon Toes block referring to the Placement Diagram for placement of colors in the block.

2. Cut two strips tan print 2 3/4" x 12 1/2"; sew a strip to two opposite sides of the pieced block. Press seams toward strips.

3. Cut two strips tan print 1 1/4" x 17"; sew a strip to opposite long sides of the bordered block. Press seams toward strips.

4. Mark the diamond quilting design on the wide tan print borders using pattern given.

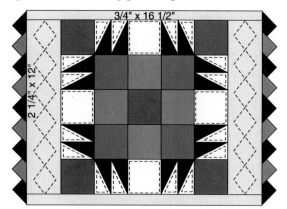

Pigeon Toes Place Mat
Placement Diagram
16 1/2" x 13 1/2" without prairie points

5. Using common template 20, cut eight rust/brown solid and 10 black solid.

6. Fold each 20 square in half on the diagonal and then in half again to form a folded triangle to make a prairie point as shown in Figure 1; press.

Figure 1
Fold each 20 square in half on the diagonal and then in half again to form a folded triangle to make a prairie point.

7. Pin the raw edge of a black prairie point to the center edge of one short side of the bordered place mat as shown in Figure 2. Pin two rust/brown and two black prairie points on each side of the center, alternating colors and pinning each one in the center of the previous one as shown in Figure 3. Baste in place. Repeat for both ends.

8. Pin the backing piece right sides together with pieced top; pin batting to the wrong side of the pieced top. Trim excess

Continued on page 102

Figure 2
Pin the raw edge of a black prairie point to the center edge of 1 side of the bordered place mat.

Wild Goose Chase Cover

Design by Judith Sandstrom

Make a photo album cover using the Wild Goose Chase block with Flying Geese borders.

PROJECT NOTE

The Wild Goose Chase block used in the album cover was cut and pieced without the use of templates. To piece one Flying Geese unit using this method: Cut a 2 3/8" x 2 3/8" square each dark and light fabrics. Cut each square on one diagonal to make triangles. Sew a light triangle to a dark triangle along diagonal edges; repeat. Join two units to complete one Flying Geese unit as shown in Figure 1. If you prefer to use this method, replace all 16 and 18 common templates in the block with the 2 3/8" x 2 3/8" squares and piece Flying Geese units as needed.

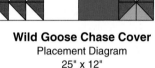

Wild Goose Chase Cover
Placement Diagram
25" x 12"

Figure 1
Join 2 units to complete 1 Flying Geese unit as shown.

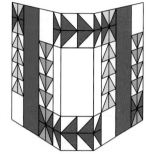

Figure 3
Complete 1 corner unit each navy and apricot prints and navy and light blue prints as shown.

PROJECT SPECIFICATIONS

Project Size: 25" x 12"

Block Size: 12" x 12"

Number of Blocks: 1

FABRIC & BATTING

- 1/8 yard each navy, light blue and apricot prints
- 1/8 yard blue print
- 1/2 yard cream print
- Batting 12 1/2" x 25 1/2"
- Lining 12 1/2" x 25 1/2"

SUPPLIES & TOOLS

- All-purpose thread to match fabrics
- Basic sewing tools and supplies

INSTRUCTIONS

1. Prepare one Wild Goose Chase block referring to the Placement Diagram for placement of colors in the block.

2. Cut two rectangles blue print 4" x 12 1/2". Sew a rectangle to opposite sides of the pieced block.

3. Piece one additional side unit each apricot and light blue prints as shown in Figure 2.

Complete one corner unit each navy and apricot prints and navy and light blue prints as shown in Figure 3.

4. Sew a navy/apricot corner unit to an apricot/cream side unit to complete an end strip. Repeat with the light blue/navy corner unit and the light blue/cream side unit. Sew these strips to the blue print sides of the pieced unit to complete the pieced top.

Continued on page 102

Figure 2
Piece 1 additional side unit each apricot and light blue prints as shown.

Bear's Paw

PIECING INSTRUCTIONS

1. Referring to the Piecing Diagram to piece one block, sew a dark 18 to a light 18 along the diagonal; repeat for 28 units.

2. Sew a light 26 to a medium 26 along the diagonal; repeat for four units.

3. Join three 18 units; sew to the medium side of a 26 unit. Join four 18 units and sew to the adjacent side of the 18-26 unit to complete a block quarter; repeat for four block quarters.

4. Join the block quarters referring to the Piecing Diagram to complete one block.

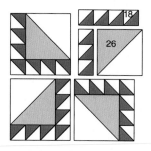

Bear's Paw

Templates needed:
18 & 26

Birds & Kites

PIECING INSTRUCTIONS

1. Referring to the Piecing Diagram to piece one block, join 2 medium and four light 29 pieces with two dark 37 pieces to complete a quarter block; repeat for four quarter units.

2. Join the quarter units to complete one block.

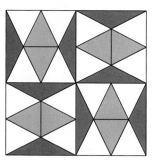

Birds & Kites

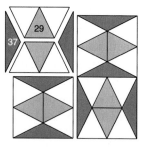

Templates needed:
29 & 37

Bird's Nest

PIECING INSTRUCTIONS

1. Referring to the Piecing Diagram to piece one block, sew a light 21 to a medium 21 along the diagonal; repeat for four units.

2. Sew a light 21 to two adjacent sides of the medium side of one 21 unit and add a dark 22 to complete a corner unit; repeat for four corner units.

3. Join two medium 27 squares with two light 28 and four light 47 triangles to make a side unit; repeat for four side units.

4. Sew a side unit to opposite sides of the dark 20 square to complete the center unit.

5. Join two corner units with a side unit; repeat. Sew one of these units to each long side of the center unit to complete one block.

Bird's Nest

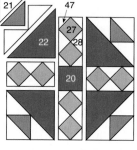

Templates needed:
20, 21, 22, 27, 28 & 47

Brown Goose

PIECING INSTRUCTIONS

1. Referring to the Piecing Diagram to piece one block, sew a light 12 to two adjacent short sides of a dark 14; repeat.

2. Join two light and two dark 14 triangles to complete the block center; sew a 12-14 unit to two opposite light sides to complete the center unit.

3. Join one light and two dark 14 triangles with two light 12 triangles to complete a long side unit; repeat for two long side units.

4. Sew a long side unit to opposite sides of the pieced center unit to complete one block.

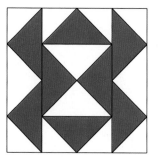

Brown Goose

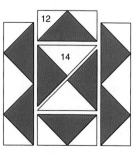

Templates needed:
12 & 14

Cats & Mice 1

PIECING INSTRUCTIONS

1. Referring to the Piecing Diagram to piece one block, join two dark and two light 5 triangles to complete a pieced unit; repeat for four units.

2. Sew a unit to a dark 7; add a light 5 to the dark 7 end. Repeat for four units.

3. Sew a pieced unit to opposite sides of a dark 7 to complete a diagonal center unit.

4. Sew a light 90 to opposite sides of the remaining two pieced units to complete large corner units.

5. Sew a large corner unit to each long side of the diagonal center unit to complete one block.

Cats & Mice 1

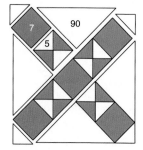

Templates needed:
5, 7 & 90

Cats & Mice 2

PIECING INSTRUCTIONS

1. Referring to the Piecing Diagram to piece one block, sew a light 5 to a medium A4 to complete a corner unit; repeat for four units.

2. Join one medium and two dark 54 triangles; sew to a medium 4 and add a light 4 to two adjacent sides to complete one side unit.

3. Sew a corner unit to each side of the dark 39; set in the side units to complete one block.

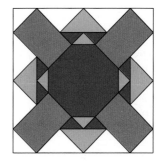

Cats & Mice 2

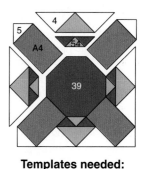

Templates needed:
4, 5, 39, 54 & A4

Claws

PIECING INSTRUCTIONS

1. Referring to the Piecing Diagram to piece one block, sew a light 10 and 10R to a medium 11 to complete a corner unit; repeat for four corner units.

2. Sew a dark 10 and 10R to opposite sides of a light 9 to complete a side unit; repeat for four side units.

3. Join two dark and two medium 3 squares to make a Four-Patch center unit.

4. Arrange the pieced units in rows referring to the Piecing Diagram. Join units in rows; join rows to complete one block.

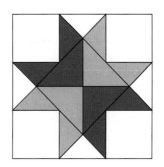

Claws

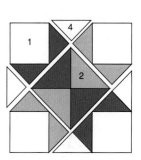

Templates needed:
3, 9, 10, 10R & 11

Country Farm

PIECING INSTRUCTIONS

1. Referring to the Piecing Diagram to piece one block, join two medium and two dark 2 triangles to complete the block center.

2. Sew two medium 4 triangles to two adjacent sides of a light 1; repeat for two units. Sew a unit to opposite sides of the block center.

3. Sew two dark 4 triangles to two adjacent sides of a light 1; repeat for two units. Sew a light 4 to the dark ends of each 1-4 unit to complete large corner units.

4. Sew a large corner unit to each long side of the previously pieced unit to complete one block.

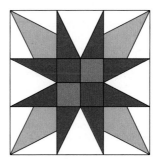

Country Farm

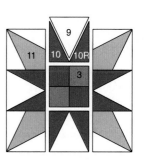

Templates needed:
1, 2 & 4

Crow's Foot 1

PIECING INSTRUCTIONS

1. Referring to the Piecing Diagram to piece one block, sew a dark 5 to a light 5 on the diagonal; repeat for 16 units.

2. Join two 5 units; repeat. Sew one unit with light sides against a dark 1 square; sew a dark 3 to the light end of the remaining pieced unit and sew to the adjacent side of the square to complete one corner unit; repeat for two units.

3. Join two 5 units; repeat. Sew one unit with dark sides against a light 1 square; sew a light 3 to the dark end of the remaining pieced unit and sew to the adjacent side of the square to complete one corner unit; repeat for two units.

4. Join the pieced units to complete one block.

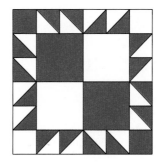

Crow's Foot 1

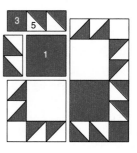

Templates needed:
1, 3 & 5

Crow's Foot 2

PIECING INSTRUCTIONS

1. Referring to the Piecing Diagram to piece one block, sew a medium 18 to two adjacent sides of a light 16; sew a light 17 to each end; repeat for four units.

2. Sew a light and medium 18 to two adjacent sides of a medium 17; repeat for two units. Sew a unit to two adjacent sides of a dark 14; sew a 16-17-18 unit to the long side of 14 to complete a side unit. Repeat for two side units.

3. Sew a light 18 to one corner of a dark 13; repeat for four corner units. Sew a corner unit to opposite ends of a side unit to complete one long side unit; repeat for two long side units.

4. Sew the remaining 16-17-18 units to the long sides of the dark 14 triangles to complete short side units.

5. Sew two medium 18 triangles to opposite sides of the remaining dark 13 square for center; set in the short side units and then add the long side units to complete the block.

Crow's Foot 2

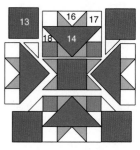

Templates needed:
13, 14, 16, 17 & 18

Crow's Nest

PIECING INSTRUCTIONS

1. Referring to the Piecing Diagram to piece one block, sew a dark 2 to a light 2 along the diagonal; repeat for four units.

2. Sew a light 4 to a dark 4 on the short sides; sew a medium 2 to the long sides to complete a side unit. Repeat for four side units.

3. Join two dark and two medium 4 triangles to complete the center unit.

4. Arrange the pieced units in rows referring to the Piecing Diagram. Join units in rows; join rows to complete one block.

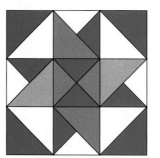

Crow's Nest

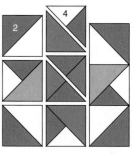

Templates needed:
2 & 4

Darting Birds

PIECING INSTRUCTIONS

1. Referring to the Piecing Diagram to piece one block, sew a dark 2 to a light 2 along the diagonal; repeat for two units.

2. Sew a light 2 to a medium 2 along the diagonal; repeat for four units.

3. Arrange the pieced units in rows with one light and two dark 1 squares referring to the Piecing Diagram. Join units in rows; join rows to complete one block.

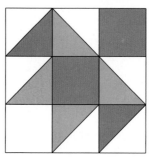

Darting Birds

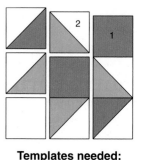

Templates needed:
1 & 2

Duck's Foot

PIECING INSTRUCTIONS

1. Referring to the Piecing Diagram to piece one block, sew a dark 21 to two adjacent sides of a medium 20 square; add a light 22 to complete a corner unit. Repeat for four corner units.

2. Sew a medium 46 between two corner units; repeat for two units.

3. Sew a dark 20 between two medium 46 pieces to complete a center unit; sew between the two pieced units to complete one block.

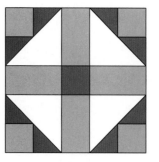

Duck's Foot

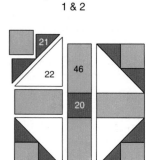

Templates needed:
20, 21, 22 & 46

Duck's Foot in the Mud

PIECING INSTRUCTIONS

1. Referring to the Piecing Diagram to piece one block, sew a light 2 to a dark 2 along the diagonal; repeat for four units.

2. Arrange the units in rows with two light and three dark 1 squares referring to the Piecing Diagram. Join units in rows; join rows to complete one block.

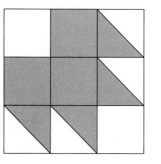

Duck's Foot in the Mud

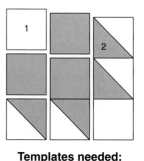

Templates needed:
1 & 2

Farm Friendliness

PIECING INSTRUCTIONS

1. Referring to the Piecing Diagram to piece one block, sew a dark 2 to a light 2 along the diagonal to complete a corner unit; repeat for four corner units.

2. Sew a light 6 to a medium 6 to complete a side unit; repeat for four side units.

3. Arrange the units in rows with one dark 1 referring to the Piecing Diagram. Join units in rows; join rows to complete one block.

Farm Friendliness

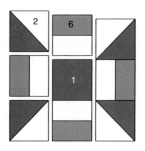
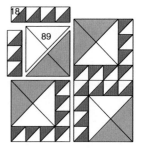

Templates needed:
1, 2 & 6

Flamingos in Flight

PIECING INSTRUCTIONS

1. Referring to the Piecing Diagram to piece one block, sew a dark 18 to a light 18 along the diagonal; repeat for 28 units.

2. Sew a light 89 to a light 89 on the short sides; sew a medium 89 to a medium 89 on the short sides. Join the two pieced units; repeat for four units.

3. Join three 18 units; sew to the light side of an 89 unit. Join four 18 units and sew to the adjacent side of the 18-89 unit to complete a block quarter; repeat for four block quarters.

4. Join the block quarters referring to the Piecing Diagram to complete one block.

Flamingos in Flight

Templates needed:
18 & 89

Fly Away Feathers

PIECING INSTRUCTIONS

1. Referring to the Piecing Diagram to piece one block, sew a dark D4 to a medium DR4; set in a light 27 and sew a light 107 to each side to complete one corner unit. Repeat for four corner units.

2. Join two corner units with a medium 44; repeat for two units.

3. Sew a dark 27 between two medium 44 pieces to make the center row; sew this row between the two pieced units to complete one block.

Fly Away Feathers

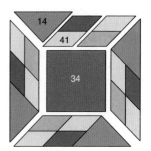

Templates needed:
27, 44, 107, D4 & DR4

Flying Bats

PIECING INSTRUCTIONS

1. Referring to the Piecing Diagram to piece one block, join one dark, one medium and two light 41 pieces to make a diamond unit; repeat for four diamond units.

2. Sew a medium 14 to one end of each diamond unit.

3. Sew the diamond units to the sides of the dark 34 square, stitching angled seams between pieces to complete one block.

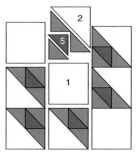

Flying Bats

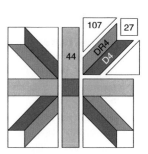

Templates needed:
14, 34 & 41

Flying Bird

PIECING INSTRUCTIONS

1. Referring to the Piecing Diagram to piece one block, join one dark and three medium 5 triangles to make a triangle unit; repeat for six units.

2. Sew a light 2 triangle to the long side of each pieced unit to complete six 2-5 units.

3. Arrange the pieced units with three light 1 squares in rows referring to the Piecing Diagram. Join units in rows; join rows to complete one block.

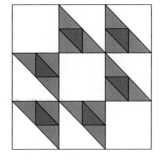

Flying Bird

Templates needed:
1, 2 & 5

Flying Crow

PIECING INSTRUCTIONS

1. Referring to the Piecing Diagram to piece one block, join two light and two medium 4 triangles to complete a side unit; repeat for four side units.

2. Arrange the side units in rows with five dark 1 squares referring to the Piecing Diagram. Join units in rows; join rows to complete one block.

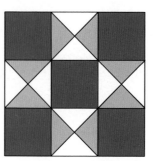

Flying Crow

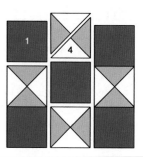

Templates needed:
1 & 4

Flying Fish 1

PIECING INSTRUCTIONS

1. Referring to the Piecing Diagram to piece one block, sew a light 16 triangle to opposite sides of a dark 59. Sew a light 16 to a medium 16 on the short sides; repeat and sew to the remaining sides of the 16-59 unit to complete a pieced unit; repeat for four units.

2. Sew a dark 57 to one side of each pieced unit to complete quarter blocks.

3. Join the quarter blocks to complete one block.

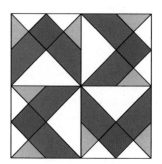

Flying Fish 1

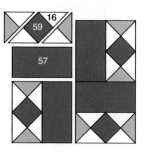

Templates needed:
16, 57 & 59

Flying Fish 2

PIECING INSTRUCTIONS

1. Referring to the Piecing Diagram to piece one block, sew a light 16 to two adjacent sides of a dark 59; repeat for four units.

2. Sew a medium 16 to a dark 93 and to a dark 93R; repeat for four of each unit.

3. Join one each units 16-93, 16-93R, 16-59 and a light 14 to complete a block quarter; repeat for four quarters.

4. Join the quarters with the light 14 triangles toward the inside to complete one block.

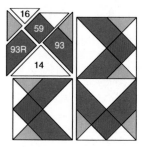

Flying Fish 2

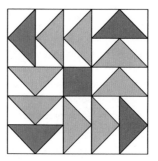

Templates needed:
14, 16, 59, 93 & 93R

Flying Geese

PIECING INSTRUCTIONS

1. Referring to the Piecing Diagram to piece one block, sew a light 21 to two adjacent sides of a dark 25; repeat for four dark units. Repeat for eight medium units.

2. Join a dark and medium unit; repeat. Join a dark and two medium units; repeat.

3. Sew a medium unit to opposite sides of a dark 20 square to make the center row.

4. Arrange the units referring to the Piecing Diagram. Join units to complete one block.

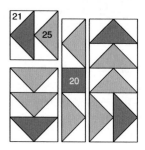

Flying Geese

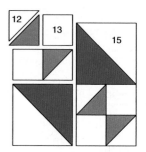

Templates needed:
20, 21 & 25

Fox & Geese

PIECING INSTRUCTIONS

1. Referring to the Piecing Diagram to piece one block, sew a light 12 to a medium 12 along the diagonal; repeat for four units.

2. Join two pieced units with two light 13 squares to complete a block quarter; repeat for two quarter units.

3. Sew a light 15 to a dark 15 along the diagonal to complete a block quarter; repeat for two quarter units.

4. Join the quarter units to complete one block.

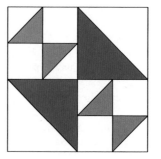

Fox & Geese

Templates needed:
12, 13 & 15

Hens & Chickens

PIECING INSTRUCTIONS

1. Referring to the Piecing Diagram to piece one block, sew a light 28 to a dark 28 along the diagonal; repeat for 20 units.

2. Join two pieced units; repeat for eight units.

3. Sew a pieced unit to one side of a light 45 square with dark pieces toward square; sew a 28 unit to one end of a two-unit unit and sew to the adjacent side of the 45 unit to complete one corner unit; repeat for four corner units.

4. Sew the light 27 between two dark 44 pieces to complete the center row. Join two corner units with a dark 44; repeat for two side units.

5. Sew the two side units to the center row to complete one block.

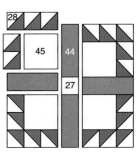

Hens & Chickens

Templates needed:
27, 28, 44 & 45

Honey Bee

PIECING INSTRUCTIONS

1. Referring to the Piecing Diagram to piece one block, sew a light 3 between two dark 3 squares to complete a row; repeat for two rows. Sew a dark 3 between two light 3 squares to complete a row. Join the rows to complete the Nine-Patch center.

2. Sew a light 57 to opposite sides of the pieced center. Sew a light 13 to each end of the remaining 57 pieces and sew these units to the remaining sides of the center to complete block piecing.

3. Pin O4 and P4 pieces to the pieced block referring to the block drawing for positioning of pieces.

4. Appliqué each piece in place with thread to match fabric to complete one block.

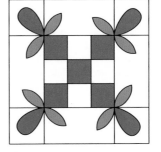

Honey Bee

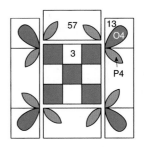

Templates needed:
3, 13, 57, O4 & P4

Kitty Corner

PIECING INSTRUCTIONS

1. Referring to the Piecing Diagram to piece one block, sew a medium 5 to each side of a dark 7 to complete a corner unit; repeat for four corner units.

2. Sew a dark 6 between two light 53 pieces to complete a side unit; repeat for four side units.

3. Arrange the pieced units in rows with a dark 1 square referring to the Piecing Diagram. Join in rows; join rows to complete one block.

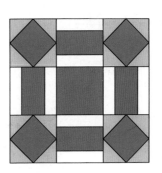

Kitty Corner

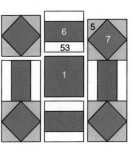

Templates needed:
1, 5, 6, 7 & 53

Old Grey Goose

PIECING INSTRUCTIONS

1. Referring to the Piecing Diagram to piece one block, sew a light 12 to a colored 12 along the diagonal to complete a corner unit; repeat for four corner units.

2. Sew a colored 12 to two adjacent sides of a light 14; repeat for six units. Join two units to complete the block center.

3. Sew a 12-14 unit to opposite sides of the block center. Sew a corner unit to each end of the remaining 12-14 units with light sides on the outside. Sew these units to the previously pieced unit to complete one block.

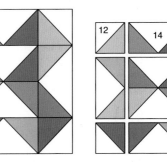

Old Grey Goose

Templates needed:
12 & 14

Pigeon Toes

PIECING INSTRUCTIONS

1. Referring to the Piecing Diagram to piece one block, sew a dark 20 between two light 20 squares to make a row; repeat for two rows. Sew a light 20 between two dark 20 squares to make a row. Join the rows to complete the Nine-Patch center.

2. Sew a light 105 to a dark 105; repeat for eight units. Join two units; repeat for four units.

3. Repeat with light and dark 105R pieces.

4. Sew a 105 and 105R unit to opposite sides of a light 20 to make a side unit; repeat for four side units.

5. Sew a side unit to opposite sides of the center unit. Sew a light 20 to each end of the remaining side units and sew to the center unit to complete one block.

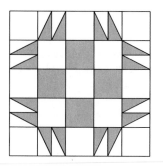

Pigeon Toes

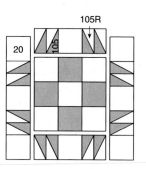

Templates needed:
20, 105 & 105R

Pigs in a Blanket

PIECING INSTRUCTIONS

1. Referring to the Piecing Diagram to piece one block, sew a light 12 to adjacent sides of a dark 36. Sew a medium and dark 12 to adjacent sides of a dark 36R. Join the two units to complete one corner unit. Repeat for four corner units.

2. Join the corner units to complete one block.

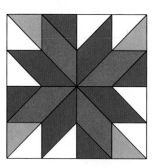

Pigs in a Blanket

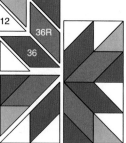

Templates needed:
12, 36 & 36R

Puss in the Corner 1

PIECING INSTRUCTIONS

1. Referring to the Piecing Diagram to piece one block, sew a light 5 to two adjacent sides of a dark 3; add a light 2 on the long side to complete a corner unit. Repeat for four corner units.

2. Sew a dark 5 to two adjacent sides of a light 4 and a light 5 to two adjacent sides of a dark 4; join the two pieced units to complete a side unit. Repeat for four side units.

3. Arrange the pieced units in rows with a light 1 square referring to the Piecing Diagram. Join units in rows; join rows to complete one block.

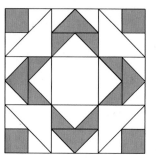

Puss in the Corner 1

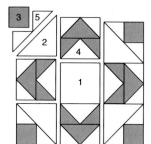

Templates needed:
1, 2, 3, 4 & 5

Puss in the Corner 2

PIECING INSTRUCTIONS

1. Referring to the Piecing Diagram to piece one block, sew a light 57 to opposite sides of the medium 34 to complete the center unit.

2. Sew a light 12 to a dark 12 along the diagonal; repeat for four units.

3. Sew a pieced 12 unit to opposite ends of each light 57 piece to complete side units.

4. Sew the side units to opposite sides of the center unit to complete one block.

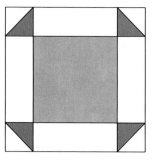

Puss in the Corner 2

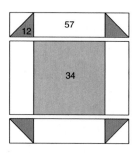

Templates needed:
12, 34 & 57

Snail's Trail

PIECING INSTRUCTIONS

1. Referring to the Piecing Diagram to piece one block, join two light and two dark 17 squares to complete a Four-Patch center.

2. Sew two light and two dark 16 triangles to the sides of the center; repeat with two dark and two light 12 triangles, then two dark and two light 14 triangles, and ending with two dark and two light 15 triangles to complete one block.

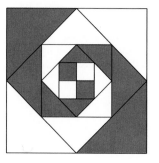

Snail's Trail

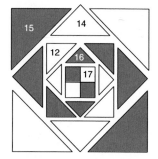

Templates needed:
12, 14, 15, 16 & 17

Spider 1

PIECING INSTRUCTIONS

1. Referring to the Piecing Diagram to piece one block, sew a light 12 to a medium or dark 12 along the diagonal; repeat for 16 units.

2. Arrange the units in rows referring to the Piecing Diagram to complete the design. Join units in rows; join rows to complete one block.

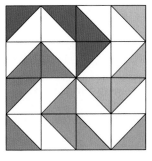

Spider 1

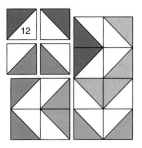

Template needed:
12

Spider 2

PIECING INSTRUCTIONS

1. Referring to the Piecing Diagram to piece one block, sew a light 2 to a dark 2 along the diagonal; repeat for nine units.

2. Arrange the pieced units in rows referring to the Piecing Diagram. Join units in rows; join rows to complete one block.

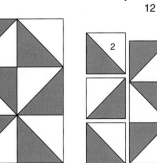

Spider 2

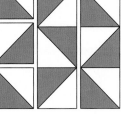

Template needed:
2

The Bat

PIECING INSTRUCTIONS

1. Referring to the Piecing Diagram to piece one block, join two dark 14 triangles on the short sides; repeat for four units.

2. Join two light 14 triangles on the short sides; repeat for four units.

3. Sew a light unit to a dark unit along the diagonal; repeat for four units.

4. Join the four units to complete the block piecing.

5. Turn under edges of the medium 94 squares; appliqué in place over the center seams of the pieced unit using thread to match fabric to complete one block.

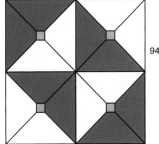

The Bat

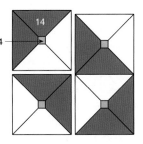

Templates needed:
14 & 94

The Crab

PIECING INSTRUCTIONS

1. Referring to the Piecing Diagram to piece one block, sew a medium K4 between a light H4 and HR4; repeat for four units.

2. Sew a dark L4 between a medium G4 and GR4; repeat for four units.

3. Join a K4-H4 unit with an L4-G4 unit to complete a side unit; repeat for four side units.

4. Sew a side unit to each side of the dark J4 square; set in light F4 pieces at the corners to complete one block.

The Crab

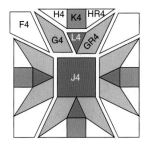

Templates needed:
F4, G4, GR4, H4, HR4,
J4, K4 & L4

The Dove

PIECING INSTRUCTIONS

1. Referring to the Piecing Diagram to piece one block, sew a light Q4 to a dark R4, matching centers and clipping curve of the R4 piece; repeat for two units.

2. Sew a dark Q4 to a light R4 as in step 1; repeat for two units.

3. Join the four pieced units referring to the Piecing Diagram to complete one block.

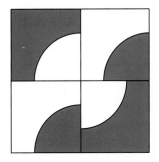

The Dove

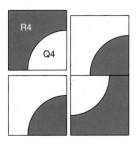

Templates needed:
Q4 & R4

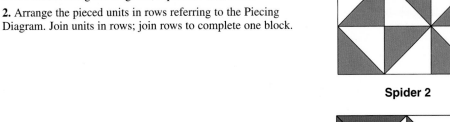

The Four-Patch Fox & Geese

PIECING INSTRUCTIONS

1. Referring to the Piecing Diagram to piece one block, sew a light 12 to a medium or dark 12 along the diagonal to complete a corner unit; repeat for four corner units.

2. Sew a medium or dark 12 to two adjacent sides of a light 14 to complete a side unit; repeat for four side units.

3. Sew four dark or medium 12 triangles to the sides of the light 19 to complete the center unit.

4. Arrange the pieced units in rows referring to the Piecing Diagram. Join units in rows; join rows to complete one block.

The Hen & Her Chicks

PIECING INSTRUCTIONS

1. Referring to the Piecing Diagram to piece one block, join two medium and two dark 68 squares to make a Four-Patch corner unit; repeat for four corner units.

2. Sew a medium 68 to each end of a lightest 8 piece; repeat for four units. Sew a light 68 to each end of a lightest 8 piece; repeat for two units.

3. Sew a dark 123 between a light 68-8 unit and a medium 68-8 unit to complete one side unit; repeat for two side units.

4. Sew a dark 123 to a medium 68-8 unit; repeat for two units. Sew a lightest 8 piece to two opposite sides of a dark 1 square.

5. Arrange the pieced units in rows referring to the Piecing Diagram. Join units in rows; join rows to complete one block.

The Owl Quilt

PIECING INSTRUCTIONS

1. Referring to the Piecing Diagram to piece one block, sew a medium E4 to each side of the dark 128, sewing angled seams as you stitch to join pieces; set in a medium 3 between E4 pieces to complete the block center.

2. Sew a medium 5 to two adjacent sides of a light 4; sew a light 3 to each end to complete a side unit; repeat for four side units.

3. Sew a side unit to opposite sides of the center unit; sew a dark 3 to each end of the remaining side units. Sew these units to the remaining sides of the center unit to complete one block.

The Swallow

PIECING INSTRUCTIONS

1. Referring to the Piecing Diagram to piece one block, sew a light 12 to a dark 12 along the diagonal; repeat for seven units.

2. Join two units; sew to one side of the medium 34 with dark sides inside. Join three 12 units; sew to the 12-34 unit.

3. Sew a dark 12 to the light end of each remaining pieced 12 unit; add a light 13 to the square end of each unit. Sew to two adjacent sides of the pieced center unit.

4. Sew a light 33 to two adjacent sides of a dark 12 to make a corner unit; sew the corner unit to the pieced center unit to complete one block.

Turkey Tracks 1

PIECING INSTRUCTIONS

1. Referring to the Piecing Diagram to piece one block, sew a light 104 to the long side of a medium C4 and CR4; join the two pieced

Continued on page 102

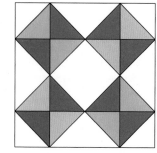
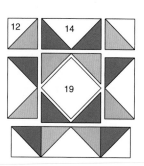

The Four-Patch Fox & Geese

Templates needed:
12, 14 & 19

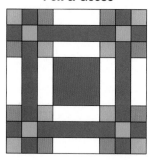
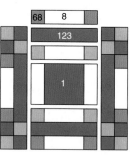

The Hen & Her Chicks

Templates needed:
1, 8, 68 & 123

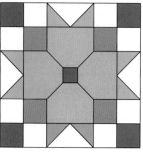
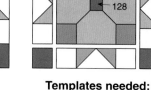

The Owl Quilt

Templates needed:
3, 4, 5, 128 & E4

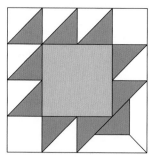
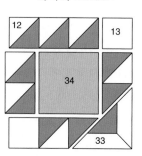

The Swallow

Templates needed:
12, 13, 33 & 34

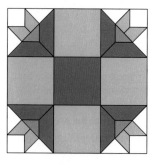
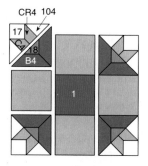

Turkey Tracks 1

Templates needed:
1, 17, 18, 104,
B4, C4 & CR4

Turkey Tracks 2

PIECING INSTRUCTIONS

1. Referring to the Piecing Diagram to piece one block, sew a light N4 and a dark NR4 to one side of a medium M4; repeat with a dark N4 and a light NR4 to complete a block quarter. Repeat for four quarter units.

2. Join the quarter units to complete one block.

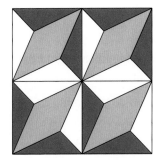

Turkey Tracks 2

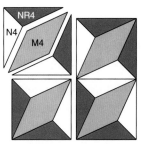

Templates needed:
M4, N4 & NR4

Wild Duck

PIECING INSTRUCTIONS

1. Referring to the Piecing Diagram to piece one block, sew a light 12 to a medium 12 along the diagonal; repeat for three units. Sew a light 12 to a dark 12 along the diagonal; repeat for five units. Sew a medium 12 to a dark 12 along the diagonal repeat for two units.

2. Arrange the pieced units in rows with four light and two medium 13 squares referring to the Piecing Diagram. Join units in rows; join rows to complete one block.

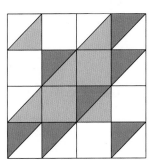

Wild Duck

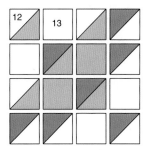

Templates needed:
12 & 13

Wild Geese

PIECING INSTRUCTIONS

1. Referring to the Piecing Diagram to piece one block, sew a light 2 to a dark 2 along the diagonal; repeat for nine units.

2. Arrange the pieced units in rows referring to the Piecing Diagram. Join units in rows; join rows to complete one block.

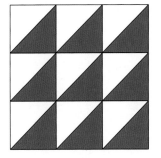

Wild Geese

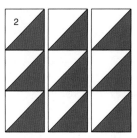

Template needed:
2

Wild Goose Chase

PIECING INSTRUCTIONS

1. Referring to the Piecing Diagram to piece one block, sew a light 18 to two adjacent sides of a dark 16; repeat for eight units. Join four units to complete a side unit; repeat for two side units.

2. Repeat step 1 with light 18 and medium 16 pieces.

3. Join two dark and two medium 16 triangles to make a corner unit; repeat for two corner units.

4. Arrange the pieced units in rows with two light 13 squares and the light 34 square referring to the Piecing Diagram. Join units in rows; join rows to complete one block.

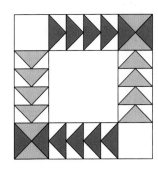

Wild Goose Chase

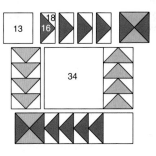

Templates needed:
13, 16, 18 & 34

Winged Square

PIECING INSTRUCTIONS

1. Referring to the Piecing Diagram to piece one block, sew a light 5 to a dark 5 on the diagonal; repeat for 24 units.

2. Join two units to make a strip; repeat to make 12 strips. Join two strips to make a side unit; repeat for two side units. Sew a side unit to opposite sides of a light 1 to make the center row.

3. Join four strips with a light 1 to make a row; repeat. Sew a row to opposite sides of the center row to complete one block.

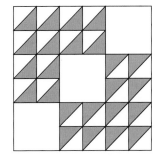

Winged Square

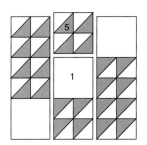

Templates needed:
1 & 5

Dad's Flannel Pillow
Continued from page 89

muslin square; pin or baste layers together to hold flat. Quilt as desired by hand or machine.

7. When quilting is complete, trim edges even; remove pins or basting.

8. Turn under one 20 1/2" edge of each backing piece 1/4"; press. Turn under again 1/2"; press and stitch to make hemmed edge.

9. Pin backing pieces to completed pillow top with wrong sides together, overlapping hemmed edges at the center back 5" as shown in Figure 2; machine-baste to hold.

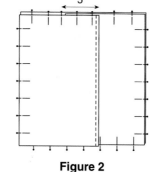

Figure 2
Pin backing pieces to completed pillow top with wrong sides together, overlapping hemmed edges at the center back as shown.

10. Bind edges of pillow using self-made or purchased binding. Insert pillow form through back opening to finish. ❖

Wild Goose Chase Album Cover
Continued from page 91

5. Cut two pieces cream print 4" x 12 1/2" for side flaps. Turn under one long edge of each piece 1/4" and press; turn under again 1/4"; press and stitch to hem.

6. Place the completed top on the batting with right side up; quilt as desired by hand or machine. Place each flap piece right sides together on the short ends of the pieced top and pin in place as shown in Figure 4.

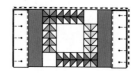

Figure 4
Place each flap piece right sides together on the short ends of the pieced top and pin in place.

7. Place the lining piece right sides together with the pieced top. Stitch all around, leaving a 4" opening on one side. Trim corners and turn right side out. Press and hand-stitch the opening closed to finish. ❖

Pigeon Toes Place Mat
Continued from page 90

backing and batting even with pieced top; stitch all around, leaving a 6" opening on one long side. Trim corners and turn right side out. Hand-stitch opening closed.

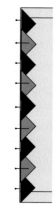

Figure 3
Pin 2 rust/brown and 2 black prairie points on each side of the center, alternating colors and pinning each 1 in the center of the previous 1 as shown.

9. Quilt on marked lines and in white-on-white print pieces 1/4" from seams using black quilting thread. Quilt remaining areas as desired to finish. ❖

Quilting Design

Turkey Tracks 1
Continued from page 100

units on the short sides and set in a light 17. Repeat for four units.

2. Sew a dark B4 to a dark B4; set in a medium 18. Repeat for four units.

3. Join one C4 unit with one B4 unit to complete one corner unit; repeat for four corner units.

4. Arrange the pieced corner units in rows with one dark and four medium 1 squares referring to the Piecing Diagram. Join units in rows; join rows to complete one block.

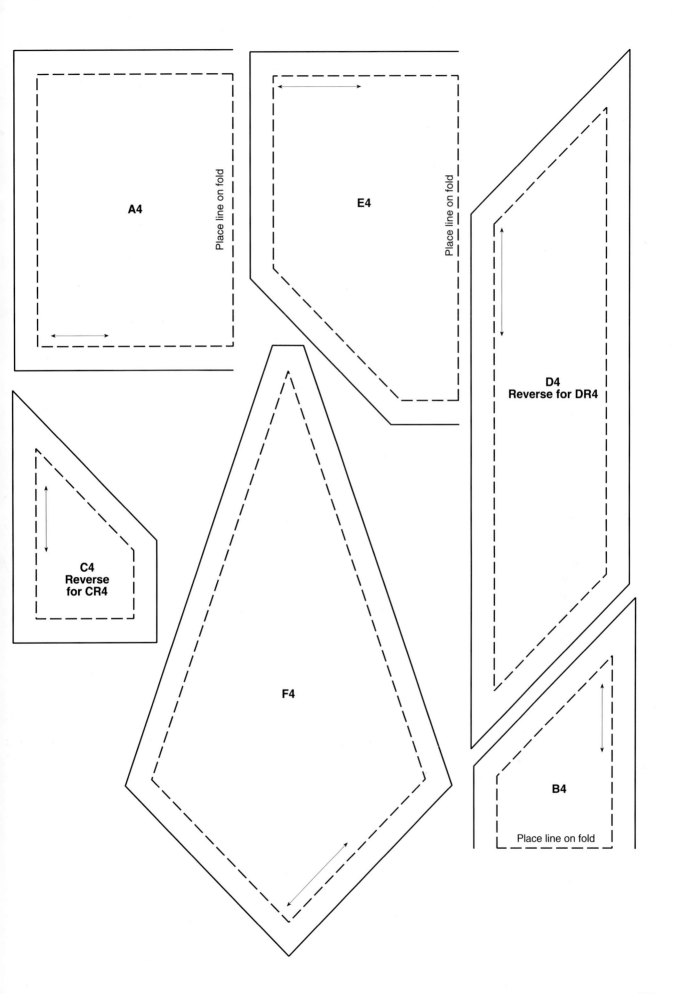

A4

E4

Place line on fold

Place line on fold

D4
Reverse for DR4

C4
Reverse
for CR4

F4

B4

Place line on fold

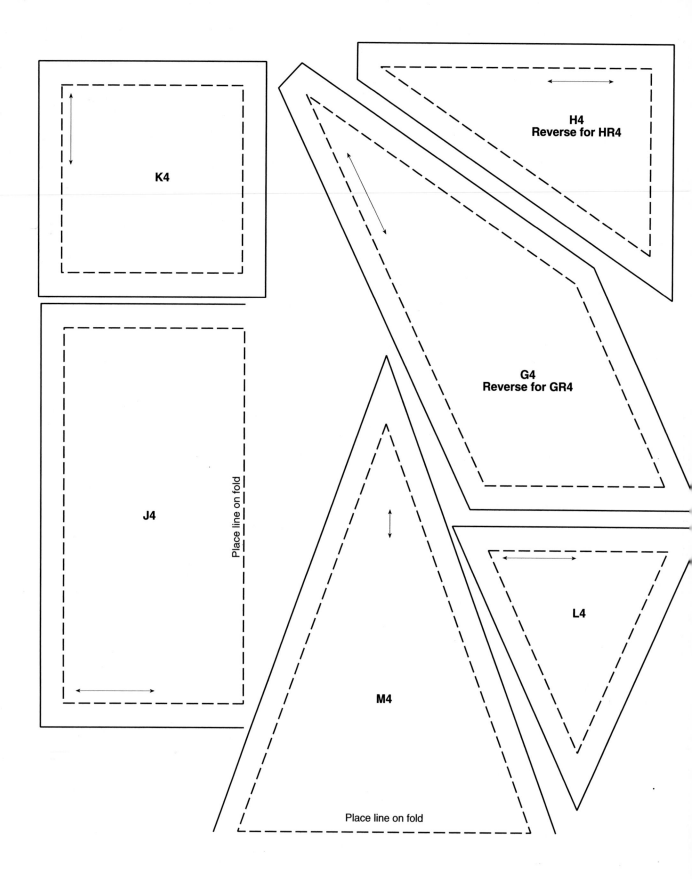

K4

H4
Reverse for HR4

G4
Reverse for GR4

Place line on fold

J4

L4

M4

Place line on fold

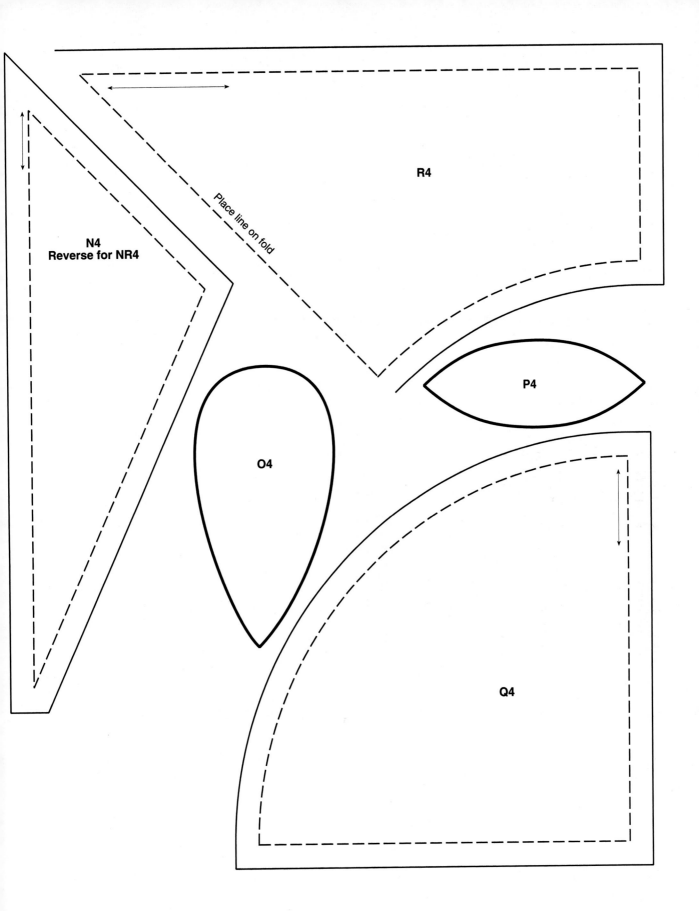

N4
Reverse for NR4

Place line on fold

R4

P4

O4

Q4

Nature's Glory

*No matter where
you live, you can enjoy
the glorious world
you see each day.
We selected these blocks
for quilters who
appreciate the beauty
all around them!
Lightning in the Hills,
Delectable Mountains,
Path Through the Woods,
Rocky Glen, Northern
Lights, Summer Winds
and Peony—all are quilt
blocks reflecting the beauty
of the world around us.*

Autumn Leaf

PIECING INSTRUCTIONS

Step 1. Referring to the Piecing Diagram to piece one block, sew a medium 28 to a light 28 along the diagonal; repeat for 16 units.

Step 2. Join two 28 units; repeat for eight 28 units.

Step 3. Sew a 28 unit to one side of a dark 45. Sew a light 27 to the dark end of a 28 unit; repeat for four units. Sew a 27-28 unit to the adjacent side of a 45-28 unit; repeat for four units.

Step 4. Join two pieced units with a medium 44; repeat. Sew a darkest 27 between two medium 44 pieces.

Step 5. Join the pieced units referring to the Piecing Diagram to complete one block.

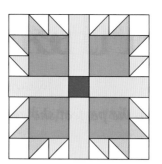

Autumn Leaf

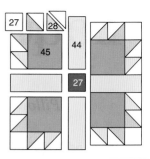

Templates needed:
27, 28, 44 & 45

Autumn Tints

PIECING INSTRUCTIONS

Step 1. Referring to the Piecing Diagram to piece one block, sew a medium 28 to a lightest 28 on the diagonal; repeat for 16 units.

Step 2. Sew a medium A5 and a medium AR5 along the angled seam; set in a dark 27. Repeat for four units.

Step 3. Join two 28 units; repeat for two units. Sew one unit to one side of an A-27 unit. Sew a lightest 27 square to the remaining 28 unit and sew to the adjacent side of the A-27-28 unit to complete one corner unit; repeat for four corner units.

Step 4. Join two corner units with a light 44 to make a row; repeat for two rows.

Step 5. Join two light 44 pieces with a dark 27 to make a row. Sew this row between the two previously pieced rows to complete one block.

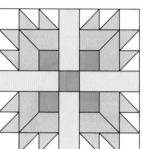

Autumn Tints

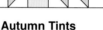

Templates needed:
27, 28, 44, A5 & AR5

Bluebell Block

PIECING INSTRUCTIONS

1. Referring to the Piecing Diagram to piece one block, sew a medium 100 to each side of a light 27, stitching seams between the 100 pieces to make a side unit; repeat for four side units.

2. Sew a lightest 99 to two adjacent sides of a dark 20 to make a corner unit; repeat for four corner units.

3. Sew the four side units to the dark 20 center square, join seams between units.

4. Set in the corner units to complete one block.

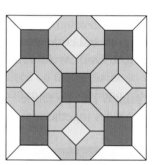

Bluebell Block

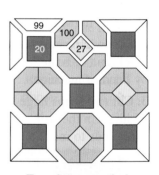

Templates needed:
20, 27, 99 & 100

Blue Heaven

PIECING INSTRUCTIONS

1. Referring to the Piecing Diagram to piece one block, sew a dark 59 between two medium 59 squares.

2. Sew a medium 59 between two dark B5 pieces; repeat. Sew the pieced 59 unit between these two units to complete the center unit.

3. Sew a light D5 and DR5 to opposite sides of a dark 59; sew a light 18 to one end of 59 to complete one corner unit. Repeat for four corner units.

4. Sew a corner unit to a lightest C5; repeat for four units.

5. Set a pieced unit into the sides of the center unit to complete one block.

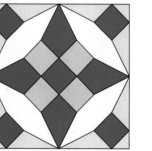

Blue Heaven

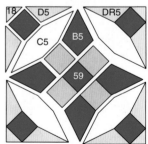

Templates needed:
18, 59, B5, C5, D5 & DR5

Buckwheat

PIECING INSTRUCTIONS

1. Referring to the Piecing Diagram to piece one block, sew a dark 5 to a medium 5; repeat for eight units. Sew a dark 4 to the medium side of four pieced units.

2. Sew a light 4 to a light 4; repeat for four units. Sew a 4-4 unit to a 4-5 unit to complete a corner unit; repeat for four corner units.

3. Sew a medium 4 to a dark 4 and a light 4 to a medium 4; repeat for two of each unit. Join one of each unit to complete a side unit. Repeat for two side units.

4. Sew a light 4 to a dark 4; repeat for two units. Join these two units to make one center unit.

5. Sew a light 4 to a dark/medium 5-5 unit; repeat for four units. Join two 4-5 units to make top and bottom units.

6. Arrange units in rows and join to complete one block.

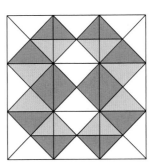

Buckwheat

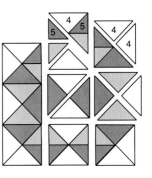

Templates needed:
4 & 5

Cobweb

PIECING INSTRUCTIONS

1. Referring to the Piecing Diagram to piece one block, sew a light 4 to a dark 4; sew this unit to a medium 2. Repeat for four units.

2. Sew a light 4 to a dark 4; repeat for two units. Join the two units to complete one center unit.

3. Join the pieced center and corner units with medium and darkest 1 pieces to make rows; join rows to complete one block.

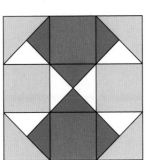

Cobweb

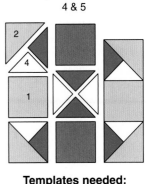

Templates needed:
1, 2 & 4

Cypress

PIECING INSTRUCTIONS

1. Referring to the Piecing Diagram to piece one block, sew a light 10 and 10R to a medium 9; repeat for four units.

2. Sew a dark 2 to a medium 2 along the diagonal; repeat for four units.

3. Arrange the pieced units in rows with the medium 1; join in rows. Join rows to complete one block.

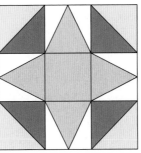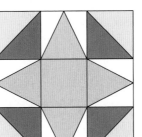

Cypress

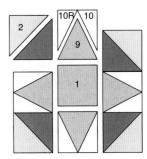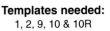

Templates needed:
1, 2, 9, 10 & 10R

Delectable Mountains

PIECING INSTRUCTIONS

1. Referring to the Piecing Diagram to piece one block, sew a light 18 to a dark 18 along the diagonal; repeat for 24 units.

2. Join six units referring to the Piecing Diagram for positioning of units; repeat for four pieced strip units. Sew a light 17 to each end of two units.

3. Join three dark and one light 18 triangles referring to the Piecing Diagram; repeat for four units. Sew a light 59 to each end of two units.

4. Sew an 18 unit to two opposite sides of a light 59. Sew the 18-59 units to the remaining sides to complete the center square.

5. Sew a dark 26 to each side of the center square.

6. Sew a strip unit to two opposite sides of the pieced center square; sew a strip unit with 17 ends to the remaining sides to complete one block.

Delectable Mountains

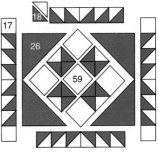

Templates needed:
17, 18, 26 & 59

Dogwood

PIECING INSTRUCTIONS

1. Referring to the Piecing Diagram to piece one block, join two light E5 pieces on the straight ends; repeat for 16 units.

2. Sew four E5 units to the sides of a dark 124; repeat for four units.

3. Join the four units with a dark 124 in the center; set in a medium 108 between units on sides to complete the center unit.

4. Sew a medium F5 to each side of the center unit to complete one block.

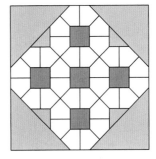

Dogwood

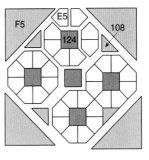

Templates needed:
108, 124, E5 & F5

Grape Basket

PIECING INSTRUCTIONS

1. Referring to the Piecing Diagram to piece one block, sew a light 21 to a medium 21 along the diagonal; repeat for 11 units.

2. Sew a light 21 to a dark 21 along the diagonal; repeat for four units.

3. Arrange pieced units in rows with light and dark 20 pieces referring to the Piecing Diagram. Join units in rows; join rows to complete one block.

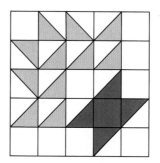

Grape Basket

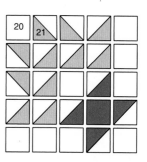

Templates needed:
20 & 21

Historic Oak Leaf

PIECING INSTRUCTIONS

1. Referring to the Piecing Diagram to piece one block, sew a light 5 to a dark 5 along the diagonal; repeat for nine units.

2. Join two 5 units to make a strip; repeat for four strips.

3. Sew one 5 strip to one side of a dark 1. Sew a third 5 unit to one end of a 5 strip and sew to the adjacent side of the dark 1 to make a corner unit.

4. Sew a dark 5 to one end of each of the remaining 5 strips; sew one of these units to each dark 2 to make a triangle unit. Sew a light 15 to each triangle unit.

5. Cut a 9 1/4" piece of 3/4"-wide dark bias for stem; appliqué in place on the center diagonal of the light 34 to complete the stem unit.

6. Join the pieced units to complete one block.

Historic Oak Leaf

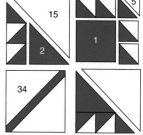

Templates needed:
1, 2, 5, 15 & 34

Indian Meadow

PIECING INSTRUCTIONS

1. Referring to the Piecing Diagram to piece one block, sew a dark 21 to two short sides of a light 25; repeat for four units.

2. Sew a dark 73 to a light 22; repeat for two units.

3. Sew a 21-25 unit to the 22 side of the 22-73 unit; sew a light 20 to the 21 end of another 21-25 unit. Sew the 20-21-25 unit to the remaining 22 side of the 22-73 unit; repeat for two units.

4. Sew a light 22 to a medium 22 along the diagonal; repeat for two units.

5. Join the pieced units using a set-in seam to complete one block.

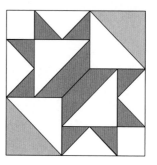

Indian Meadow

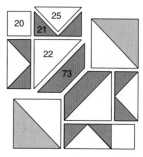

Templates needed:
20, 21, 22, 25 & 73

July's Summer Sky

PIECING INSTRUCTIONS

1. Referring to the Piecing Diagram to piece one block, sew a medium 5 to a lightest 122; add a light GR5 and a lightest 77 to complete a pieced unit.

2. Repeat with lightest 5, light 122R, dark G5 and medium 77R. Join the two pieced units to complete one unit; repeat for four units.

3. Join the four pieced units to complete one block.

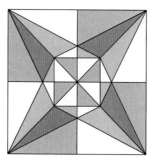

July's Summer Sky

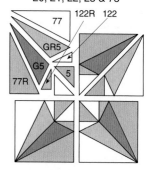

Templates needed:
5, 77, 77R, 122, 122R,
G5 & GR5

Lightning in the Hills

PIECING INSTRUCTIONS

1. Referring to the Piecing Diagram to piece one block, sew a light 5 to a medium 5 along the diagonal; repeat for 20 units.

2. Sew a dark 5 to a darkest 5 along the diagonal; repeat for eight units.

3. Sew a light 5 to a dark 5 along the diagonal; repeat for four units.

4. Arrange the pieced units in rows with the light 3 pieces referring to the Piecing Diagram. Join units in rows; join rows to complete one block.

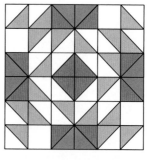

Lightning in the Hills

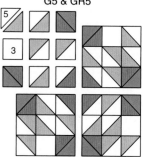

Templates needed:
3 & 5

Maple Leaf 2

PIECING INSTRUCTIONS

1. Referring to the Piecing Diagram to piece one block, sew a light 28 to a medium 28 along the diagonal; repeat for 16 units.

2. Cut a 3" piece of dark 1/4"-wide bias tape for stem; appliqué to four light 27 squares for stem corner.

3. Arrange four pieced units with light and dark 27 squares in rows referring to the Piecing Diagram; join pieces in rows. Join rows to complete one corner unit; repeat to make four corner units.

4. Join two corner units with a light 44 to make a row; repeat. Join two light 44 pieces with a dark 27 to make the center row.

5. Join the rows to complete one block.

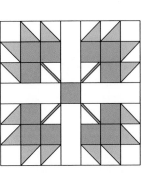

Maple Leaf 2

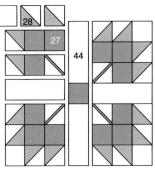

Templates needed:
27, 28 & 44

Meadow Flower

PIECING INSTRUCTIONS

1. Referring to the Piecing Diagram to piece one block, sew a medium 130 to a dark H5; repeat for four units. Sew a medium 130 to a darkest H5; repeat for four units.

2. Join a dark 130-H5 unit and a darkest 130-H5 unit to make a corner unit; repeat for four corner units.

3. Sew a medium 130 to two opposite sides of two lightest and two light J5 pieces. Sew a medium 54 to one remaining side.

4. Join these pieces with the 54 triangles toward the center to complete the center unit.

5. Sew a corner unit to each side of the center unit to complete one block.

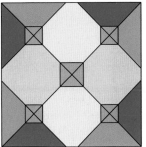

Meadow Flower

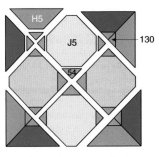

Templates needed:
54, 130, H5 & J5

Morning

PIECING INSTRUCTIONS

1. Referring to the Piecing Diagram to piece one block, sew a medium 5 to a light 5 on the diagonal; repeat for eight units.

2. Join two 5 units with a light and medium 3 to make a corner unit; repeat for four corner units.

3. Sew a light 5 to the angled sides of a dark 87 to complete one side unit; repeat for four side units.

4. Arrange pieced units in rows with the dark 1 square referring to the Piecing Diagram. Join units in rows; join rows to complete one block.

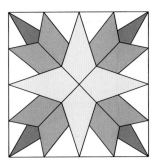

Morning

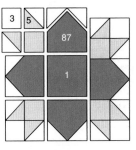
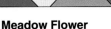

Templates needed:
1, 3, 5 & 87

Morning Star

PIECING INSTRUCTIONS

1. Referring to the Piecing Diagram to piece one block, sew a light M5 to a dark LR5 and a light MR5 to a dark L5; join these two units on the L piece sides. Repeat for four units.

2. Sew a light O5 and OR5 to the sides of a darkest N5; repeat for four units.

3. Set an O-N unit into a L-M unit to complete one corner unit; repeat for four corner units.

4. Join a corner unit with two medium R5 pieces; repeat for two units. Join these units. Set the remaining corner units into the pieced unit to complete one block.

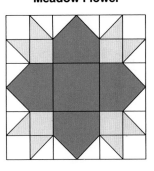

Morning Star

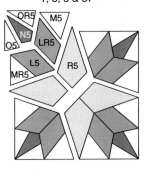

Templates needed:
L5, LR5, M5, MR5, N5,
O5, OR5 & R5

Northern Lights

PIECING INSTRUCTIONS

1. Referring to the Piecing Diagram to piece one block, sew a lightest P5 to a dark KR5; add a light 95. Repeat with a lightest PR5, a medium K5 and a dark 95R.

2. Join the two units to make a corner unit; repeat for four corner units.

3. Join the four corner units to complete one block.

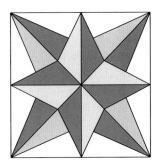

Northern Lights

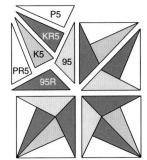

Templates needed:
95, 95R, K5, KR5, P5 & PR5

Old Snowflake

PIECING INSTRUCTIONS

1. Referring to the Piecing Diagram to piece one block, sew a light 12 to opposite sides of a medium S5 to complete one corner unit; repeat for four corner units.

2. Join two darkest, one dark and one light 4 triangles referring to the Piecing Diagram to complete one side unit; repeat for four side units.

3. Arrange the pieced units in rows with a medium 1 referring to the Piecing Diagram. Join units in rows; join rows to complete one block.

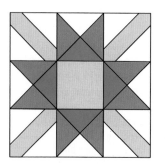

Old Snowflake

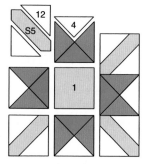

Templates needed:
1, 4, 12 & S5

Over & Under

PIECING INSTRUCTIONS

1. Referring to the Piecing Diagram to piece one block, sew a light 84 to a light 84R; set in a medium 3 to make a corner unit. Repeat for four corner units.

2. Sew a medium 8 to a dark 69; repeat for four units.

3. Arrange the pieced units in rows with a lightest 1 referring to the Piecing Diagram. Join units in rows; join rows to complete one block.

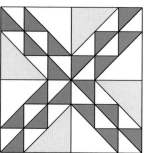

Over and Under

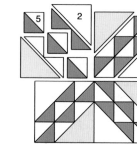

Templates needed:
1, 3, 8, 69, 84 & 84R

Path Through the Woods

PIECING INSTRUCTIONS

1. Referring to the Piecing Diagram to piece one block, sew a light 5 to a dark 5 along the diagonal; repeat for 12 units.

2. Join four pieced units with two light and two dark 5 pieces to make one pieced strip referring to the Piecing Diagram; repeat for four pieced strips.

3. Sew a medium 2 to one side of one pieced unit and a light 2 to the opposite side; repeat for four units.

4. Join the four pieced units referring to the Piecing Diagram to complete one block.

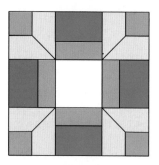

Path Through the Woods

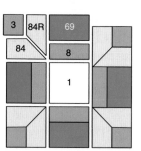

Templates needed:
2 & 5

Paths & Stiles

1. Referring to the Piecing Diagram to piece one block, sew a lightest 2 to a dark 2 along the diagonal to complete one corner unit; repeat for four corner units.

2. Sew a darkest 8 between two light 8 pieces to complete one side unit; repeat for four side units.

3. Arrange the side and corner units in rows with the medium 1 square referring to the Piecing Diagram. Join units in rows; join rows to complete one block.

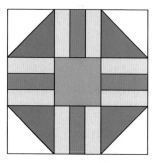

Paths & Stiles

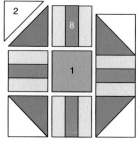

Templates needed:
1, 2 & 8

Peony

PIECING INSTRUCTIONS

1. Referring to the Piecing Diagram to piece one block, set a medium W5 into a light X5; repeat for four units.

2. Sew a light T5 to a medium U5; repeat for four units.

3. Sew a T-U unit to a W-X unit; sew a dark V5 to the T-U side of the unit. Repeat for four units.

4. Join two pieced units referring to the Piecing Diagram; repeat. Join the two pieced units to complete one block.

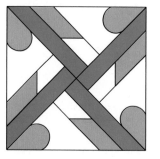

Peony

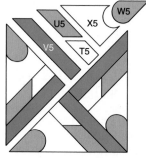

Templates needed:
T5, U5, V5, W5 & X5

Perpetual Motion

PIECING INSTRUCTIONS

1. Referring to the Piecing Diagram to piece one block, sew a light 125R to a medium 125R along the longest seam; repeat for four units.

2. Sew a light 80R to the medium 125R side of the pieced unit and a dark 80R to the light 125R side; repeat for four units.

3. Join the units with the dark 80 pieces toward the center to complete one block.

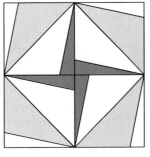

Perpetual Motion

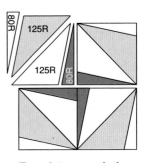

Templates needed:
80R & 125R

Rain or Shine

PIECING INSTRUCTIONS

1. Referring to the Piecing Diagram to piece one block, sew a light 16 to a lightest Y5 to a medium Z5 to complete a side unit; repeat for four side units.

2. Sew a lightest BB5 and BBR5 to a dark AA5; add a light CC5 and a lightest DD5 to complete a corner unit; repeat for four corner units.

3. Join the pieced units with the medium EE5 to complete one block.

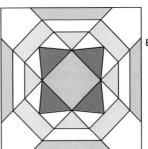

Rain or Shine

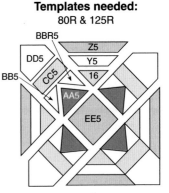

Templates needed:
16, Y5, Z5, AA5, BB5, BBR5,
CC5, DD5 & EE5

Rocky Glen

PIECING INSTRUCTIONS

1. Referring to the Piecing Diagram to piece one block, sew a light 18 to a dark 18 along the diagonal; repeat for 28 units.

2. Join four pieced units to make a row; repeat for four four-unit rows. Join three pieced units to make a row; repeat for four three-unit rows.

3. Sew a medium 26 to a light 26 along the diagonal; repeat for four units.

4. Sew a three-unit row to one medium side of one unit 26 and a four-unit row to the adjacent side of one unit 26 referring to the Piecing Diagram; repeat for four pieced units.

5. Join the pieced units to complete one block.

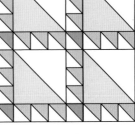

Rocky Glen

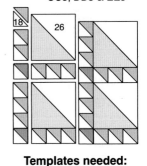

Templates needed:
18 & 26

Rocky Mountain Puzzle

PIECING INSTRUCTIONS

1. Referring to the Piecing Diagram to piece one block, sew a dark FF5 to each side of a light 13, finishing the beginning seam after all pieces have been added to complete the center unit.

2. Sew a light 12 to a medium 12 along the diagonal; repeat for 10 units.

3. Join three 12 units to make a row; add a light 13. Repeat for two three-unit rows. Join two 12 units; repeat for two two-unit rows.

4. Sew a two-unit row to opposite sides of the pieced center.

5. Sew a three-unit row to the remaining sides of the pieced center to complete one block.

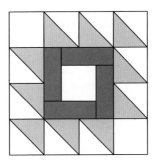

Rocky Mountain Puzzle

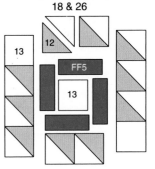

Templates needed:
12, 13 & FF5

Rolling Stone

PIECING INSTRUCTIONS

1. Referring to the Piecing Diagram to piece one block, sew one dark and three medium 5 pieces to the sides of a light 7 to complete one corner unit; repeat for four corner units.

2. Sew a light 6 to a dark 6 to complete one side unit; repeat for four side units.

3. Arrange the side and corner units in rows with the light 1 referring to the Piecing Diagram. Join units in rows; join rows to complete one block.

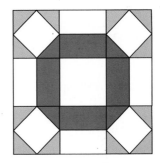

Rolling Stone

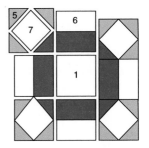

Templates needed:
1, 5, 6 & 7

Snowball Variation

PIECING INSTRUCTIONS

1. Referring to the Piecing Diagram to piece one block, sew a light 2 to a dark 2 along the diagonal to make a corner unit; repeat for four corner units.

2. Arrange the corner units in rows with light and dark 1 pieces referring to the Piecing Diagram.

3. Join units and pieces in rows; join rows to complete one block.

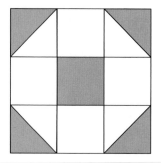

Snowball Variation

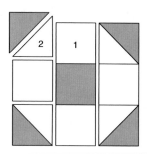

Templates needed:
1 & 2

Spider's Den

PIECING INSTRUCTIONS

1. Referring to the Piecing Diagram to piece one block, sew a dark 79 between two light 79 squares; repeat for two units. Sew a light 79 between two dark 79 squares.

2. Sew the dark/light/dark unit between the two light/dark/light units to complete one Nine-Patch unit; repeat for four Nine-Patch units.

3. Sew a light HH5 between two dark HH5 pieces; add a light JJ5 to complete one side unit. Repeat for four side units.

4. Sew a light GG5 to a dark GG5; repeat for four units. Repeat to make four GGR5 units.

5. Sew a light 104 to a dark 104 along the diagonal; repeat for four units.

6. Join a Nine-Patch unit with a GG5 and GGR5 unit and 104 unit to complete one corner unit; repeat for four corner units.

7. Arrange the side and corner units in rows with the light 13 referring to the Piecing Diagram. Join units in rows; join the rows to complete one block.

Spider's Den

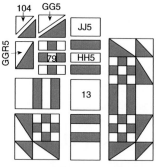

Templates needed:
13, 79, 104, GG5,
GGR5, HH5 & JJ5

Spring Has Come

PIECING INSTRUCTIONS

1. Referring to the Piecing Diagram to piece one block, sew a light 59 between two medium 59 squares; repeat. Sew a medium 59 between two light 59 squares; sew this unit between the two previously pieced units to complete the center Nine-Patch section of the block. Sew a dark 26 to each side of the pieced center.

2. Sew a lightest 18 to a dark or medium 18 along the diagonal; repeat for 16 units. Join two units; repeat for eight joined units. Sew a lightest 17 to the dark/medium end of four of the units.

3. Sew a medium or dark 18 to the short sides of a lightest 16; repeat for four units.

4. Sew a 17-18 unit to each side of a 16-18 unit; repeat. Sew a pieced 18 unit to each side of the remaining two 16-18 units. Sew these units to opposite sides of the pieced center; sew the longer pieced units to the remaining sides to complete one block.

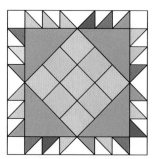

Spring Has Come

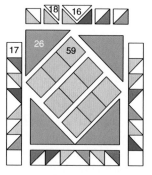

Templates needed:
16, 17, 18, 26 & 59

Storm at Sea

PIECING INSTRUCTIONS

1. Referring to the Piecing Diagram to piece one block, sew a light 16 to each side of a dark 13. Sew a medium 12 to each side of the 13-16 unit to complete the center unit; set aside.

2. Sew light 58 and 58R to the sides of a medium 83 to complete a side unit; repeat for four side units.

3. Sew a dark 18 to each side of a light 59 to complete one corner unit; repeat for four corner units.

4. Arrange pieced units in rows referring to the Piecing Diagram. Join units in rows; join rows to complete one block.

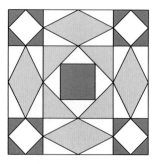

Storm at Sea

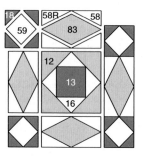

Templates needed:
12, 13, 16, 18,
58, 58R, 59 & 83

Storm Signal

PIECING INSTRUCTIONS

1. Referring to the Piecing Diagram to piece one block, sew a light 4 to a medium 4 along the diagonal; repeat for four units.

2. Sew a light 5 to a medium 5 on a short side; repeat for two units. Join the two units to complete the center square.

3. Arrange the pieced 4 units with light and medium 7 squares and the center square in rows to make center unit referring to the Piecing Diagram. Join units in rows; join rows.

4. Sew a dark 15 to each side of the pieced center unit to complete one block.

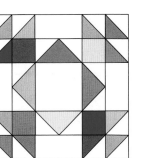

Storm Signal

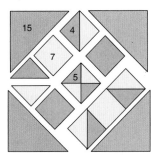

Templates needed:
4, 5, 7 & 15

Summer Winds

PIECING INSTRUCTIONS

1. Referring to the Piecing Diagram to piece one block, sew a light 5 to a colored 5 along the diagonal; repeat for 12 units.

2. Join three 5-5 units with one colored 3 to complete a corner unit; repeat for four corner units.

3. Sew a light 5 to adjacent short sides of a colored 4; repeat for four units. Sew a light 6 to each unit to complete a side unit; repeat for four side units.

4. Arrange pieced units in rows with the light 1 referring to the Piecing Diagram. Join units in rows; join rows to complete one block.

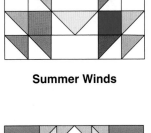

Summer Winds

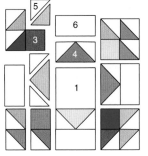

Templates needed:
1, 3, 4, 5 & 6

Summer's Dream

PIECING INSTRUCTIONS

1. Referring to the Piecing Diagram to piece one block, sew a dark 3 between two darkest 3 squares. Sew a darkest 3 between two dark 3 squares; repeat. Join these units to complete the center Nine-Patch unit.

2. Sew a lightest 14 to each side of the pieced Nine-Patch unit to complete the center unit.

3. Sew a light 18 to a medium 18 along the diagonal; sew a medium 18 to two adjacent sides of the light side; repeat for eight pieced triangle units.

4. Sew a triangle unit to two adjacent sides of a dark 13 to make a corner triangle; repeat for four corner triangles.

5. Sew a corner triangle to each side of the center unit to complete one block.

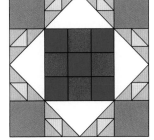

Summer's Dream

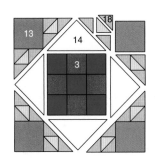

Templates needed:
3, 13, 14 & 18

Sunburst

PIECING INSTRUCTIONS

1. Referring to the Piecing Diagram to piece one block, sew a medium 68 between two dark 68 squares; repeat. Sew a dark 68 between two medium 68 squares. Join these pieced units to complete a Nine-Patch center unit.

2. Sew MM5 and MMR5 to opposite sides of 8 to complete a side unit; repeat for four side units.

3. Sew a light LL5 to a dark LLR5 to complete a corner unit; repeat for four corner units.

4. Arrange pieced units in rows referring to the Piecing Diagram. Join units in rows; join rows to complete pieced center.

5. Set a light KK5 and a dark KKR5 into each side of the pieced center to complete one block.

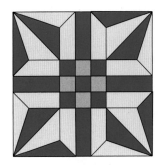

Sunburst

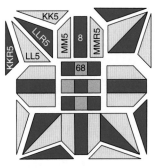

Templates needed:
8, 68, KK5, KKR5, LL5, LLR5, MM5 & MMR5

Sunset Star

PIECING INSTRUCTIONS

1. Referring to the Piecing Diagram to piece one block, sew a lightest OO5 and OOR5 to two adjacent sides of a dark NN5 to make a side unit; repeat for four side units.

2. Sew a light 127 into a medium PP5 to make one corner unit; repeat for four corner units.

3. Sew a side unit between two corner units; repeat.

4. Sew the remaining side units to opposite sides of a medium 3.

5. Sew the pieced side/corner units to opposite sides of the side/center unit to complete one block.

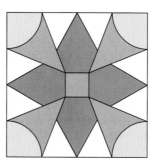

Sunset Star

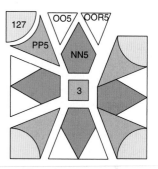

Templates needed:
3, 127, NN5, OO5,
OOR5 & PP5

Sunshine

PIECING INSTRUCTIONS

1. Referring to the Piecing Diagram to piece one block, sew a medium 2 to a dark 2 along the diagonal to make a corner unit; repeat for four corner units.

2. Sew a light QQ5 and QQR5 to the sides of a dark 9 to complete one side unit; repeat for four side units.

3. Join the side units and set in the corner units to complete one block.

Sunshine

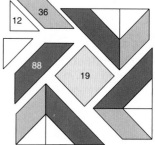

Templates needed:
2, 9, QQ5 & QQR5

Symmetry in Motion

PIECING INSTRUCTIONS

1. Referring to the Piecing Diagram to piece one block, sew a lightest 12 to a dark 88; repeat for four units.

2. Sew a lightest 12 to a medium 36; repeat for four units.

3. Join a 12-88 unit to a 12-36 unit referring to the Piecing Diagram; repeat for four units.

4. Sew the pieced units to the light 19, finishing the beginning seam after all seams are stitched to complete one block.

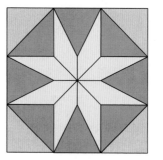

Symmetry in Motion

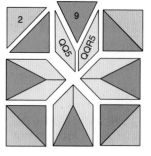

Templates needed:
12, 19, 36 & 88

Time & Tide

PIECING INSTRUCTIONS

1. Referring to the Piecing Diagram to piece one block, sew a lightest 10 and 10R to a dark 9 to make a side unit; repeat. Repeat with medium 9 pieces to complete four side units.

2. Sew a light 10 and 10R to a darkest 11 to make a corner unit; repeat for four corner units.

3. Join two dark and two medium 4 triangles referring to the Piecing Diagram to complete the center unit.

4. Arrange the pieced units in rows referring to the Piecing Diagram. Join units in rows; join rows to complete one block.

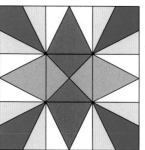

Time & Tide

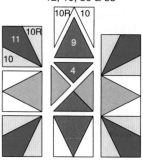

Templates needed:
4, 9, 10, 10R & 11

Tumbleweed

PIECING INSTRUCTIONS

1. Referring to the Piecing Diagram to piece one block, sew a dark 31 to one angled end of a light RR5; repeat for four units.

2. Sew a medium 120 to each 31-RR5 unit.

3. Sew a medium 4 to a light RR5; repeat for four units. Sew a dark 14 to each unit referring to the Piecing Diagram for positioning.

4. Sew a 4-14-RR5 unit to a 120-31-RR5 unit to make a square unit; repeat for four square units.

5. Join the square units to complete one block.

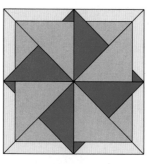

Tumbleweed

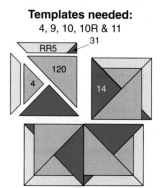

Templates needed:
4, 14, 31, 120 & RR5

Weathervane

PIECING INSTRUCTIONS

1. Referring to the Piecing Diagram to piece one block, sew a light 6 to opposite sides of the dark 1. Sew a medium 3 to each end of the remaining two light 6 pieces; sew to remaining sides of the dark 1 to complete the center unit.

2. Join two lightest and one light 4 triangle to make a strip; sew a medium 5 to each end to complete a side strip; repeat for four side strips.

3. Sew a side strip to opposite sides of the center unit. Sew a lightest 3 to each end of the remaining side strips. Sew these strips to the remaining sides of the pieced unit to complete one block.

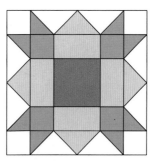

Weathervane

Templates needed:
1, 3, 4, 5 & 6

Woodland Path

PIECING INSTRUCTIONS

1. Referring to the Piecing Diagram to piece one block, sew a light 47 to two adjacent sides of a colored 28; repeat for 16 units.

2. Join four 28-47 units to complete a side unit; repeat for four side units.

3. Sew a dark 47 to each side of the medium 27 to complete the center unit.

4. Sew a light 22 to a dark 22 on the diagonal to make a corner unit; repeat for four corner units.

5. Arrange pieced units in rows referring to the Piecing Diagram. Join units in rows; join rows to complete one block.

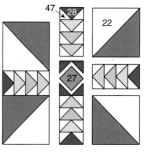

Woodland Path

Templates needed:
22, 27, 28 & 47

Autumn Leaf Vest
Continued from page 113

adhesive. Following manufacturer's instructions, bond fusible adhesive pieces to tan solid pieces; remove paper backing.

2. Prepare one Maple Leaf 2 block referring to the Placement Diagram for placement of colors in the block and fusing tan solid stem pieces in place on 27 pieces. Machine satin-stitch stems in place using thread to match fabric.

3. Prepare pieces for a second block, eliminating the center row 27 and 44 pieces. Join pieces to complete two end rows.

4. Cut the following size strips from the 5/8"-wide ribbon and 5/8"-wide fusible adhesive: 2—13 1/4"; 6—12 1/2"; and 4—6 3/8".

5. Following manufacturer's instructions, bond same-size fusible adhesive to ribbon lengths; remove paper backing.

6. Center the whole block on the vest back referring to the Placement Diagram for positioning; pin or baste in place.

7. Center the 12 1/2" ribbon strips over the top and bottom edges of the block and the 13 1/4" ribbon strips on the remaining sides. When satisfied with arrangement, fuse in place.

8. Using thread to match the ribbon, topstitch both sides of the ribbon in place. Machine satin-stitch corners to create squares as shown in Figure 1.

9. Position a half block section on each vest front referring to the Placement Diagram for positioning; pin or baste in place. Center the 12 1/2" ribbon strips on opposite long sides and 6 3/8" ribbon strips on the top and bottom. When satisfied with arrangement, fuse in place. Stitch in place as in step 8.

10. Using thread to match fabric, stitch in the ditch around leaf shapes to secure block to vest base to finish. ❖

Figure 1
Machine satin-stitch corners to create squares as shown.

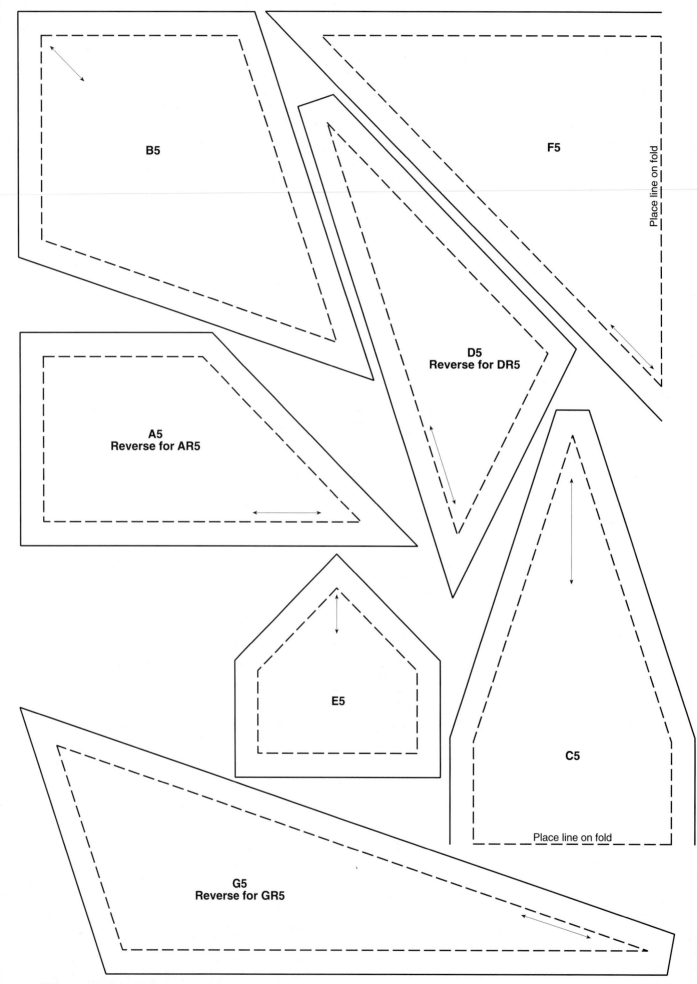

B5

F5

Place line on fold

A5
Reverse for AR5

D5
Reverse for DR5

E5

C5

Place line on fold

G5
Reverse for GR5

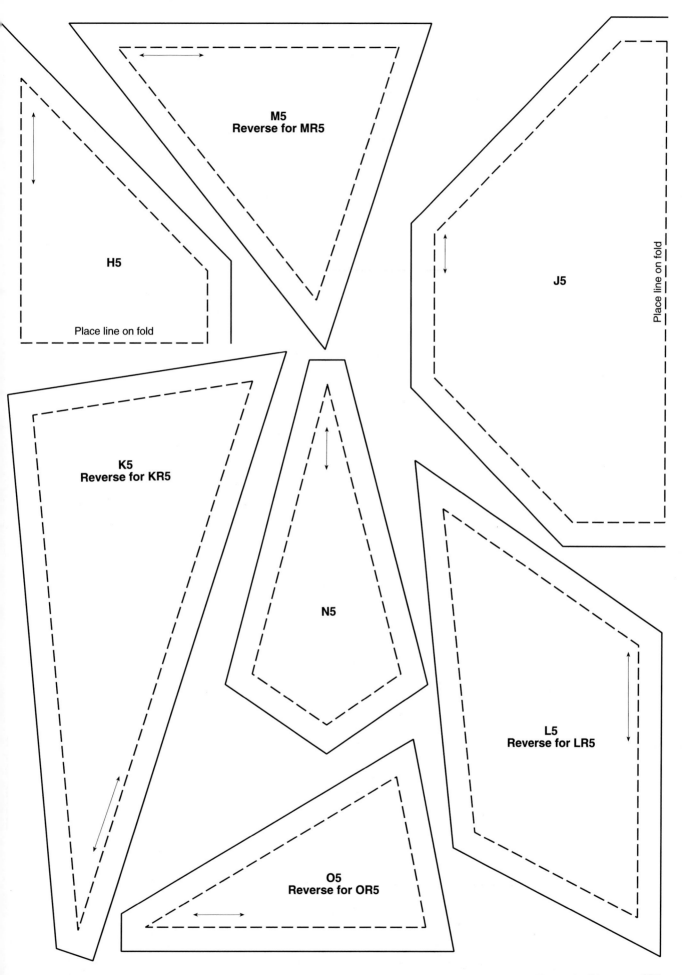

M5
Reverse for MR5

H5

Place line on fold

J5

Place line on fold

K5
Reverse for KR5

N5

L5
Reverse for LR5

O5
Reverse for OR5

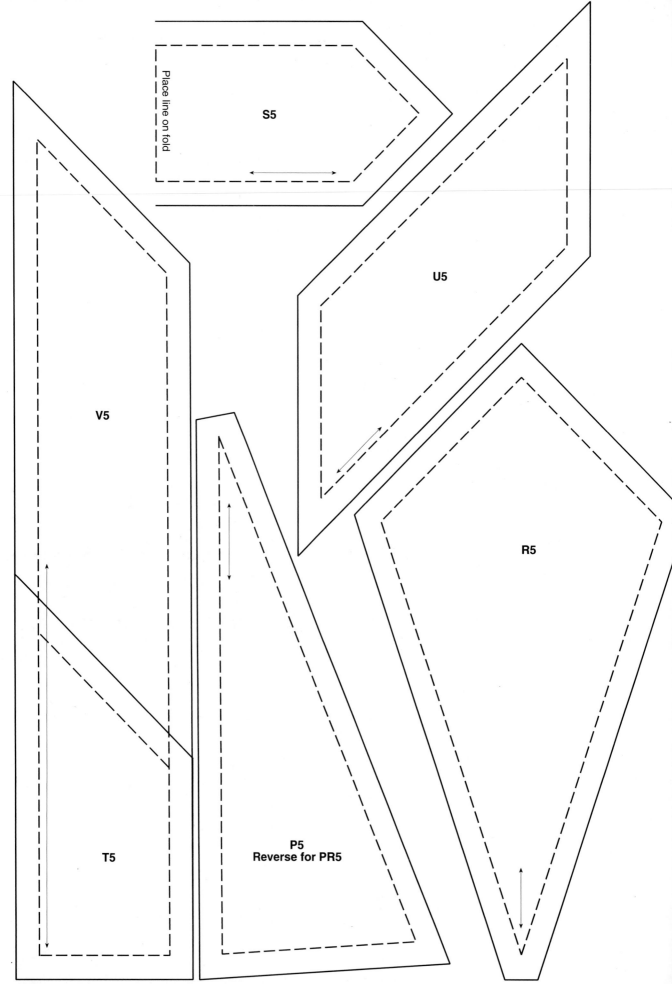

Place line on fold

S5

U5

V5

R5

T5

P5
Reverse for PR5

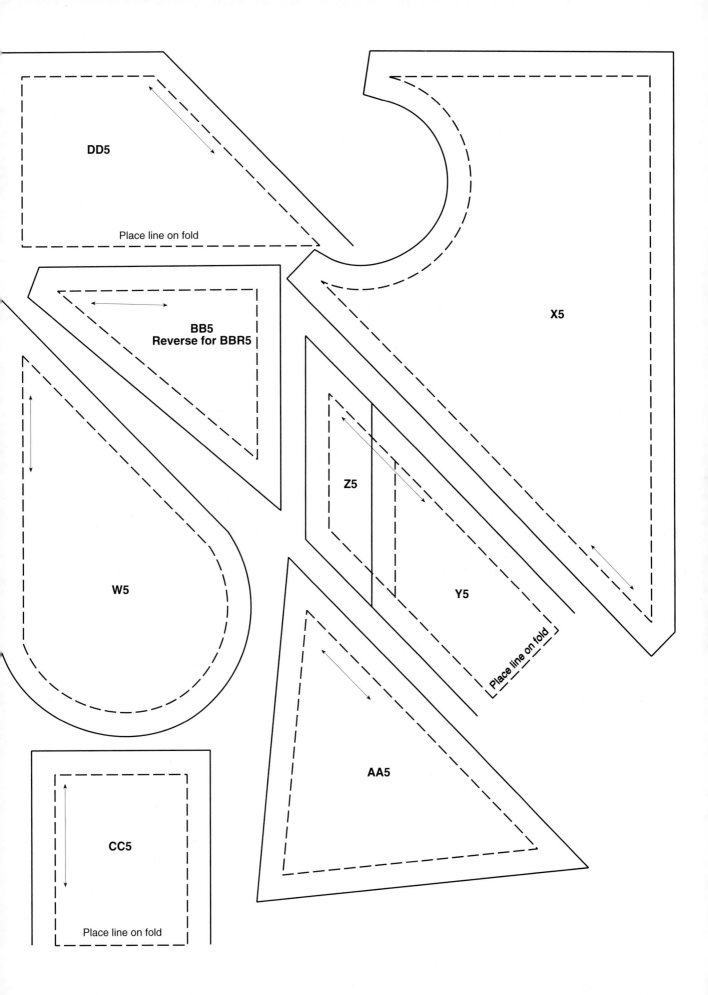

DD5

Place line on fold

X5

BB5
Reverse for BBR5

Z5

Y5

W5

Place line on fold

AA5

CC5

Place line on fold

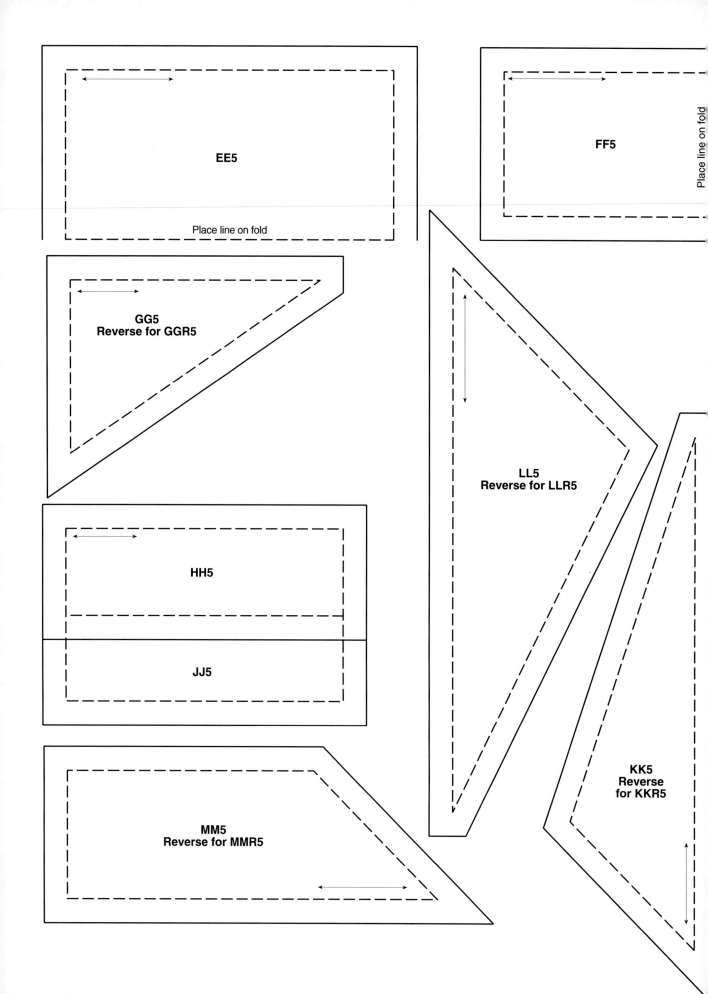

EE5

Place line on fold

FF5

Place line on fold

GG5
Reverse for GGR5

LL5
Reverse for LLR5

HH5

JJ5

KK5
Reverse
for KKR5

MM5
Reverse for MMR5

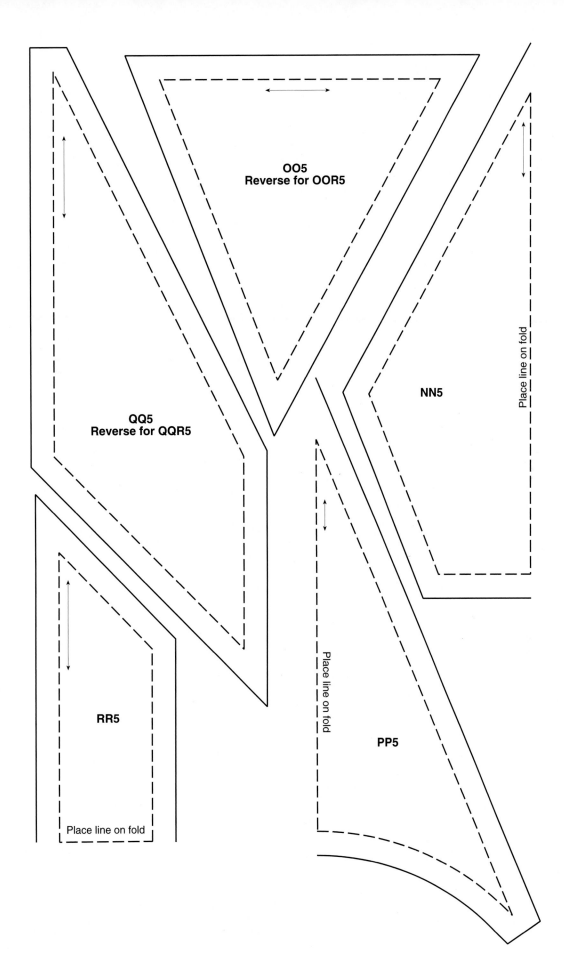

OO5
Reverse for OOR5

NN5

Place line on fold

QQ5
Reverse for QQR5

Place line on fold

RR5

Place line on fold

PP5

Beneath the Stars

*All quilters appreciate
the intricacy and
splendor of the stars.
The blocks in this chapter
show the diversity
of stars a quilter can
stitch and enjoy!
Although some of the
blocks do not have
the word star as part
of their name,
nevertheless, they have
the look of a star!*

Beneath the Stars Sampler

By Johanna Wilson

Red, cream and blue fabrics create a sampler with a patriotic flair.

Setting Block
12" x 12" Block

PROJECT SPECIFICATIONS
Project Size: 60" x 60"

Block Size: 12" x 12"

Number of Blocks: 9

FABRIC & BATTING
- 1/2 yard total red prints
- 3/4 yard red mottled
- 3/4 yard total cream prints
- 1/2 yard red-cream-and-blue stripe
- 2 yards blue print
- Batting 64" x 64"
- Batting 64" x 64"
- 7 yards self-made or purchased binding

SUPPLIES & TOOLS
- All-purpose thread to match fabrics
- Basic sewing tools and supplies

INSTRUCTIONS
1. Complete five blocks as desired, referring to the Placement Diagram for positioning of colors within blocks. Blocks used in the sample shown are Grandma's Star, Skyrocket, Exploding Star, Braced Star and Fizzle. *Note: You may choose any five blocks from this chapter or from other chapters in this book.*

2. Square up blocks to 12 1/2" x 12 1/2"; set aside.

3. Cut two 12 7/8" x 12 7/8" squares red-cream-and-blue stripe; cut each square on one diagonal to make two large triangles from each square. *Note:*

Place the squares on top of each other with stripes aligned for cutting to keep stripes going the same way in all triangles.

4. Cut one square each red mottled and blue print 13 1/4" x 13 1/4"; cut each square on both diagonals to make four triangles from each square.

5. Sew a red mottled triangle to a blue print triangle as shown in Figure 1; sew a stripe triangle to the pieced unit as shown in Figure 2 to complete a Setting block. Repeat for four Setting blocks.

Figure 1
Sew a red mottled triangle
to a blue print triangle.

Figure 2
Sew a stripe triangle to
the pieced unit as shown.

6. Arrange the pieced blocks in rows with the Setting blocks referring to the Placement Diagram for positioning of blocks; join blocks in rows. Join rows to complete the pieced center; press seams in one direction.

7. Cut two strips each 3 1/2" x 36 1/2" and 3 1/2" x 42 1/2" blue print. Sew the shorter strips to opposite sides of the pieced center; press seams toward strips. Sew the longer strips to the remaining sides; press seams toward strips.

8. Cut 56 common template 12 triangles red mottled and 56 common template 16 triangles each cream and blue prints. Cut four 12 triangles each cream and blue prints.

9. Sew a cream print 16 to a blue print 16 as shown in Figure 3; sew to a red mottled 12 to complete one border unit as shown in Figure 4. Repeat for 56 border units.

Figure 3
Sew a cream print 16 to a
blue print 16 as shown.

Figure 4
Sew to a red mottled 12 to
complete 1 border unit as shown.

10. Join seven border units as shown in Figure 5;

Beneath the Stars Sampler
Placement Diagram
60" x 60"

repeat with seven more border units to make a reverse strip, again referring to Figure 5. Join the two pieced strips as shown in Figure 6 to make a side strip; repeat for four side strips. Press seams toward darker fabrics.

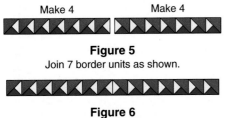

Make 4   Make 4

Figure 5
Join 7 border units as shown.

Figure 6
Join the 2 pieced strips as shown.

11. Sew a pieced strip to two opposite sides of the pieced center; press seams toward blue print strips.

12. Sew a cream print 12 to a blue print 12 as shown in Figure 7 to make a corner unit. Sew a corner unit to each end of the remaining two pieced strips as shown in Figure 8; sew these strips to the remaining sides of the pieced center. Press seams toward blue print strips.

Figure 7
Sew a cream print 12 to a blue print 12 to make a corner unit.

Continued on page 148

King's Star Basket Cover

By Chris Malone

One 12" block makes the perfect combination cover/pincushion for your sewing basket.

PROJECT SPECIFICATIONS
Project Size: 12" x 12"

Block Size: 12" x 12"

Number of Blocks: 1

FABRIC & BATTING
- 1/8 yard each 3 different yellow prints
- 1/4 yard green print
- 1 yard red floral
- 14" x 36" batting

SUPPLIES & TOOLS
- All-purpose thread to match fabrics
- Yellow and red quilting thread
- 12" x 25" x 3/16" foam board
- 12"-square basket without handles
- Permanent fabric adhesive
- 2" red tomato pincushion
- 4 (7/8") green buttons
- Basic sewing tools and supplies and craft knife

INSTRUCTIONS
1. Prepare one King's Star block referring to the Placement Diagram for placement of colors in the block.

2. Cut a 12 1/2" x 12 1/2" square batting and red floral for backing. Place backing right side up on batting square. Place the pieced block right side down on the backing square; pin layers together to secure.

3. Sew all around leaving a 4" opening on one side. Trim batting close to seam; trim corners. Turn right side out; press. Hand-stitch opening closed.

4. Quilt block as desired by hand or machine. *Note: The sample was hand-quilted in the ditch of seams with yellow quilting thread.*

5. Sew a green button in the center of each 72 square.

6. To make basket lid, cut a square of foam board to fit the quilted top. Cut a second piece of foam board to fit the basket inside opening. Round corners and trim as necessary until the second piece of foam board fits inside basket top.

King's Star
Basket Cover
Placement Diagram
12" x 12"

7. To cover large piece of foam board, cut a 17" x 17" square red floral. Lay fabric wrong side up on work surface; center foam board on fabric. Fold and glue each corner up over board as shown in Figure 1; fold and glue side edges, forming miters.

8. To cover smaller piece of foam board, cut a piece of batting the same size as the piece;

Figure 1
Fold and glue each corner up over board as shown.

Continued on page 148

Stars of Stripes Chair Pad

By Chris Malone

Dress up a chair back with a padded patchwork block.

PROJECT SPECIFICATIONS

Project Size: 15" x 15"

Block Size: 12" x 12"

Number of Blocks: 1

FABRIC & BATTING

- 1/8 yard dark blue print
- 1/8 yard cream print 1
- 1/4 yard cream print 2
- 1/2 yard red print
- Batting 15 1/2" x 15 1/2"

SUPPLIES & TOOLS

- All-purpose thread to match fabrics
- Ecru quilting thread
- 4 yards 1"-wide cream grosgrain ribbon
- Basic sewing tools and supplies

INSTRUCTIONS

1. Prepare one Stars of Stripes block referring to the Placement Diagram for placement of colors in the block. *Note: The 74 pieces may be strip pieced by cutting one strip each 1 3/8" by fabric width from red and blue prints and cream print 1. Stitch these strips with right sides together in a red/cream/blue order; press seams in one direction. Place the 74 template*

on the strip, matching lines on template with seam lines as shown in Figure 1; cut eight 74 pieces.

2. Cut two strips blue print 2" x 12 1/2"; sew a strip to opposite sides of the pieced block. Press seams toward strips. Cut two strips red print 2" x 15 1/2"; sew a strip to each remaining side of the pieced block. Press seams toward strips.

3. Cut 1"-wide grosgrain ribbon into four 1-yard lengths. Fold one ribbon piece in half and place folded edge on raw edge of right side of one red border strip a generous 1/4" from the corner as shown in Figure 2; baste in place. Repeat with remaining ribbon pieces as shown in Figure 3 for placement.

Figure 1
Place the 74 template
on the strip as shown.

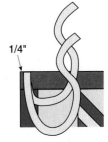

1/4"

Figure 2
Place folded edge on raw edge
of right side of 1 red border strip
a generous 1/4" from the
adjacent corner.

Continued on page 148

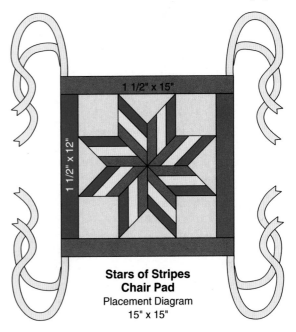

1 1/2" x 15"

1 1/2" x 12"

**Stars of Stripes
Chair Pad**
Placement Diagram
15" x 15"

Mexican Star Basket

By Julie Weaver

Turn a square block into a fabric basket to hold a plastic bowl liner which can be used to hold candy, a flower arrangement or sewing supplies.

PROJECT SPECIFICATIONS

Project Size: Approximately 5 1/2" x 5 1/2" x 5 1/2"

Block Size: 12" x 12"

Number of Blocks: 1

FABRIC & BATTING

- 1/8 yard red mottled
- 1/4 yard fall print
- 1/4 yard muslin
- Batting 16" x 16"
- Backing 16" x 16"
- 1 1/2 yards self-made or purchased binding

SUPPLIES & TOOLS

- All-purpose thread to match fabrics
- Basic sewing tools and supplies

INSTRUCTIONS

1. Prepare one Mexican Star block referring to Figure 1 for placement of colors in the block.

Figure 1
Piece 1 block placing colors as shown.

2. Sandwich batting between completed block and backing piece; pin or baste layers together.

3. Quilt as desired by hand or machine. *Note: The large muslin areas were machine-quilted in a 1" crosshatch design using red all-purpose thread on the sample shown.*

4. When quilting is complete, trim edges even; remove pins or basting. Bind edges with self-made or purchased binding.

5. Place block right side down on a flat surface. Pull the muslin 1 squares in so that the side points of the corner units touch and a V shape is formed as shown in Figure 2; pin to hold. Repeat this process on the three other muslin 1 squares to make a basket shape. Adjust the formed V shapes to make uniform.

Figure 2
Pull the muslin 1 squares in so that the side points of the corner units touch and a V shape is formed as shown.

6. Sew along each pinned V to make a tuck in each side approximately 3" long as shown in Figure 3.

7. Hand-stitch each tuck to the inside of the formed basket to finish. Insert plastic liner, if desired. ❖

Figure 3
Sew along each pinned V to make a tuck in each side approximately 3" long as shown.

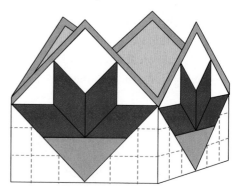

Mexican Star Basket
Placement Diagram
Approximately 5 1/2" x 5 1/2" x 5 1/2"

Morning or Evening Star Mat

By Connie Kauffman

One block makes the perfect-size mat on which to center your favorite-scented candle.

PROJECT SPECIFICATIONS
Project Size: 12" x 12"
Block Size: 12" x 12"
Number of Blocks: 1

FABRIC & BATTING
- 1/8 yard cream metallic solid
- 1/8 yard cream-with-metallic print
- 1/8 yard white-with-gold dots
- 1/8 yard gold metallic solid
- Backing 12 1/2" x 12 1/2"
- Batting 12 1/2" x 12 1/2"

SUPPLIES & TOOLS
- All-purpose thread to match fabrics
- Gold metallic thread
- 1 1/4 yards cream 1/4"-wide braided trim
- Basic sewing tools and supplies

INSTRUCTIONS
1. Prepare one Morning or Evening Star block referring to the Placement Diagram for placement of colors in the block. Leave off the 49 corner triangles to create an octagon shape.

2. Pin 1/4"-wide braided trim around edges, overlapping beginning and end as shown in Figure 1; baste in place.

Figure 1
Pin braided trim around edges,
overlapping beginning and end as shown.

3. Place backing square on the batting square with wrong side of backing against batting; lay the pieced block right sides together with backing. Stitch all around, leaving a 4" opening.

4. Turn right side out; press. Hand-stitch opening closed.

5. Quilt as desired by hand or machine. *Note: The sample was machine-quilted in the ditch of seams and in star shapes using gold metallic thread in the top of the machine and all-purpose thread in the bobbin.* ❖

Morning or Evening Star Mat
Placement Diagram
12" x 12"

Amish Star

PIECING INSTRUCTIONS

1. Referring to the Piecing Diagram to piece one block, sew a light 5 to a dark 5 along the diagonal; repeat for eight units.

2. Join two 5 units with two dark 3 squares to make a corner unit; repeat for four corner units.

3. Sew a light 5 to two adjacent sides of a dark 4; repeat for four units.

4. Sew a light 6 to a 4-5 unit on the 4 side to make a side unit; repeat for four side units.

5. Arrange the units with a light 1 square in rows referring to the Piecing Diagram. Join units in rows; join rows to complete one block.

Braced Star

PIECING INSTRUCTIONS

1. Referring to the Piecing Diagram to piece one block, join two light and one each dark and medium 4 triangles to make a side unit; repeat for four units.

2. Sew a light 5 to each side of a medium 7 to complete the center unit.

3. Arrange the units with four dark 1 squares in rows referring to the Piecing Diagram. Join units in rows; join rows to complete one block.

Card Basket

PIECING INSTRUCTIONS

1. Referring to the Piecing Diagram to piece one block, sew a dark 2 to a medium 2 along the diagonal to make a corner unit; repeat for four corner units.

2. Join two light, one medium and one dark 4 triangles to complete one side unit; repeat for four side units.

3. Sew a medium 5 to each side of a light 7 to complete the center unit.

4. Arrange the units in rows referring to the Piecing Diagram. Join units in rows; join rows to complete one block.

Christmas Star

PIECING INSTRUCTIONS

1. Referring to the Piecing Diagram to piece one block, sew a light 21 to a medium 21 along the diagonal; repeat for 16 units.

2. Join four units referring to the Piecing Diagram to make a corner unit; repeat for four corner units.

3. Sew a light 20 to a dark 20 to make a side unit; repeat for two side units.

4. Join two corner units with a side unit to make a row; repeat for two rows.

5. Sew a light 20 to each end of a dark 75 to make a center row;

6. Join the rows with the center row to complete one block.

Danish Star

PIECING INSTRUCTIONS

1. Referring to the Piecing Diagram to piece one block, join two dark and two light 3 squares to make a Four-Patch corner unit; repeat for four units.

2. Sew a light 54 to two adjacent sides of a dark 64; sew a medium 5 to the opposite sides to complete a side unit. Repeat for four side units.

3. Sew a light 31 to two adjacent sides of a medium 54; add a light 3. Sew a medium K6 and KR6 to opposite sides of this pieced unit to complete one star unit; repeat for four star units.

4. Sew a side unit to each star unit. Join the four star units with a light 3 square in the center, stitching angled seams between units.

5. Set a Four-Patch corner unit into each corner to complete one block.

Amish Star

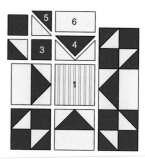

Templates needed:
1, 3, 4, 5 & 6

Braced Star

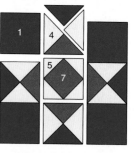

Templates needed:
1, 4, 5 & 7

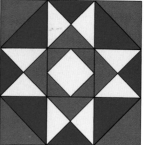

Card Basket

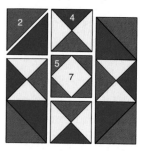

Templates needed:
2, 4, 5 & 7

Christmas Star

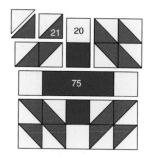

Templates needed:
20, 21 & 75

Danish Star

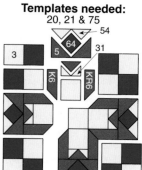

Templates needed:
3, 5, 31, 54, 64, K6 & KR6

Diamond Chain

PIECING INSTRUCTIONS

1. Referring to the Piecing Diagram to piece one block, join four light 101 pieces on square sides; repeat for nine units.

2. Join the pieced units with colored 121 pieces.

3. Set in colored 60 pieces around edges to complete one block.

Diamond Chain

Templates needed:
60, 101 & 121

Double Star

PIECING INSTRUCTIONS

1. Referring to the Piecing Diagram to piece one block, sew a medium L6 to a dark L6; repeat for four L6 and four LR6 units.

2. Join an L6 and LR6 unit and set in a light 19 square between the points to complete a quarter square; repeat for four quarter squares.

3. Join the quarter squares and set in light 35 triangles at sides to complete one block.

Double Star

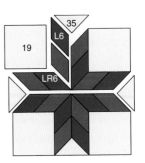

Templates needed:
19, 35, L6 & LR6

Eccentric Star

PIECING INSTRUCTIONS

1. Referring to the Piecing Diagram to piece one block, sew a light 2 to a dark 2 along the diagonal; repeat for eight units.

2. Arrange the pieced units with one medium 1 square in rows referring to the Piecing Diagram. Join units in rows; join rows to complete one block.

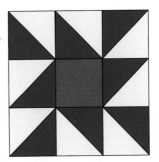

Eccentric Star

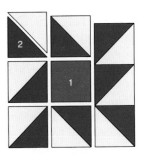

Templates needed:
1 & 2

Exploding Stars

PIECING INSTRUCTIONS

1. Referring to the Piecing Diagram to piece one block, sew a light 24 to a dark 24 to a light 24 to a dark 24; repeat for four units. Join the units to complete the block center.

2. Sew a medium 5 to two adjacent sides of a light 4; repeat for four units. Sew a unit to opposite sides of the block center.

3. Sew a light 3 to each end of the remaining two 4-5 units and sew to the remaining sides of the block center.

4. Sew a medium 10 and 10R to a dark A6 to complete a side unit; repeat for four side units.

5. Sew a side unit to opposite sides of the pieced center unit. Sew a dark 3 to each end of the remaining side units; sew these units to the remaining sides of the pieced center to complete one block.

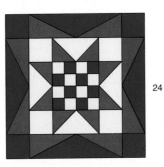

Exploding Stars

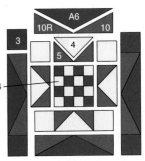

Templates needed:
3, 4, 5, 10, 10R, 24 & A6

Fizzle

PIECING INSTRUCTIONS

1. Referring to the Piecing Diagram to piece one block, sew a dark 2 to a light 2 along the diagonal to make a corner unit; repeat for four corner units.

2. Sew a dark 10 and 10R to two medium and two light 9 pieces to complete side units.

3. Join two medium and two light 4 triangles to make the center unit.

4. Arrange the units in rows referring to the Piecing Diagram. Join units in rows; join rows to complete one block.

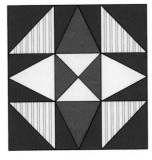

Fizzle

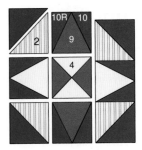

Templates needed:
2, 4, 9, 10 & 10R

Four-X

PIECING INSTRUCTIONS

1. Referring to the Piecing Diagram to piece one block, sew a light 2 to a medium 2 along the diagonal to make a corner unit; repeat for four corner units.

2. Join two light and two dark 4 triangles to make a side unit; repeat for four side units.

3. Arrange the units in rows with a medium 1 square referring to the Piecing Diagram. Join units in rows; join rows to complete one block.

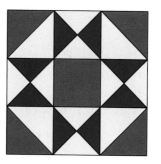

Four-X

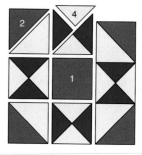

Templates needed:
1, 2 & 4

Friendship Star

PIECING INSTRUCTIONS

1. Referring to the Piecing Diagram to piece one block, sew a dark 51 to each side of the light 7 square to complete the center unit.

2. Sew two light 4 triangles to two adjacent sides of a dark 1 square to make a corner unit; repeat for four corner units. Sew one of these units to two opposite sides of the center unit.

3. Sew a medium 4 to each light 4 side of each remaining corner unit to complete two large corner units.

4. Sew a large corner unit to the remaining sides of the pieced center unit to complete one block.

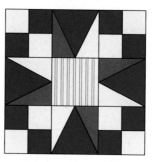

Friendship Star

Templates needed:
1, 4, 7 & 51

Grandma's Star

PIECING INSTRUCTIONS

1. Referring to the Piecing Diagram to piece one block, join two light and two dark 3 squares to make a Four-Patch corner unit; repeat for four corner units.

2. Sew a medium 10 and a light 10R to the sides of a dark 9 to make a side unit; repeat for four side units.

3. Arrange the units in rows with a light 1 square referring to the Piecing Diagram. Join units in rows; join rows to complete one block.

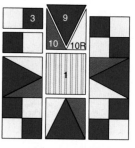

Grandma's Star

Templates needed:
1, 3, 9, 10 & 10R

Indian Star

PIECING INSTRUCTIONS

1. Referring to the Piecing Diagram to piece one block, join two light and two dark 13 squares to make the center Four-Patch unit.

2. Sew a medium 12 to two adjacent sides of a light 14; repeat for four units. Sew a unit to two opposite sides of the center unit.

3. Sew a dark 13 to each end of the remaining two 12-14 units; sew these units to the remaining sides of the center unit to complete one block.

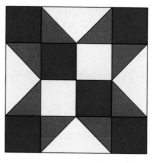

Indian Star

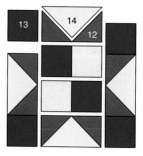

Templates needed:
12, 13 & 14

Kansas Star

PIECING INSTRUCTIONS

1. Referring to the Piecing Diagram to piece one block, sew a light 5 to each side of a medium 7 to complete a corner unit; repeat for four corner units and one center unit.

2. Sew a dark 5 to each side of a light 7 to complete a side unit; repeat for four side units.

3. Arrange the units in rows referring to the Piecing Diagram. Join units in rows; join rows to complete one block.

Kansas Star

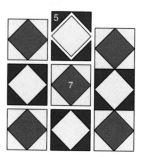

Templates needed:
5 & 7

King's Star

PIECING INSTRUCTIONS

1. Referring to the Piecing Diagram to piece one block, sew a dark D6 to a medium C6; repeat for four units. Sew a medium D6 to a dark C6; repeat for four units.

2. Sew dark B6 pieces to the medium C6 units and the light B6 pieces to the dark C6 units. Join the pieced units to complete a star shape.

3. Set in light 72 pieces to make corners and light 49 triangles to make sides to complete one block.

King's Star

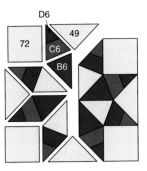

Templates needed:
49, 72, B6, C6 & D6

Lena's Choice

PIECING INSTRUCTIONS

1. Referring to the Piecing Diagram to piece one block, sew a light 40 to a light 40R; repeat for four units.

2. Join the four units to make a star unit; set in four dark 16 triangles. Sew a medium 18 to a dark 18 along the diagonal; repeat for four units. Set these units into the corners of the pieced unit to complete the block center.

3. Sew a medium 40 and 40R to a dark 16; repeat for eight units; sew a light 16 to 40 edge of each unit. Join two units to complete a side unit; repeat for four side units.

4. Arrange the pieced units with the light 13 squares in rows referring to the Piecing Diagram. Join units in rows; join rows to complete one block.

Lena's Choice

Templates needed:
13, 16, 18, 40 & 40R

Mexican Star

PIECING INSTRUCTIONS

1. Referring to the Piecing Diagram to piece one block, sew a medium E6 to a dark ER6; sew a dark E6 to a medium ER6. Join the two units; set in a light 27 and two light 126 triangles. Add a dark T6 to complete one corner unit; repeat for four corner units.

2. Arrange the units in rows with one dark and four light 1 squares referring to the Piecing Diagram. Join units in rows; join rows to complete one block.

Mexican Star

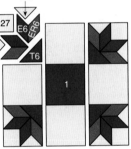

Templates needed:
1, 27, 126, E6, ER6 & T6

Miller's Daughter

PIECING INSTRUCTIONS

1. Referring to the Piecing Diagram to piece one block, sew a dark 85 to a dark 85R; sew a light 5 to opposite sides of the pieced unit. Set in a light 3 to complete one corner unit. Repeat for four corner units.

2. Sew a medium 6 to a light 6 to complete one side unit; repeat for four side units.

3. Arrange the units in rows with the dark 1 square referring to the Piecing Diagram. Join units in rows; join rows to complete one block.

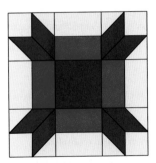

Miller's Daughter

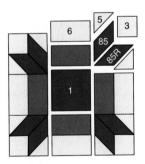

Templates needed:
1, 3, 5, 6, 85 & 85R

Morning or Evening Star

PIECING INSTRUCTIONS

1. Referring to the Piecing Diagram to piece one block, sew a dark F6 to each long side of a medium F6; repeat for eight units.

2. Sew the pieced F units onto the light G6, stitching seams between units as you go.

3. Sew a light 49 to corners to complete one block.

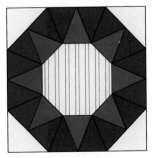

Morning or Evening Star

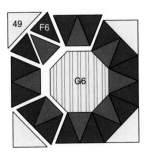

Templates needed:
49, F6 & G6

Mother's Fancy

PIECING INSTRUCTIONS

1. Referring to the Piecing Diagram to piece one block, sew a light 24 between two dark 24 squares; repeat for two units. Sew a dark 24 between two light 24 squares. Join the units to complete a corner Nine-Patch corner unit; repeat for four corner units.

2. Sew a dark 65 between two light 65 pieces to complete one side unit; repeat for four side units.

3. Sew a medium 18 to two adjacent sides of a light 16; repeat for four units. Sew a unit to two opposite sides of the medium 13. Sew a light 17 to each end of the remaining two 18-16 units and sew to the remaining sides of pieced unit to complete the center unit.

4. Arrange the units in rows referring to the Piecing Diagram. Join units in rows; join rows to complete one block.

Ohio Star

PIECING INSTRUCTIONS

1. Referring to the Piecing Diagram to piece one block, join one light, one dark and two medium 4 triangles to make a side unit; repeat for four side units.

2. Arrange pieced units in rows with light 1 squares referring to the Piecing Diagram. Join units in rows; join rows to complete one block.

Pinwheel Star

PIECING INSTRUCTIONS

1. Referring to the Piecing Diagram to piece one block, sew a dark 30 to a medium 30R and a dark 30R to a medium 30; join the two pieced units on the dark sides; repeat for four units.

2. Set in a light 3 and two light 54 triangles; add a light 5 to the medium sides to complete one corner unit; repeat for four corner units.

3. Join a dark MR6 and a medium M6; set in a light N6. Repeat for four units.

4. Join the M-N units to make a star shape; set in a light 5 between the M points.

5. Sew a medium 4 to each N6 side of the pieced unit to complete the center.

6. Sew a corner unit to each side of the center to complete one block.

Ribbon Quilt

PIECING INSTRUCTIONS

1. Referring to the Piecing Diagram to piece one block, sew a light 5 to a dark 5 along the diagonal; repeat for 32 units.

2. Arrange the pieced units in rows with light 3 squares to form four corner units; join in rows. Join corner units to complete one block.

Salem

PIECING INSTRUCTIONS

1. Referring to the Piecing Diagram to piece one block, sew two medium 5 and two light 5 triangles to the sides of a light 7 to complete one corner unit; repeat for four corner units.

2. Sew a light 5 to two adjacent sides of a dark 4; repeat for four units. Sew a dark 5 to two adjacent sides of a light 4; repeat for four units. Join one of each unit to complete a side unit; repeat for four side units.

3. Sew a dark 5 to each side of a light 7 to complete the center unit.

4. Arrange the pieced units in rows referring to the Piecing Diagram. Join units in rows; join rows to complete one block.

Mother's Fancy

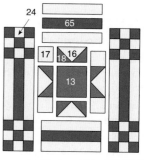

Templates needed:
13, 16, 17, 18, 24 & 65

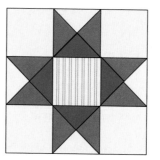

Ohio Star

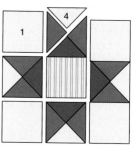

Templates needed:
1 & 4

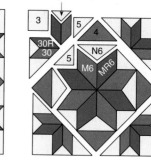

Pinwheel Star

Templates needed:
3, 4, 5, 30, 30R,
54, M6, MR6 & N6

Ribbon Quilt

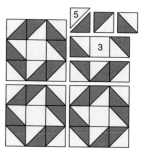

Templates needed:
3 & 5

Salem

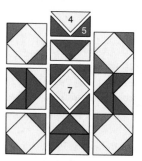

Templates needed:
4, 5 & 7

Sandhills Star

PIECING INSTRUCTIONS

1. Referring to the Piecing Diagram to piece one block, sew a medium 41 to a dark 41R; sew a dark 41 to a medium 41R. Join these two pieced units on the dark sides.

2. Set in a light 13 and two light 16 triangles to complete one corner unit; repeat for four corner units.

3. Join two dark and two light 59 squares to make a Four-Patch center unit.

4. Sew a corner unit onto each side of the center unit, join seams at sides to complete one block.

Shooting Star

PIECING INSTRUCTIONS

1. Referring to the Piecing Diagram to piece one block, sew two dark H6 and two dark HR6 pieces to the sides of a light 83; repeat for two units.

2. Sew two light H6 and two light HR6 pieces to the sides of a dark 83; repeat for two units.

3. Join the four pieced units to complete one block.

Skyrocket

PIECING INSTRUCTIONS

1. Referring to the Piecing Diagram to piece one block, sew a dark 95 and 95R to opposite sides of a medium 116 to make a corner unit; repeat for four corner units.

2. Sew a light 54 to the angled sides of a medium 114; repeat for four units.

3. Sew a 54-114 unit to two opposite sides of the light 7. Sew a dark 7 to opposite sides of each of the remaining 54-114 units; sew these units to the remaining sides of the light 7 to complete the center unit.

4. Sew a corner unit to each side of the center unit to complete one block.

Spinning Stars

PIECING INSTRUCTIONS

1. Referring to the Piecing Diagram to piece one block, sew a light 12 to a dark 36; repeat for four units. Sew a light 12 to a medium 36; repeat for four units.

2. Join two 12-36 units with a light 14 to make a pieced triangle unit; repeat for four units.

3. Join these units to complete one block.

Star

PIECING INSTRUCTIONS

1. Referring to the Piecing Diagram to piece one block, sew a dark 40 to a dark 40R; repeat for 12 units.

2. Join two 40 units with two light 18 triangles, two light 17 squares and one light 16 to make a side unit; repeat for four side units.

3. Sew a light 18 to a dark 18 along the diagonal; repeat for four units.

4. Join four 40 units to make the star center; set in four white 16 triangles. Set in the four 18 units at the corners to complete the center unit.

5. Arrange the pieced units in rows with dark 13 squares referring to the Piecing Diagram. Join units in rows; join rows to complete one block.

Sandhills Star

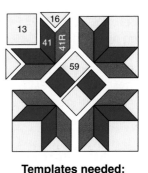

Templates needed:
13, 16, 41, 41R & 59

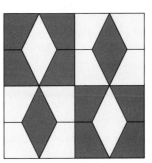

Shooting Star

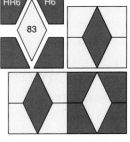

Templates needed:
83, H6 & HR6

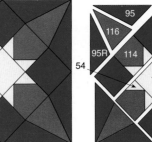

Skyrocket

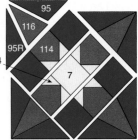

Templates needed:
7, 54, 95, 95R, 114 & 116

Spinning Stars

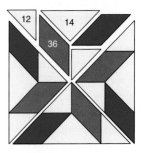

Templates needed:
12, 14 & 36

Star

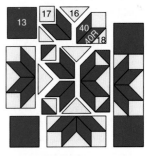

Templates needed:
13, 16, 17, 18, 40 & 40R

Star & Square

PIECING INSTRUCTIONS

1. Referring to the Piecing Diagram to piece one block, sew a light 36 and 36R to adjacent sides of a medium 14 to complete one side unit; repeat for four side units.

2. Sew a side unit to each side of a dark 34, sewing corner seams to complete one block.

Star of Spring

PIECING INSTRUCTIONS

1. Referring to the Piecing Diagram to piece one block, sew a light 51 between a dark 5 and a dark 81; sew a medium 80 to a light 125.

2. Join the two pieced units to complete a block quarter; repeat for four block quarters.

3. Join the block quarters to complete one block.

Starry Lane

PIECING INSTRUCTIONS

1. Referring to the Piecing Diagram to piece one block, sew a dark 32 to one side of a light 3. Sew a light 24 to one end of another dark 32; sew to the adjacent side of the 3-32 unit to complete a corner unit. Repeat for four corner units.

2. Sew a medium 12 to two adjacent sides of a light 14 to complete a side unit; repeat for four side units.

3. Sew a light 5 to a medium 5 along the diagonal; repeat for four units; join the units to make a pinwheel center unit. Sew a dark 53 to two opposite sides of the center unit; sew a light 24 to each end of a dark 53. Sew the 24-53 units to the remaining sides of the center unit.

4. Arrange the pieced units in rows referring to the Piecing Diagram. Join units in rows; join rows to complete one block.

Starry Pavement

PIECING INSTRUCTIONS

1. Referring to the Piecing Diagram to piece one block, appliqué a medium R6 piece onto each long side of 39 to complete the center unit.

2. Sew a dark 5 to a medium 115, to a light 114; sew a dark 54 to each angled side of 114 to complete one corner unit; repeat for four corner units.

3. Sew a light 5 to opposite short sides of medium S6 to complete a side unit; repeat for four side units.

4. Sew side and corner units to the center unit, stitching seams between units as you go to complete one block.

Starry Sky

PIECING INSTRUCTIONS

1. Referring to the Piecing Diagram to piece one block, sew a medium 5 to a light 5 on the diagonal; repeat for eight units.

2. Join two units with a light 3 and a dark 3 to complete one corner unit; repeat for four corner units.

3. Sew a light 56 to two adjacent sides of a medium 121; repeat for four units. Sew an I6 and IR6 to the long sides of the pieced units. Sew a light 5 to each remaining corner to complete a side unit; repeat for four side units.

4. Arrange the pieced units in rows with a light 1. Join units in rows; join rows to complete one block.

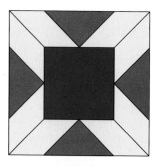

Star & Square

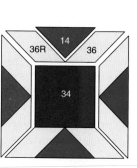

Templates needed:
14, 34, 36 & 36R

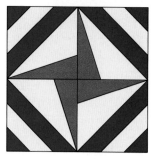

Star of Spring

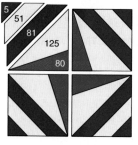

Templates needed:
5, 51, 80, 81 & 125

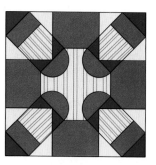

Starry Lane

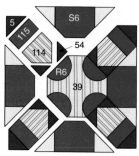

Templates needed:
3, 5, 12, 14, 24, 32 & 53

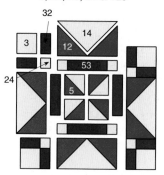

Starry Pavement

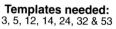

Templates needed:
5, 39, 54, 114, 115, R6 & S6

Starry Sky

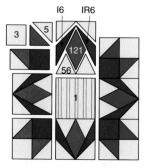

Templates needed:
1, 3, 5, 56, 121, I6 & IR6

Stars of Stripes

PIECING INSTRUCTIONS

1. Referring to the Piecing Diagram to piece one block, cut a 74 foundation piece. Sew a light strip between dark and medium strips on the 74 foundation piece to make a star unit; repeat for eight star units.

2. Join the star units to create the block center.

3. Set in light 72 squares at each corner and light 49 triangles on each side to complete one block.

Stars of Stripes

Templates needed:
49, 72 & 74

Stars Over Tennessee

PIECING INSTRUCTIONS

1. Referring to the Piecing Diagram to piece one block, sew a dark 28 to a medium 28 on the diagonal; repeat for eight units.

2. Sew one unit to a light 43; sew a second unit to a medium 27. Join a 27-28 and 28-43 unit; repeat for four units.

3. Sew a light J6 and JR6 to the pieced units to complete a corner unit.

4. Join two corner units with a medium 44; repeat for two units.

5. Sew a light 27 between two medium 44 pieces to make a row. Sew this row between the two pieced units to complete one block.

Stars Over Tennessee

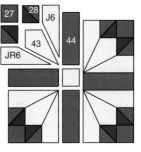

Templates needed:
27, 28, 43, 44, J6 & JR6

Twin Star

PIECING INSTRUCTIONS

1. Referring to the Piecing Diagram to piece one block, sew a dark 4 to a light 4 on the short sides; sew a medium 2 to the joined unit to complete a side unit. Repeat for four side units.

2. Arrange the pieced units with five light 1 squares in rows referring to the Piecing Diagram. Join units in rows; join rows to complete one block.

Twin Star

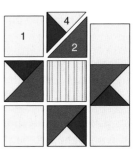

Templates needed:
1, 2 & 4

Twin Stars

PIECING INSTRUCTIONS

1. Referring to the Piecing Diagram to piece one block, join four dark 42 pieces to make the center star unit; set in light O6 pieces to complete the center unit.

2. Sew medium 81 pieces to each side of the center unit, stitching corner seams as you sew.

3. Sew a light P6 and PR6 to each side of a dark Q6 to complete one corner unit; repeat for four corner units.

4. Sew a corner unit to each side of the center unit to complete one block.

Twin Stars

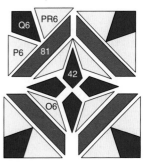

Templates needed:
42, 81, O6, P6, PR6 & Q6

Utah Star

PIECING INSTRUCTIONS

1. Referring to the Piecing Diagram to piece one block, sew a light 58 to a dark 58; sew a light 58R to a medium 58R. Join the two units; repeat. Join these two units to complete a side unit; repeat for four side units.

2. Sew a medium 58 and 58R to a dark 37; repeat for two units. Sew a pieced unit to opposite long sides of 57 to complete the center unit.

3. Arrange the pieced units in rows with the four light 13 squares referring to the Piecing Diagram. Join units in rows; join rows to complete one block.

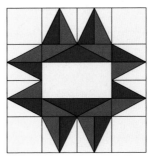

Utah Star

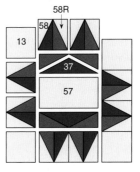

Templates needed:
13, 37, 57, 58 & 58R

Beneath the Stars Sampler
Continued from page 135

Figure 8
Sew a corner unit to each end of the
remaining 2 pieced strips as shown.

13. Cut and piece two strips each 6 1/2" x 48 1/2" and
6 1/2" x 60 1/2" blue print. Sew the shorter strips to
opposite sides of the pieced center; press seams

toward strips. Sew the longer strips to the remaining
sides; press seams toward strips.

14. Sandwich batting between the completed top and
prepared backing piece; pin or baste to hold.

15. Hand- or machine-quilt as desired. *Note: The
sample shown was machine-quilted using thread to
match fabrics and in a variety of quilting designs.*

16. Trim edges even with top. Bind edges with self-
made or purchased binding to finish. ❖

King's Star Basket Cover
Continued from page 136

glue to one side of the foam board. Cut a red floral
square 2" larger than the foam board. Using doubled
thread, sew a long gathering stitch 1/4" from outside
edge of fabric.

9. Place the foam board in the center of the fabric
square with batting side of board on wrong side of
fabric; pull thread to gather fabric over edge of foam
board. Knot thread and clip.

10. Place a small amount of glue under fabric edges to
secure cover. Center and glue the small foam board to
the large foam board with fabric sides out.

11. Cut two 3 1/2" by fabric width strips green print.
Join strips together on short ends to make a tube. Fold
in half with right side out; sew two lines of machine

gathering stitches close to raw edge. Divide tube in
four sections.

12. Pin one section to each side of
the quilted top; pull gathering
stitches until each side fits, adjust-
ing gathers as necessary.

13. Glue gathered ruffle around
outer edge of lid, overlapping lid
edge 3/8" as shown in Figure 2.

Figure 2
Glue gathered ruffle
around outer edge of lid,
overlapping lid edge 3/8"

14. Cut an 11" x 11" square batting; place on top of lid. Lay the
quilted block, right side up, on
top of the batting. Using red quilting thread, whipstitch
the edge of the quilted block to the ruffle.

15. Glue the pincushion to the top center of the block
to finish. ❖

Stars of Stripes Chair Pad
Continued from page 137

4. Pin ribbon ends to pieced block to keep away from
edges. Cut a 15 1/2" x 15 1/2" square red print for
backing; place right sides together with pieced block,
keeping ribbon ends between layers. Place the pinned
layers with the pieced block on the batting. Sew all
around, leaving a 4" opening on one side.

5. Trim batting close to seam; clip corners. Turn right
side out through opening; press seam and hand-stitch
opening closed.

6. Quilt as desired by hand or machine. *Note: The
sample was hand-quilted in the ditch of seams with
ecru quilting thread.*

7. Trim ribbon ends in a V shape as shown in Figure 4
to finish. ❖

Figure 3
Place folded ribbon pieces
at each corner as shown.

Figure 4
Trim ribbon ends
in a V shape.

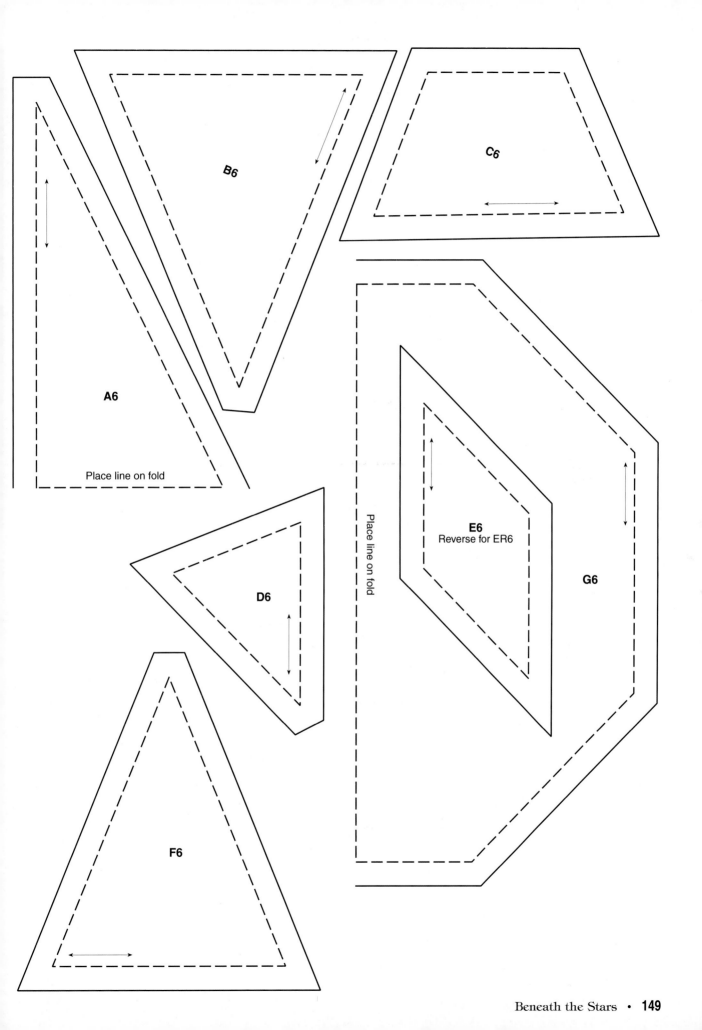

B6

C6

A6

Place line on fold

D6

Place line on fold

E6
Reverse for ER6

G6

F6

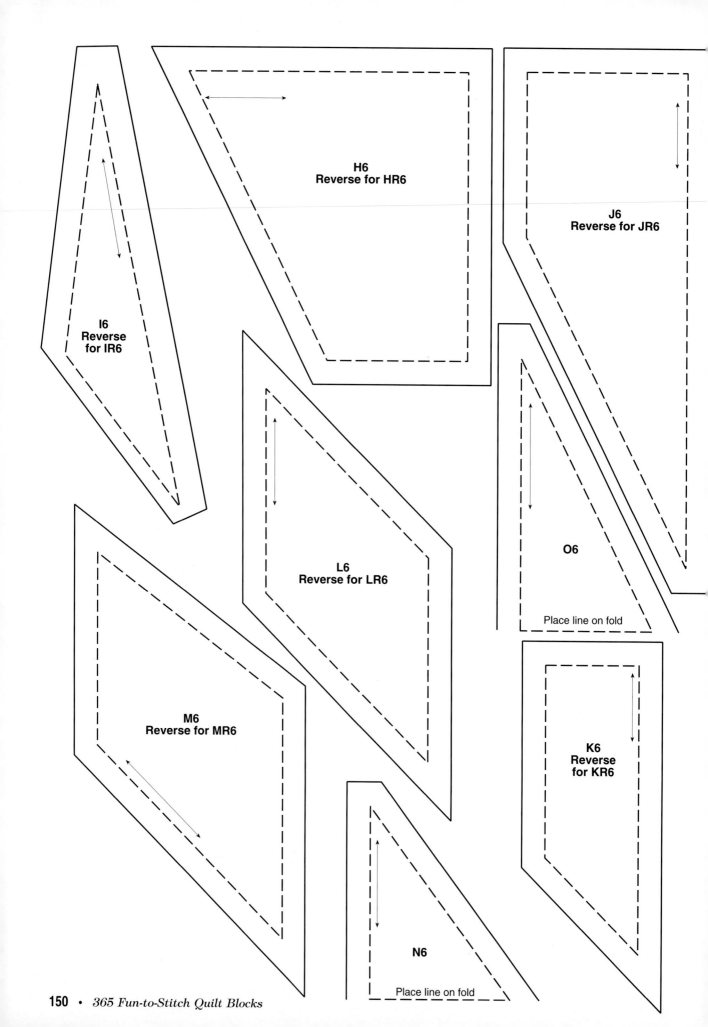

H6
Reverse for HR6

J6
Reverse for JR6

I6
Reverse
for IR6

L6
Reverse for LR6

O6

Place line on fold

M6
Reverse for MR6

K6
Reverse
for KR6

N6

Place line on fold

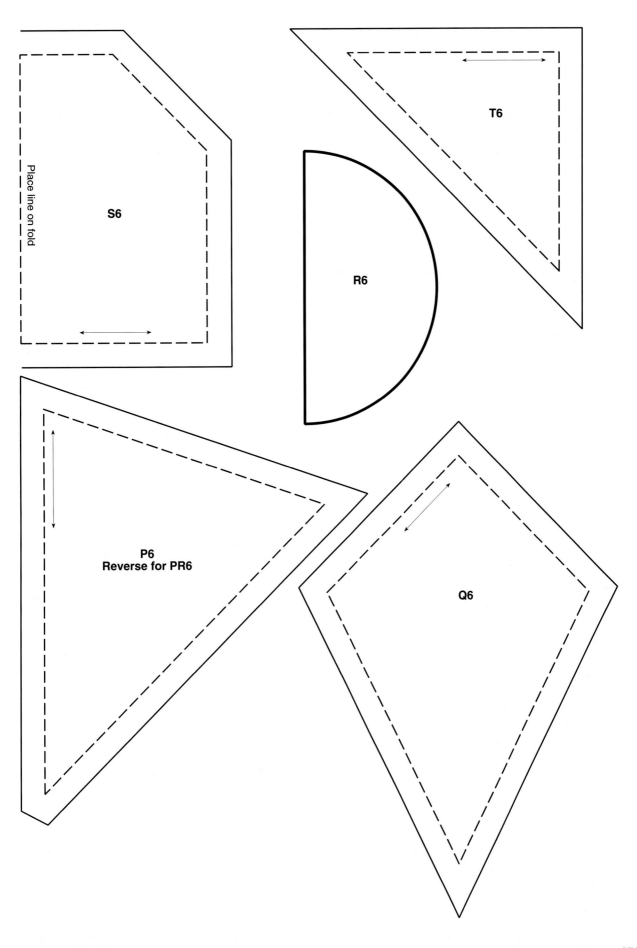

S6

Place line on fold

T6

R6

P6
Reverse for PR6

Q6

Around the World

*Although quilting
is an American tradition,
it is easy to see from the
blocks in this chapter
that quilters come from
a wide variety of
nationalities!
Quilters named their
blocks after places
where they lived
and places they
wanted to visit.*

Around the World Sampler

By Holly Daniels

Take a trip around the world, choosing blocks with place names. Strip-pieced sashing combines with nine pieced blocks to make an interesting setting.

PROJECT SPECIFICATIONS
Quilt Size: 57" x 57"
Block Size: 12" x 12"
Number of Blocks: 9

FABRIC & BATTING
- 3/4 yard each red, gold and green mottleds
- 3/4 yard brown mottled
- 1 1/4 yards blue batik
- 2 1/2 yards cream mottled
- Backing 61" x 61"
- Batting 61" x 61"
- 6 3/4 yards self-made or purchased binding

SUPPLIES & TOOLS
- All-purpose thread to match fabrics
- Cream quilting thread
- Basic sewing tools and supplies, rotary cutter, mat and ruler

INSTRUCTIONS
1. Complete nine blocks as desired referring to the Placement Diagram for positioning of colors within blocks. Blocks used in the sample are Roman Roads, London Roads, Alaska, Formosa Tea Leaf, Philippine Islands, Judy in Arabia, Alabama, Road to Paris and Rocky Road to Dublin. *Note: You may choose any nine blocks from this chapter or from other chapters in this book.*

2. Square up blocks to 12 1/2" x 12 1/2".

3. Cut eight strips each cream and brown mottled 2" by fabric width. Sew a brown strip to a cream strip with right sides together along length; press seam toward darker strip; repeat for eight strip sets.

4. Subcut each strip set into 12 1/2" segments for sashing; you will need 24 sashing strips.

5. Cut two strips brown mottled 3 1/2" by fabric width; subcut into 3 1/2" square segments for sashing squares. You will need 16 sashing squares.

6. Join four sashing squares with three sashing strips to make a row as shown in Figure 1; repeat for four sashing rows.

Figure 1
Join 4 sashing squares with 3
sashing strips to make a row.

7. Join three blocks with four sashing strips to make a row as shown in Figure 2 and referring to the Placement Diagram for positioning of blocks and strips; press seams toward strips. Repeat for three rows.

Figure 2
Join 3 blocks with 4 sashing
strips to make a row.

8. Join the block rows with the sashing rows to complete the pieced center.

9. Cut and piece two strips each 2" x 48 1/2" and 2" x 51 1/2" cream mottled. Sew the shorter strips to opposite sides and longer strips to the top and bottom of the pieced center; press seams toward strips.

10. Cut and piece two strips each 3 1/2" x 51 1/2" and 3 1/2" x 57 1/2" blue batik. Sew the shorter strips to opposite sides and longer strips to the top and bottom of the pieced center; press seams toward strips.

11. Sandwich batting between the completed top and prepared backing piece; pin or baste layers together to hold.

12. Quilt as desired by hand or machine. *Note: The sample shown was machine-quilted in diagonal grid using cream quilting thread.*

13. When quilting is complete, trim edges even; remove pins or basting.

14. Bind edges with self-made or purchased binding to finish. ❖

3" x 57"

1 1/2" x 51"

3" x 51"

1 1/2" x 48"

Around the World Sampler
Placement Diagram
57" x 57"

St. Louis Tote Bag

By Barbara Clayton

Carry your summer quilting supplies around in this large denim tote bag.

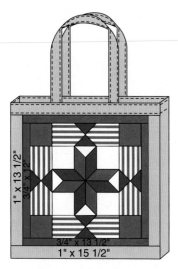

St. Louis Tote Bag
Placement Diagram
15 1/2" x 15 1/2" x 4"

PROJECT SPECIFICATIONS

Project Size: 15 1/2" x 15 1/2" x 4"

Block Size: 12" x 12"

Number of Blocks: 1

FABRIC & BATTING

- 1/8 yard blue print
- 1/8 yard blue mottled
- 1/8 yard red-and-white stripe
- 1/4 yard red solid
- 1/2 yard white solid
- 1 yard 60"-wide denim
- Batting 16" x 16"

SUPPLIES & TOOLS

- All-purpose thread to match fabrics
- Blue quilting thread
- Clear nylon monofilament
- Basic sewing tools and supplies

INSTRUCTIONS

1. Prepare one St. Louis block referring to the Placement Diagram for placement of colors in the block.

2. Cut two strips each 1 1/4" x 12 1/2" and 1 1/4" x 14" red solid. Sew the shorter strips to opposite sides and longer strips to remaining sides; press seams toward strips.

3. Cut two strips each denim 1 1/2" x 14" and 1 1/2" x 16". Sew the shorter strips to opposite sides and longer strips to remaining sides; press seams toward strips.

4. Cut a 16" x 16" white solid backing square. Sandwich batting between the bordered block and the backing square; pin or baste layers together.

5. Quilt as desired by hand or machine. ***Note:*** *The project shown was machine-quilted in the ditch of seams using clear nylon monofilament in the top of the machine and all-purpose thread in the bobbin. The white solid pieces were hand-quilted 1/4" from seams using blue quilting thread.*

6. When quilting is complete, remove pins or basting; trim edges even.

7. Cut three squares denim 16" x 16". Cut two strips denim 4 1/2" x 48". Sew a long strip around three sides of the quilted top, clipping corners as you

Continued on page 172

Texas Cactus Basket Pillow

By Chris Malone

Desert colors and a Western novelty print work together to make this unusual pillow.

print for pillow back and two 15" x 17 1/2" rectangles for front border ends.

4. Sew a 15" x 17 1/2" rectangle to two opposite sides of the pieced block as shown in

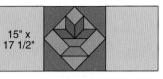

Figure 1
Sew a 15" x 17 1/2" rectangle to 2 opposite sides of the pieced block.

Figure 1; press seams toward rectangles.

5. Pin the pieced front to the 46" x 17 1/2" backing piece with right sides together. Sew along both long sides; press.

6. Press each end under 1/4"; press under 1/4" again and stitch to hem.

7. Fold each end inside 7" to cover seams and press; hand-stitch in place.

8. On one end, measure and mark three evenly spaced dots 3" from seam line for button and snap placement. Sew a snap at each of these spots on the inside to hold the pillow flaps together. Sew a large button on the front, covering snap stitching. To finish back, sew a small tan button over stitches.

9. On the opposite end, measure and mark as before but sew only buttons to pillow flaps, sewing through all layers with large buttons on top and small buttons on back.

10. Slide the pillow form inside cover from snapped end, centering it behind the pieced block to finish. ❖

PROJECT SPECIFICATIONS
Project Size: 31 1/2" x 17"

Block Size: 12" x 12"

Number of Blocks: 1

FABRIC & BATTING
- 1/4 yard each green, salmon and tan prints
- 1/3 yard blue print
- 1 1/4 yards Western novelty print

SUPPLIES & TOOLS
- All-purpose thread to match fabrics
- 16" pillow form
- 3 (size 4) snaps
- 6 (1 1/4") brown buttons
- 6 (5/8"–1") tan buttons
- Basic sewing tools and supplies

INSTRUCTIONS
1. Prepare one Texas Cactus Basket block referring to the Placement Diagram for placement of colors in the block.

2. Cut two 9 3/8" x 9 3/8" squares blue print; cut each square on one diagonal to make triangles. Sew a triangle to each side of the pieced block; press seams toward triangles.

3. Cut one 46" x 17 1/2" piece Western novelty

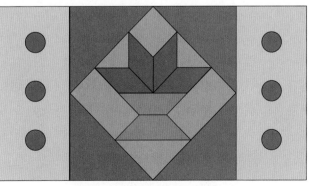

Texas Cactus Basket Pillow
Placement Diagram
31 1/2" x 17"

Chinese Lanterns Tea Cozy

By Chris Malone

Border three sides of a block to create the perfect-size tea cozy.

PROJECT SPECIFICATIONS

Project Size: 15" x 13 3/4" (without prairie points)

Block Size: 12" x 12"

Number of Blocks: 1

FABRIC & BATTING

- 1/4 yard each 2 different red-and-black prints
- 1/4 yard black-with-red print
- 1/2 yard dark red print
- 2 (15 1/2" x 14") pieces low-loft batting
- 1 yard self-made or purchased narrow black binding

SUPPLIES & TOOLS

- All-purpose thread to match fabrics
- Red quilting thread
- Basic sewing tools and supplies

INSTRUCTIONS

1. Prepare one Chinese Lanterns block referring to the Placement Diagram for placement of colors in the block.

2. Cut one strip 2" x 15 1/2" and two strips 2" x 12 1/2" dark red print.

3. Sew the shorter strips to opposite sides of the

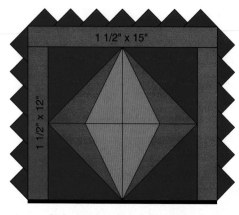

Chinese Lanterns Tea Cozy
Placement Diagram
15" x 13 3/4" (without prairie points)

pieced block; sew the longer strip to the top. Press seams toward strips.

4. Cut three 14" x 15 1/2" rectangles dark red print for backing and lining.

5. To make tea cozy front, place one backing piece right side up on one piece of batting; place the pieced block right side down on the backing. Sew around the three bordered sides, leaving bottom edge open.

6. Trim batting close to seam; trim corners. Turn right side out; press. Machine-baste bottom edges together along raw edges. Trim batting close to stitching.

7. To make tea cozy back, layer the second piece of batting and the two remaining dark red lining pieces and sew as in step 5. Turn and baste bottom edge as in step 6.

8. Quilt front and back layers as desired by hand or machine. ***Note:*** *The front of the sample was hand-quilted in the ditch of seams using red quilting thread. The back of the sample was hand-quilted in the Chinese Lantern design using red quilting thread.*

9. Cut 19 squares black-with-red print 3" x 3". Fold each square on one diagonal with wrong sides together; fold a second time to form a prairie point as shown in Figure 1; repeat for all squares.

10. Pin six prairie points

Figure 1
Fold each square on 1 diagonal with wrong sides together; fold a second time to form a prairie point.

Continued on page 172

Broken Windows Monitor Cover

By Connie Kauffman

Make a quilted monitor cover using fabrics to coordinate with your home-office space.

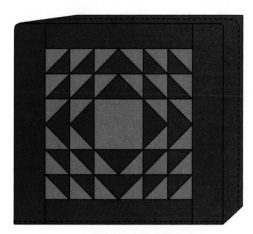

**Broken Windows
Monitor Cover**
Placement Diagram
17" x 14 3/4" x 5 3/4"

PROJECT NOTE

Computer monitors vary in size. The instructions are given for a monitor that measures 14" wide by 16" high from outside edge to outside edge. If your monitor is a different size, measure the front of the monitor from edge to edge and top edge to bottom edge (not screen size). Subtract 12" for the pieced block. Divide in half for border strips and add 1/2". Top and bottom strips may be different from side strips.

Depending on the shape of your monitor, the monitor cover may fit better if a length of elastic is run through the outside-edge seam. Make the elastic long enough to fit completely around the monitor, extending along the bottom of the monitor. Overlap and sew the ends of the elastic together.

PROJECT SPECIFICATIONS

Project Size: 17" x 14 3/4" x 5 3/4"

Block Size: 12" x 12"

Number of Blocks: 1

FABRIC & BATTING

- 1/4 yard computer print
- 3/4 yard purple mottled
- Muslin 13" x 13"
- Batting 13" x 13"

SUPPLIES & TOOLS

- All-purpose thread to match fabrics
- Purple metallic thread
- Basic sewing tools and supplies

INSTRUCTIONS

1. Prepare one Broken Windows block referring to the Placement Diagram for placement of colors in the block.

2. Sandwich batting between the completed block and the muslin backing; pin or baste layers together to hold. Quilt as desired by hand or machine. *Note: The sample was machine-quilted in the ditch of seams using purple metallic thread in the top of the machine and all-purpose thread in the bobbin.*

3. When quilting is complete, trim edges even; remove pins or basting.

4. Cut two strips each 2" x 12 1/2" and 3" x 15 1/2" purple mottled.

Continued on page 172

Pride of Italy Centerpiece

By Barbara Clayton

Blue-and-white dishes look wonderful when used with this table centerpiece.

PROJECT SPECIFICATIONS

Project Size: 16" x 16" (without loops)

Block Size: 12" x 12"

Number of Blocks: 1

FABRIC & BATTING

- 1/8 yard dark blue solid
- 1/8 yard light blue print
- 1/4 yard medium blue print
- 3/4 yard white-with-blue print
- Batting 16 1/2" x 16 1/2"

SUPPLIES & TOOLS

- All-purpose thread to match fabrics
- Blue quilting thread
- Clear nylon monofilament
- 7 yards 1/4" cord
- Large safety pin
- Basic sewing tools and supplies and lightweight cardboard

INSTRUCTIONS

1. Prepare one Pride of Italy block referring to the Placement Diagram for placement of colors in the block.

2. Cut two strips each 1 1/4" x 12 1/2" and 1 1/4" x 14" medium blue print. Sew the shorter strips to opposite sides of the pieced block and the longer strips to the remaining sides; press seams toward strips.

3. Cut two strips each 1 3/4" x 14" and 1 3/4" x 16 1/2" white-with-blue print. Sew the shorter strips to opposite sides of the pieced block and the longer strips to the remaining sides; press seams toward strips.

4. Cut 1 1/2"-wide bias strips from the white-with-blue print to create at least 210" in strips. Fold each strip in half along length with right sides together; stitch along raw edges. Turn right side out.

5. Using the large safety pin, feed cord into bias tubes, cutting lengths as needed to fit tubes. Cut

into 4" lengths: you will need 48 corded bias tubes.

6. Evenly space and pin 12 bias tubes to one side of the quilted square referring to Figure 1, beginning and ending 1/4" from the edges and evenly overlapping loops to fit across edge. Baste in place; repeat on remaining sides.

7. Pin the backing piece right sides together with the

Continued on page 172

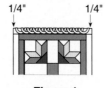

Figure 1
Evenly space and pin 12 bias tubes to 1 side of the quilted square, beginning and ending 1/4" from the edges and evenly overlapping loops to fit across edge.

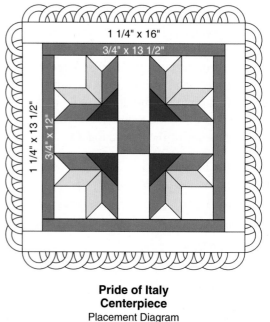

1 1/4" x 16"

3/4" x 13 1/2"

1 1/4" x 13 1/2"

3/4" x 12"

Pride of Italy Centerpiece
Placement Diagram
16" x 16" (without loops)

Alabama

PIECING INSTRUCTIONS

1. Referring to the Piecing Diagram to piece one block, sew a light 68 to a dark 68 to a light 68. Sew a dark 68 to a light 68 to a dark 68; repeat. Join these pieced units to make the center Nine-Patch unit.

2. Sew a medium 8 to opposite sides of the pieced center unit. Sew a dark 68 to each end of two 8 pieces; sew these units to the remaining sides of the pieced center.

3. Sew a light 123 to opposite sides of the pieced center unit. Sew a dark 68 to each end of two 123 pieces; sew these units to the remaining sides of the pieced center.

4. Sew a darkest A7 to opposite sides of the pieced center unit. Sew a dark 68 to each end of two A7 pieces; sew these units to the remaining sides of the pieced center to complete one block.

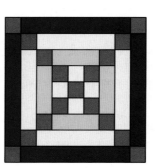

Alabama

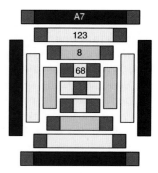

Templates needed:
8, 68, 123 & A7

Alaska

PIECING INSTRUCTIONS

1. Referring to the Piecing Diagram to piece one block, join two light and two darkest 54 triangles to make the center unit. Sew a dark 2 to opposite sides.

2. Sew a light 5 to a darkest 5 along the diagonal; repeat for four units. Sew a unit to each end of the remaining two dark 2 squares; sew these pieced units to the remaining sides of the pieced center unit.

3. Sew a darkest D7 and a DR7 to adjacent sides of a light C7; sew a medium B7 and BR7 to the sides of the pieced unit to complete a side unit. Repeat for four side units.

4. Sew a side unit to each side of the pieced center unit sewing corner seams to complete one block.

Alaska

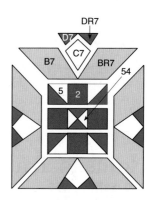

Templates needed:
2, 5, 54, B7, BR7,
C7, D7 & DR7

Albany

PIECING INSTRUCTIONS

1. Referring to the Piecing Diagram to piece one block, sew a medium 41R and a darkest 41 to short sides of a light 12; repeat for two units. Sew a medium 41 and a darkest 41R to short sides of a light 12; repeat for two units.

2. Sew a darkest 16 to the medium sides and a medium 16 to the darkest sides of each pieced unit; add a light 12 to the 16 end of each unit to make corner units.

3. Sew a medium 16 to adjacent sides of a light 59; repeat for two side units. Sew a darkest 16 to adjacent sides of a light 59; repeat for two side units.

4. Join two medium 59 squares with two dark 59 squares to make a Four-Patch center unit.

5. Join the pieced units referring the to Piecing Diagram to complete one block.

Albany

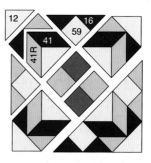

Templates needed:
12, 16, 41, 41R & 59

All Points

PIECING INSTRUCTIONS

1. Referring to the Piecing Diagram to piece one block, sew a light 8 to a dark 8 to a medium 8 to make a side unit; repeat for four side units.

2. Sew a light 4 to a medium 4 on one short side; sew this unit to a dark 2 to complete one corner unit; repeat for four corner units.

3. Sew a light JJ7 between two darkest 12 triangles to make the center unit.

4. Arrange the pieced units in rows referring to the Piecing Diagram. Join units in rows; join rows to complete one block.

All Points

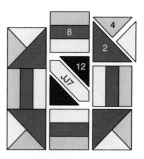

Templates needed:
2, 4, 8, 12 & JJ7

Arizona

PIECING INSTRUCTIONS

1. Referring to the Piecing Diagram to piece one block, sew a dark 5 to a light 5 along the diagonal; repeat for 12 units.

2. Join three 5 units with a light 3 to make a corner unit referring to the Piecing Diagram for positioning; repeat for four corner units.

3. Sew a dark 5 to two adjacent sides of a light 4; sew this to a light 6 to complete a side unit. Repeat for four side units.

4. Arrange the pieced units in rows with the dark 1 square referring to the Piecing Diagram. Join units in rows; join rows to complete one block.

Arizona

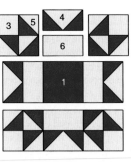

Templates needed:
1, 3, 4, 5 & 6

Arkansas Traveler 1

PIECING INSTRUCTIONS

1. Referring to the Piecing Diagram to piece one block, sew a medium 6 to a lightest 9; sew a lightest 10 and 10R to the short ends of the 6 part of the unit to complete one side unit. Repeat for four side units.

2. Join two dark, one light and one darkest KK7 pieces to make a diamond unit; repeat for four diamond units.

3. Join the side units with the diamond units to complete one block.

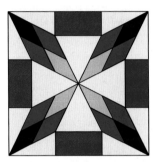

Arkansas Traveler 1

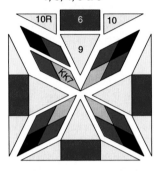

Templates needed:
6, 9, 10, 10R & KK7

Arkansas Traveler 2

PIECING INSTRUCTIONS

1. Referring to the Piecing Diagram to piece one block, sew a dark 108 to a light LL7; repeat for eight units.

2. Sew a medium 14 to a pieced unit on the short sides; repeat for two units. Join the units to complete a quarter block; repeat for four quarter blocks.

3. Join the quarter blocks to complete one block.

Arkansas Traveler 2

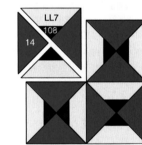

Templates needed:
14, 108 & LL7

Balkan Puzzle

PIECING INSTRUCTIONS

1. Referring to the Piecing Diagram to piece one block, sew all dark and medium 12 triangles to a light 12 triangle on the diagonal.

2. Arrange the pieced units in rows referring to the Piecing Diagram. Join units in rows; join rows to complete one block.

Balkan Puzzle

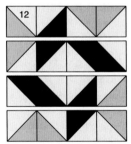

Template needed:
12

Baton Rouge

PIECING INSTRUCTIONS

1. Referring to the Piecing Diagram to piece one block, sew a dark 41 to a medium 41R along long sides; repeat for four units. Sew a medium 41 to a dark 41R; repeat for four units.

2. Join two 41 units with a light 59 to complete a side unit; repeat for four side units.

3. Sew a side unit to each side of the darkest 34 square, joining the 41 units with an angled seam.

4. Sew a light 12 to each corner to complete one block.

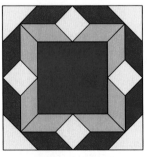

Baton Rouge

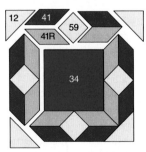

Templates needed:
12, 34, 41, 41R & 59

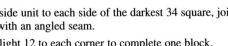

Boise

PIECING INSTRUCTIONS

1. Referring to the Piecing Diagram to piece one block, sew a light 14 to a medium 14 on one short side; repeat. Join these two units to complete the center square.

2. Sew a dark 57 piece to opposite light sides of the center unit.

3. Join a dark 14 to each short side of a medium 14; sew a light 12 triangle to each end to complete one side strip; repeat for two side strips.

4. Sew the side strips to opposite sides of the center unit with the medium 14 triangles on the inside edge to complete one block.

Boise

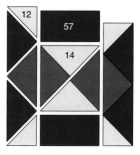

Templates needed:
12, 14 & 57

Broken Windows

PIECING INSTRUCTIONS

1. Referring to the Piecing Diagram to piece one block, sew a light 5 to a dark 5 along the diagonal; repeat for 16 units.

2. Join four pieced 5 units referring to the Piecing Diagram to make a corner unit; repeat for four corner units.

3. Sew a light 5 to two adjacent short sides of a dark 4; repeat for eight units. Join two units to make a side unit; repeat for four side units.

4. Arrange side and corner units with the light 1 square in rows referring to the Piecing Diagram. Join units in rows; join rows to complete one block.

Broken Windows

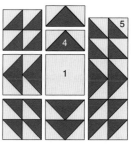

Templates needed:
1, 4 & 5

Castle Wall

PIECING INSTRUCTIONS

1. Referring to the Piecing Diagram to piece one block, sew a medium 3 to a light E7; repeat for eight units.

2. Sew a dark 49 to the E7 side of four 3-E7 units. Sew a dark F7 and FR7 to two sides of these units to complete the corner units.

3. Sew a 3-E7 unit to every other side of the light G7 center. Set in the corner units to complete one block.

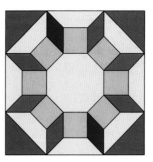

Castle Wall

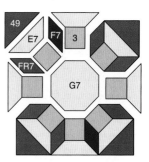

Templates needed:
3, 49, E7, F7, FR7 & G7

Chinese Lanterns

PIECING INSTRUCTIONS

1. Referring to the Piecing Diagram to piece one block, sew a darkest 77R to a medium PPR7 to a light 15; repeat for two units. Sew a dark 77 to a darkest PP7 to a light 15; repeat for two units.

2. Join the units to complete one block.

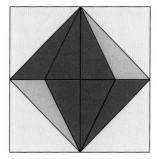

Chinese Lanterns

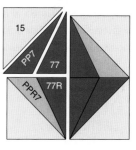

Templates needed:
15, 77, 77R, PP7 & PPR7

Dublin Steps

PIECING INSTRUCTIONS

1. Referring to the Piecing Diagram to piece one block, sew a light 5 to a dark 5 along the diagonal; repeat for four units.

2. Join two units with one light and one dark 3 square to make a corner unit; repeat for two corner units.

3. Join two light and two darkest 3 squares to make a Four-Patch unit; repeat for three Four-Patch units.

4. Sew a medium 2 to a dark 2 along the diagonal to make side units; repeat for four side units.

5. Arrange pieced units in rows referring to the Piecing Diagram. Join units in rows; join rows to complete one block.

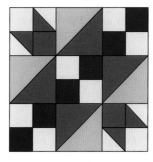

Dublin Steps

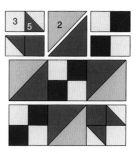

Templates needed:
2, 3 & 5

Dutch Puzzle

PIECING INSTRUCTIONS

1. Referring to the Piecing Diagram to piece one block, sew a light RR7 to opposite sides of a dark SS7; repeat for eight units.

2. Join two units with a dark TT7 to make a corner unit; repeat for four corner units.

3. Sew a light 65 between two dark 65 pieces to complete one side unit; repeat for four side units.

4. Sew one side unit to two opposite sides of the light 34 center square.

5. Sew a corner unit to each end of the remaining side units; sew these units to the remaining sides of the center square to complete one block.

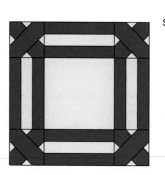
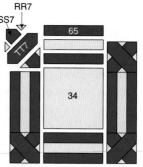

Dutch Puzzle

Templates needed:
34, 65, RR7, SS7 & TT7

Far Horizons

PIECING INSTRUCTIONS

1. Referring to the Piecing Diagram to piece one block, sew a medium 18 to each side of the light 59 square to complete block center.

2. Sew a light 16 triangle to each side of the block center.

3. Sew a light 18 to a medium 102; repeat for four units. Sew an 18-102 unit to each side of the pieced center unit.

4. Sew a darkest 18 to adjacent short sides of a light 16; add a darkest 18 to opposite ends and a darkest 16 to a long side. Repeat for four units.

5. Sew a 16-18 unit to each side of the pieced center to make the center square.

6. Sew a medium 41 and 41R to two adjacent short sides of a light 12. Add a dark 102 and a light 18 to the 41 edge to complete one corner unit; repeat for four corner units.

7. Sew a corner unit to each side of the center square to complete one block.

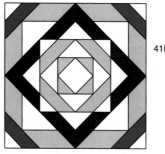
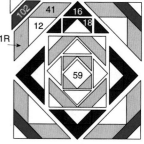

Far Horizons

Templates needed:
12, 16, 18, 41,
41R, 59 & 102

Formosa Tea Leaf

PIECING INSTRUCTIONS

1. Referring to the Piecing Diagram to piece one block, join two darkest, three dark and four light QQ7 pieces to make one diamond unit; repeat for four diamond units.

2. Join these units with four medium 74 pieces to make a star unit.

3. Set in the lightest 72 squares and lightest 49 triangles to complete one block.

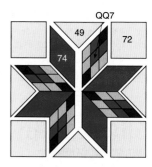

Formosa Tea Leaf

Templates needed:
49, 72, 74 & QQ7

Georgia

PIECING INSTRUCTIONS

1. Referring to the Piecing Diagram to piece one block, join two medium 66 pieces on the angled end; set in a light 20. Sew a dark 21 triangle to the 66 end to complete one corner unit; repeat for four corner units.

2. Sew a light 20 to a dark 20; repeat for four units. Join two units with a medium 20 referring to the Piecing Diagram for positioning of colors.

3. Join two corner units with a 20-20 unit; repeat. Join these two units with the long 20 unit to complete one block.

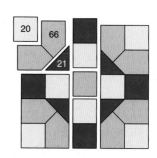

Georgia

Templates needed:
20, 21 & 66

Greek Square

PIECING INSTRUCTIONS

1. Referring to the Piecing Diagram to piece one block, sew a light 2 to a dark 2 along the diagonal to make corner units; repeat for four corner units.

2. Sew a light 6 to a dark 6 along length to make a side unit; repeat for four side units.

3. Arrange the pieced units in rows with the dark 1 square referring to the Piecing Diagram. Join units in rows; join rows to complete one block.

Greek Square

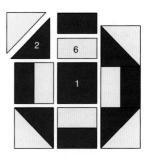

Templates needed:
1, 2 & 6

Hither & Yon

PIECING INSTRUCTIONS

1. Referring to the Piecing Diagram to piece one block, sew a light 16 to a dark 16 along the diagonal; repeat for eight units.

2. Join four 16 units to make a square; repeat for two square units. Sew three light and one medium 12 triangles to the sides of each pieced square unit.

3. Sew a light 12 to a darkest 12 along the diagonal; repeat for six units.

4. Join three 12 units with a darkest 13 referring to the Piecing Diagram; repeat for two units.

5. Arrange the pieced units referring to the Piecing Diagram. Join units in rows; join rows to complete one block.

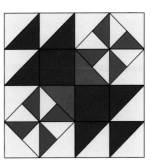

Hither & Yon

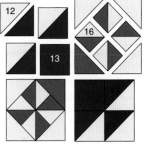

Templates needed:
12, 13 & 16

Japanese Poppy

PIECING INSTRUCTIONS

1. Referring to the Piecing Diagram to piece one block, sew a medium 47 triangle to each side of a light 27 square.

2. Sew a dark 105 and 105R to sides of a darkest NN7; repeat for four units. Sew one of these units to two opposite sides of the 27-47 unit. Sew a light 20 square to each end of the remaining two 105-NN7 units; sew these units to the remaining sides of the 27-47 unit to complete the center unit.

3. Join one darkest, two light and two lightest NN7 pieces. Sew a medium 105 and 105R to the ends to complete a side unit; repeat for four units. Sew a side unit to two opposite sides of the center unit.

4. Sew a mediun 21 to a lightest 21 on the diagonal to make a corner unit; repeat for four corner units.

5. Sew a corner unit to each end of the remaining two side units; sew these units to the previously pieced unit to complete one block.

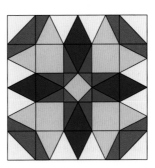

Japanese Poppy

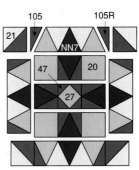

Templates needed:
20, 21, 27, 47,
105, 105R & NN7

Judy in Arabia

PIECING INSTRUCTIONS

1. Referring to the Piecing Diagram to piece one block, sew a light 2 to a medium 2 along the diagonal to make a corner unit; repeat for four corner units.

2. Sew a light 10 and 10R to the angled sides of a dark 9 to make a side unit; repeat for four side units.

3. Sew a light 3 to a dark 3; repeat. Join the 3 units to make the Four-Patch center unit.

4. Arrange the units in rows referring to the Piecing Diagram. Join units in rows; join rows to complete one block.

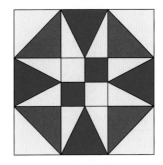

Judy in Arabia

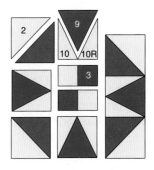

Templates needed:
2, 3, 9, 10 & 10R

Kansas

PIECING INSTRUCTIONS

1. Referring to the Piecing Diagram to piece one block, sew a light K7 to a dark KR7; repeat for eight units. Join two units; repeat for four units.

2. Set in a medium 20 and two medium L7 triangles.

3. Sew a dark 104 to two M7 pieces and a light 107 to two M7 pieces. Sew an M7-104 unit to each pieced unit to complete four units.

4. Join the four units referring to the Piecing Diagram to complete one block.

Kansas

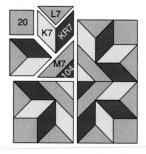

Templates needed:
20, 104, K7, KR7, L7 & M7

London Roads

PIECING INSTRUCTIONS

1. Referring to the Piecing Diagram to piece one block, join a light 4 with a colored 4 along the short sides; add a light 2 to make a corner unit. Repeat for four corner units.

2. Sew a light 8 between two colored 8 pieces to make a side unit; repeat for four side units.

3. Arrange the pieced units in rows with the light 1 square referring to the Piecing Diagram. Join units in rows; join rows to complete one block.

London Roads

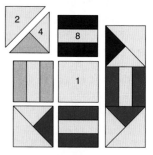

Templates needed:
1, 2, 4 & 8

Mississippi

PIECING INSTRUCTIONS

1. Referring to the Piecing Diagram to piece one block, sew a light 5 to opposite sides of a dark OO7 to make a side unit; repeat for four side units.

2. Arrange the side units with the one light and four dark 1 squares in rows. Join units in rows; join rows to complete one block.

Mississippi

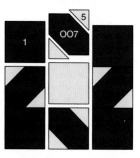

Templates needed:
1, 5 & OO7

Missouri Puzzle

PIECING INSTRUCTIONS

1. Referring to the Piecing Diagram to piece one block, sew a light P7 between two dark P7 squares. Sew a dark P7 between two light P7 squares; repeat. Join these pieced units to complete a Nine-Patch unit; repeat for four Nine-Patch units.

2. Sew a light O7 strip between two dark O7 strips; repeat for four units. Sew a unit to two opposite sides of the light 1.

3. Sew a Nine-Patch unit to each end of the remaining O7 strips; sew these units to the remaining sides of the center square.

4. Sew a dark 5 to each angled end of a light N7; repeat for four units. Sew one of these units to two opposite sides of the pieced center unit.

5. Sew a light 3 to each end of the remaining 5-N7 units; sew these units to the remaining sides of the pieced unit to complete one block.

Missouri Puzzle

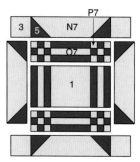

Templates needed:
1, 3, 5, N7, O7 & P7

Missouri Windmills

PIECING INSTRUCTIONS

1. Referring to the Piecing Diagram to piece one block, sew a dark 12 to a medium 12 along the diagonal to make a corner unit; repeat for four corner units.

2. Sew a lightest 12 to a dark 12 along the diagonal; repeat for eight units. Join two 12 units to make a side unit; repeat for four side units.

3. Sew a light VV7 to a medium UU7; repeat for four units. Sew a dark VV7 to a medium UU7; repeat for four units. Join the units to complete the center unit.

4. Arrange the pieced units in rows referring to the Piecing Diagram. Join units in rows; join rows to complete one block.

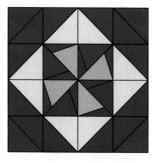

Missouri Windmills

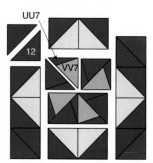

Templates needed:
12, UU7 & VV7

Nebraska Windmills

PIECING INSTRUCTIONS

1. Referring to the Piecing Diagram to piece one block, sew a dark 68 between two medium 68 squares; repeat. Sew a medium 68 between two dark 68 squares. Join these pieced units to complete the center Nine-Patch unit.

2. Sew a medium Q7 to a darkest QR7; set in a light S7. Add a light R7 to the medium Q7 end; repeat for four units.

3. Sew a unit to each side of the pieced center, leaving one seam unstitched until all units have been added to complete one block.

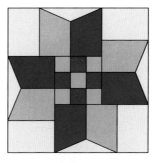

Nebraska Windmills

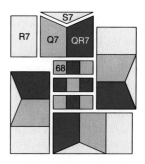

Templates needed:
68, Q7, QR7, R7 & S7

Norway Pine

PIECING INSTRUCTIONS

1. Referring to the Piecing Diagram to piece one block, sew a light 21 to a dark 21 along the diagonal; repeat for 14 units.

2. Arrange the pieced units in rows with the light 20 squares; join pieces to make rows.

3. Join two light 14 triangles with a medium T7; sew a dark U7 to the longest side.

4. Join the pieced units and rows referring to the Piecing Diagram to complete one block.

Norway Pine

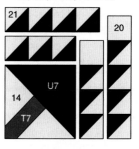

Templates needed:
14, 20, 21, T7 & U7

Oriental Star

PIECING INSTRUCTIONS

1. Referring to the Piecing Diagram to piece one block, sew darkest V7 and W7 pieces to the medium X7.

2. Sew a light 12 to each V7 to complete the center unit.

3. Sew a dark 41 and 41R to short sides of a light 16 to make a side unit; repeat for four side units. Sew a unit to each side of the pieced center.

4. Sew a medium 12 to each corner to complete one block.

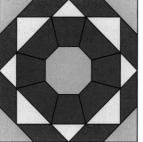

Oriental Star

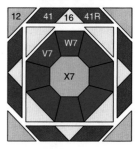

Templates needed:
12, 16, 41, 41R,
V7, W7 & X7

Ozark Trails

PIECING INSTRUCTIONS

1. Referring to the Piecing Diagram to piece one block, sew a colored 16 to two adjacent short sides of a light 13 square; repeat for four units.

2. Sew a colored WW7 and WWR7 to two adjacent sides of a medium XX7; repeat for two units.

3. Join the two units; sew to one 13-16 unit to complete one corner unit; repeat for four corner units.

4. Sew a pieced unit to two opposite sides of a light 19.

5. Sew a light 14 to opposite sides of each remaining pieced unit; sew these units to opposite sides of the long pieced unit to complete one block.

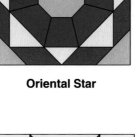

Ozark Trails

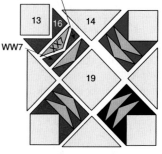

Templates needed:
13, 14, 16, 19,
WW7, WWR7 & XX7

Philadelphia Pavement

PIECING INSTRUCTIONS

1. Referring to the Piecing Diagram to piece one block, sew a light 21 to a dark 21 on the diagonal; repeat for four units. Join two 21 units with a light 20; repeat. Sew a dark 20 between two light 20 squares.

2. Sew the 20 unit between the two 20-21 units to complete the center square.

3. Sew a medium 75 to two opposite sides of the center square.

4. Sew a light 20 to opposite ends of a medium 75; repeat. Sew to the remaining sides of the center square to complete one block.

Philadelphia Pavement

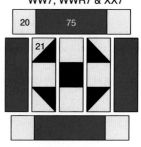

Templates needed:
20, 21 & 75

Philippine Islands

PIECING INSTRUCTIONS

1. Referring to the Piecing Diagram to piece one block, sew two lightest 18 triangles to the point of a darkest BB7; repeat for four units.

2. Sew a lightest 18 to each end of a medium CC7; repeat for four units.

3. Sew an 18-CC7 unit to an 18-BB7 unit to complete one side unit; repeat for four side units.

4. Join two dark and two light 35 triangles referring to the Piecing Diagram; sew to a lightest AA7. Sew a lightest 35 to the dark 35 end to complete one corner unit; repeat for four corner units.

5. Join the side and corner units with angled seams, being very careful to match center points as you stitch to complete one block.

Phillippine Islands

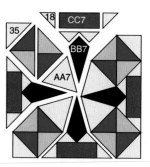

Templates needed:
18, 35, AA7, BB7 & CC7

Phoenix

PIECING INSTRUCTIONS

1. Referring to the Piecing Diagram to piece one block, sew a medium 60 to two opposite long sides of a dark 110; repeat.

2. Sew a dark 110 to two opposite sides of a light 64. Sew the pieced 60-110 units to the remaining sides of the 64-110 unit to complete the center unit.

3. Sew a light 54 to two adjacent sides of a dark 64; sew this unit to a short side of a medium 4; repeat for four units.

4. Sew a light 4 and medium 4 on short sides; repeat for four units.

5. Sew a 4-4 unit to a 4-54-64 unit to complete a side unit; repeat for four side units.

6. Sew a light 2 to a darkest 2 along the diagonal to complete one corner unit; repeat for four corner units.

7. Arrange the pieced units in rows referring to the Piecing Diagram. Join the units in rows; join the rows to complete one block.

Phoenix

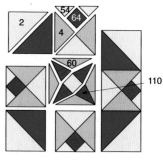

Templates needed:
2, 4, 54, 60, 64 & 110

Pride of Italy

PIECING INSTRUCTIONS

1. Referring to the Piecing Diagram to piece one block, sew a light 129 to a darkest 129R; set in a light 28. Sew a darkest 129 to a light 129R; set in a light 28.

2. Join the two pieced units with a light 20. Sew a darkest 21 on the angled end to complete one corner unit; repeat for four corner units.

3. Join two corner units with a medium 46; repeat.

4. Sew a dark 20 between two medium 46 pieces; sew between the two pieced units to complete one block.

Pride of Italy

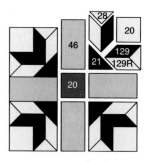

Templates needed:
20, 21, 28, 46, 129 & 129R

Rhode Island

PIECING INSTRUCTIONS

1. Referring to the Piecing Diagram to piece one block, sew a light 54 to two adjacent short sides of a dark 5; repeat for four units.

2. Sew a 5-54 unit to two opposite sides of the light 7. Sew a dark 64 to each end of the remaining two 5-54 units. Sew these units to the remaining sides of the 5-54-7 unit to complete the center unit.

3. Sew a light 4 to two adjacent sides of a medium 1; repeat for four units. Sew a unit to two opposite sides of the pieced center unit.

4. Sew a darkest 4 to the light 4 ends of the remaining 1-4 units to make a corner unit; repeat for two corner units.

5. Sew a corner unit to each remaining side of the pieced center unit to complete one block.

Rhode Island

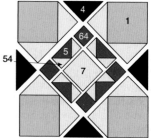

Templates needed:
1, 4, 5, 7, 54 & 64

Richmond

PIECING INSTRUCTIONS

1. Referring to the Piecing Diagram to piece one block, sew a lightest 2 to a dark 2 along the diagonal to make a corner unit; repeat for four corner units.

2. Join two lightest and two medium 64 squares to make a Four-Patch unit; sew a light 5 to each side of the pieced unit to complete one side unit. Repeat for four side units.

3. Sew a darkest 5 to each side of a lightest 7 to complete one center unit.

4. Arrange the pieced units in rows referring to the Piecing Diagram. Join the units in rows; join the rows to complete one block.

Richmond

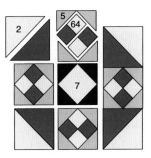

Templates needed:
2, 5, 7 & 64

Road to Paris

PIECING INSTRUCTIONS

1. Referring to the Piecing Diagram to piece one block, sew a colored EE7 to each side of the light DD7 to complete the center unit.

2. Sew a light FF7 and FFR7 to each end of a colored EE7; repeat for four units. Sew a unit to each side of the center unit.

3. Sew a light 108 to each end of a colored 99; sew a light 107 to the longer side of piece 99 to complete one corner unit. Repeat for four corner units.

4. Sew a corner unit to each side of the center unit to complete one block.

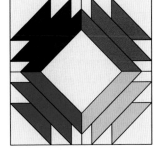

Road to Paris

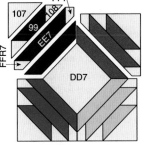

Templates needed:
99, 107, 108, DD7,
EE7, FF7 & FFR7

Rocky Road to Dublin

PIECING INSTRUCTIONS

1. Referring to the Piecing Diagram to piece one block, sew a medium 5 to a light 5 along the diagonal; repeat for four units. Join two units with two light 3 squares to make a corner unit; repeat for two corner units.

2. Join two medium and two light 3 squares to make a Four-Patch unit; repeat for three Four-Patch units.

3. Sew a medium 5 to two adjacent sides of a light 3; sew a dark 2 to this unit to complete a side unit. Repeat for four side units.

4. Arrange the pieced units in rows referring to the Piecing Diagram. Join units in rows; join rows to complete one block.

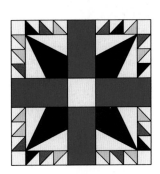

Rocky Road to Dublin

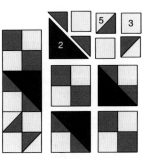

Templates needed:
2, 3 & 5

Roman Roads

PIECING INSTRUCTIONS

1. Referring to the Piecing Diagram to piece one block, sew a light 47 to a colored 47 along the diagonal; repeat for 24 units.

2. Join three units to make a row; repeat for eight units.

3. Sew a light Z7 and ZR7 to a dark Y7; repeat for four units.

4. Sew a 47 unit to one side of a Z-Y unit. Sew a light 52 to one end of a 47 unit; sew this unit to the pieced 47-Z-Y unit to complete one corner unit. Repeat for four corner units.

5. Join two corner units with a medium 46; repeat for two rows.

6. Sew a light 20 between two medium 46 rectangles to make a row; join the previously pieced rows to complete one block.

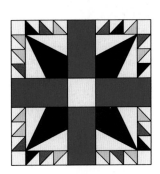

Roman Roads

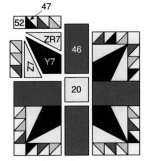

Templates needed:
20, 46, 47, 52, Y7, Z7 & ZR7

South Dakota

PIECING INSTRUCTIONS

1. Referring to the Piecing Diagram to piece one block, sew a light 54 to a dark 54 along the diagonal; repeat for 20 units.

2. Join four 54 units to complete a pinwheel unit; repeat for five pinwheel units.

3. Join the pinwheel units with medium 7 squares to make the center unit.

4. Sew a light 5 to a darkest 5 along the diagonal; join with two light 3 squares and three medium 5 triangles to make a corner unit; repeat for four corner units.

5. Sew a corner unit to each side of the center unit to complete one block.

South Dakota

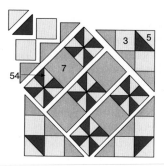

Templates needed:
3, 5, 7 & 54

St. Louis

PIECING INSTRUCTIONS

1. Referring to the Piecing Diagram to piece one block, sew a medium 129 to a medium 129R; repeat for four units.

2. Join the four units; set in a light 28 between points and a light 20 in each corner to complete the center unit.

3. Sew a light 28 to one angled end of a dark 66; repeat for eight units. Join two units to complete a side unit; repeat for four side units.

4. Sew a side unit to two opposite sides of the pieced center. Sew a light 20 to each end of the remaining two side units. Sew these units to the remaining sides of the pieced center to complete one block.

St. Louis

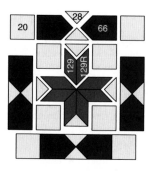

Templates needed:
20, 28, 66, 129 & 129R

Texas Cactus Basket

PIECING INSTRUCTIONS

1. Referring to the Piecing Diagram to piece one block, sew a dark 74 to a medium 74R; sew a medium 74 to a dark 74R. Join the two units; set in two light 49 triangles and one light 72.

2. Sew the darkest HH7 to the bottom edge of the pieced unit.

3. Sew the light 62 to the darkest MM7 piece; sew this unit to the HH7 side of the pieced unit.

4. Set in the light GG7 pieces to complete one block.

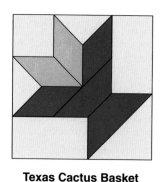

Texas Cactus Basket

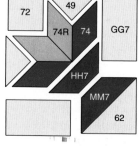

Templates needed:
49, 62, 72, 74, 74R,
GG7, HH7 & MM7

To Market, To Market

PIECING INSTRUCTIONS

1. Referring to the Piecing Diagram to piece one block, sew a dark 16 to a medium 16 on short sides; repeat for two units. Sew a darkest 16 to a medium 16 on short sides; repeat for two units.

2. Sew a pieced 16 unit to each side of the light 19 to complete the center unit.

3. Sew a medium 12 to a dark 12 along the diagonal; repeat for four units. Sew a medium 12 to a darkest 12 along the diagonal; repeat for four units. Join a medium and dark unit to make side units referring to the Piecing Diagram; repeat for four side units.

4. Sew a side unit to two opposite sides of the center unit.

5. Sew a dark and darkest 13 to each end of the remaining two side units; sew these units to the pieced center unit to complete one block.

To Market, To Market

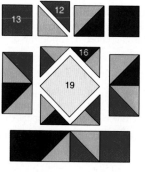

Templates needed:
12, 13, 16 & 19

Vermont

PIECING INSTRUCTIONS

1. Referring to the Piecing Diagram to piece one block, join four light 42 pieces with four dark 92 pieces to complete the center unit.

2. Join one light and two dark 92 pieces with medium 91 and 91R pieces; sew a medium 2 to one side; repeat for four units. Sew two of these units to opposite sides of the pieced center unit.

3. Sew a light 4 to the 91 ends of the remaining two pieced units to make corner units. Sew the two corner units to the pieced center unit to complete one block.

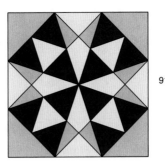

Vermont

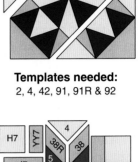

Templates needed:
2, 4, 42, 91, 91R & 92

Virginia

PIECING INSTRUCTIONS

1. Referring to the Piecing Diagram to piece one block, sew a medium YY7 to a light H7; sew a medium J7 to the adjacent side to complete one corner unit; repeat for four corner units referring to the Piecing Diagram for proper positioning of pieces.

2. Sew a dark 5 to one long side of medium 38 and 38R; join the two units at the angled seam; set in a light 4 to complete a side unit. Repeat for four side units.

3. Arrange the pieced units with a light 1 square referring to the Piecing Diagram. Join the units in rows; join rows to complete one block.

Virginia

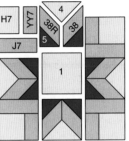

Templates needed:
1, 4, 5, 38, 38R, H7, J7 & YY7

West Virginia

PIECING INSTRUCTIONS

1. Referring to the Piecing Diagram to piece one block, sew a light 18 to a dark 40 and a light 18 to a darkest 40R; sew a light 17 to the 18 end. Repeat for four dark 40 units and four darkest 40R units.

2. Sew a 17-18-40 and a 17-18-40R unit to two adjacent sides of a medium 13 to complete a corner unit; repeat for four corner units.

3. Sew a dark 40 and darkest 40R to two adjacent sides of a light 59; repeat on remaining sides of 59. Sew a light 18 to two angled sides of the 40-59 unit to complete one side unit; repeat for four side units.

4. Join the four side units on angled center sides.

5. Set in corner units referring to the Piecing Diagram to complete one block.

West Virginia

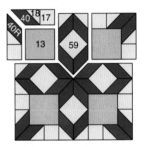

Templates needed:
13, 17, 18, 40, 40R & 59

Wyoming Valley

PIECING INSTRUCTIONS

1. Referring to the Piecing Diagram to piece one block, sew a light 5 to a dark 5 along the diagonal; repeat for 12 units.

2. Join three units with a light 3 to complete one corner unit referring to the Piecing Diagram; repeat for four corner units.

3. Sew a medium 38 and 38R to two adjacent side of a light 4; repeat for four units. Sew a light 5 to the 38 sides of a 4-38 pieced unit to complete one side unit; repeat for four side units.

4. Sew a dark 5 to each side of the light 7 to complete the center unit.

5. Arrange the pieced units in rows referring to the Piecing Diagram. Join the units in rows; join rows to complete one block.

Wyoming Valley

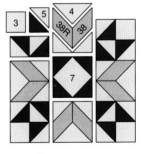

Templates needed:
3, 4, 5, 7, 38 & 38R

St. Louis Tote Bag
Continued from page 156

stitch; trim off excess at ends when stitching is complete as shown in Figure 1.

8. Sew a denim square to the other edge of the strip; press seams open. Repeat with remaining strip and denim squares for lining.

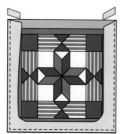

Figure 1
Trim off excess at ends when stitching is complete.

9. Cut two 4" x 19" strips denim for handles. Fold the strips with right sides together along length; stitch to make a tube. Turn right side out; press with seams flat on one side. Topstitch 1/4" from each long edge.

10. Pin a handle to each side of the open edge of the bag top as shown in Figure 2; baste in place.

11. Insert denim lining inside bag top with wrong sides together.

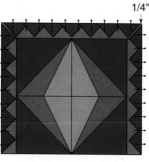

Figure 2
Pin a handle to each side of the open edge of the bag top as shown.

12. Cut one 1 3/4" x 39 1/2" strip denim; join together on short ends to make a tube. Press one raw edge under 1/4". Pin remaining raw edge to the right side of the bag front. *Note: If the strip does not fit, adjust size at seams. Stitch all around.*

13. Turn the strip to the inside; press. Topstitch in place 1/4" from top edge and along bottom edge of the top denim border to catch the inside strip and hold in place to finish. ❖

Chinese Lanterns Tea Cozy
Continued from page 158

to each side of the quilted top and seven across the top edge, with folded edges facing the same direction, with points overlapping about 1/2" and leaving 1/4" on each end for seams as shown in Figure 2; machine-baste in place.

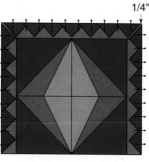

1/4"

Figure 2
Pin 6 prairie points to each side and 7 across the top edge, with folded edges facing the same direction, with points overlapping about 1/2" and leaving 1/4" on each end for seams as shown.

11. Pin the quilted front and back pieces right sides together; sew along sides and across top. Carefully trim corners; overcast or zigzag along seams to keep from fraying. Turn right side out.

12. Bind bottom edges using self-made or purchased narrow black binding to finish. ❖

Broken Windows Monitor Cover
Continued from page 159

5. Sew a 2" x 12 1/2" strip to the top and bottom of the quilted block and the 3" x 15 1/2" strips to the opposite sides; press seams toward strips. Finish inside seam edges with a zigzag stitch to keep from fraying.

6. Hold the bordered block up to your monitor to check size. Trim off any excess beyond 1/4" on the outside edges.

←1/2"

Figure 1
Make curve at corners to eliminate tucks.

7. Measure both sides and the top to get the correct length for the outside border. Cut and piece one strip purple mottled 12" by this measured length plus 1".

8. Pin the strip in place around sides and top with right sides together, leaving 1/2" extending at each end and curving strip at corners to create side strips without tucks as shown in Figure 1; stitch. Trim corners; press.

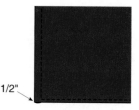

1/2"

Figure 2
Leave 1/2" open on both bottom corners to insert elastic if necessary.

9. Fold under outer edge of strip 1/4"; press. Fold the strip to the inside to cover the seam line; hand-stitch in place.

10. Turn up the bottom edge 1/4" and 1/4" again and press; stitch to hem. Topstitch around sides and top 1/2". *Note: Referring to Figure 2, leave 1/2" open on both bottom corners to insert elastic if needed to keep cover on your monitor.* ❖

Pride of Italy Table Centerpiece
Continued from page 160

quilted block with bias loops; place on top of batting. Sew all around, leaving a 4" opening on one side. Turn right side out; hand-stitch opening closed.

8. Quilt as desired by hand or machine. *Note: The project shown was machine-quilted in the ditch of seams using clear nylon monofilament in the top of the machine and all-purpose thread in the bobbin. The white solid pieces were hand-quilted 1/4" from seams using blue quilting thread.* ❖

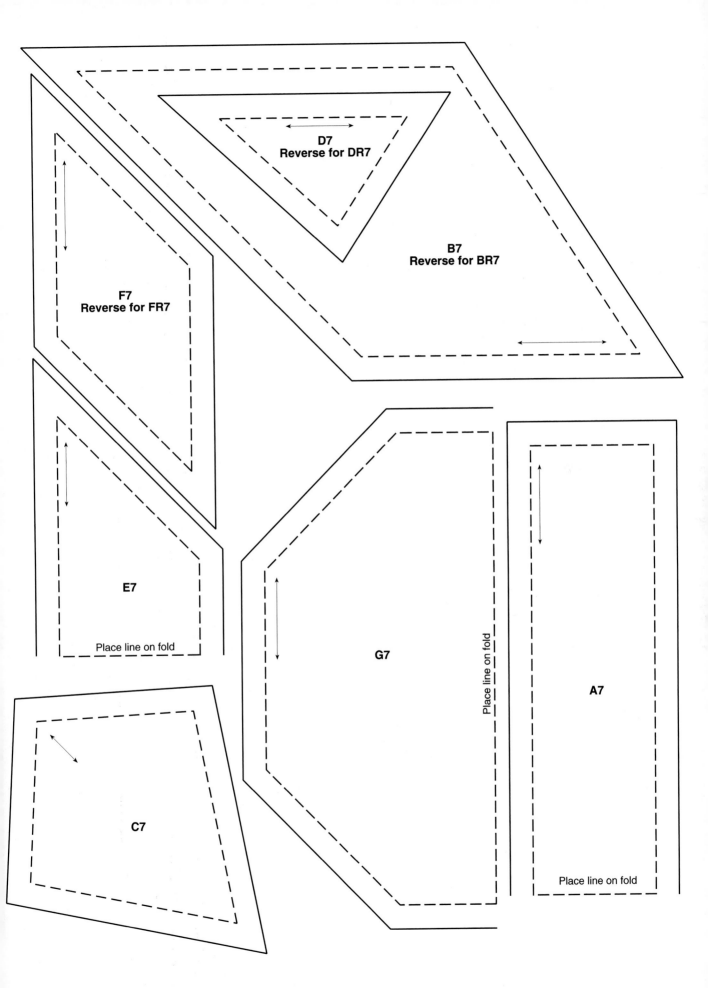

D7
Reverse for DR7

B7
Reverse for BR7

F7
Reverse for FR7

E7

Place line on fold

G7

Place line on fold

A7

Place line on fold

C7

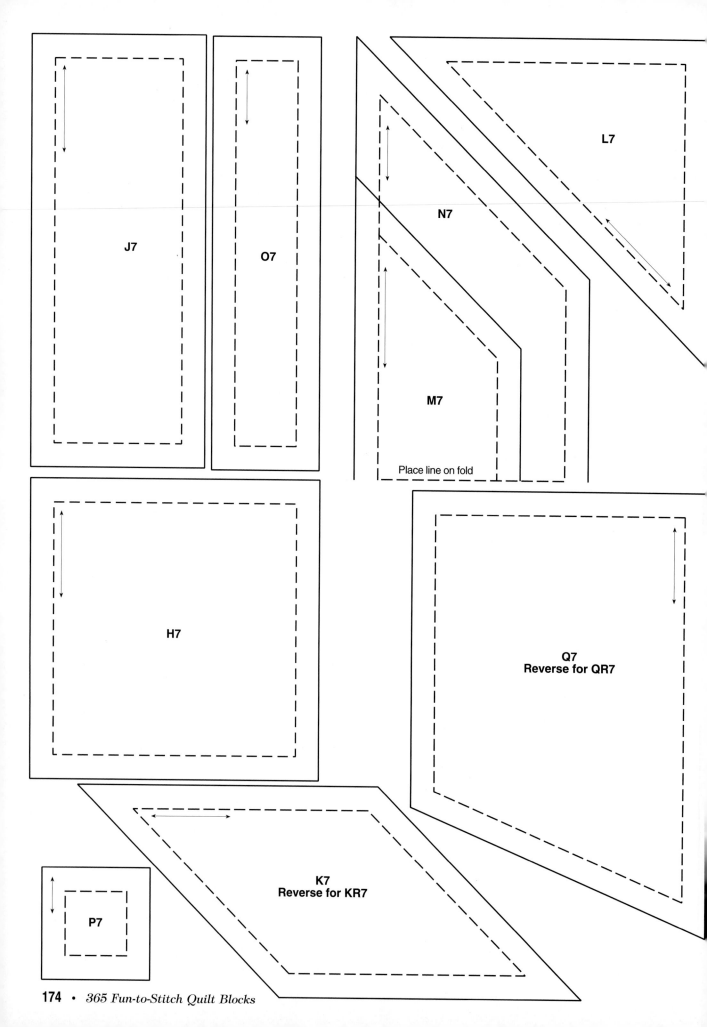

J7

O7

L7

N7

M7

Place line on fold

H7

Q7
Reverse for QR7

K7
Reverse for KR7

P7

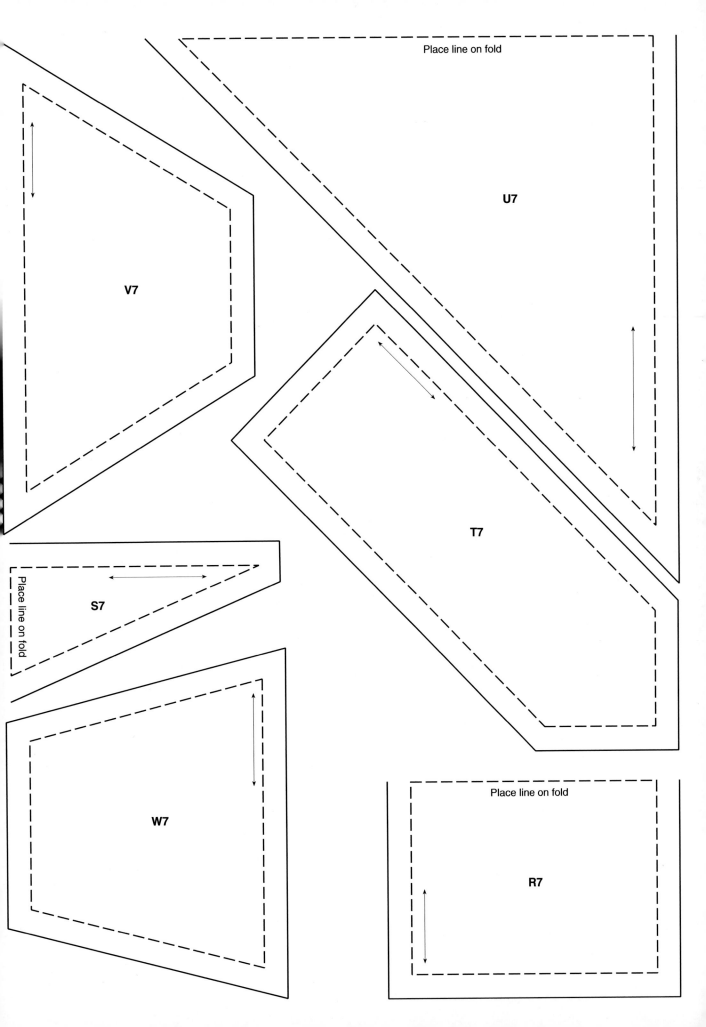

Place line on fold

U7

V7

T7

Place line on fold

S7

W7

Place line on fold

R7

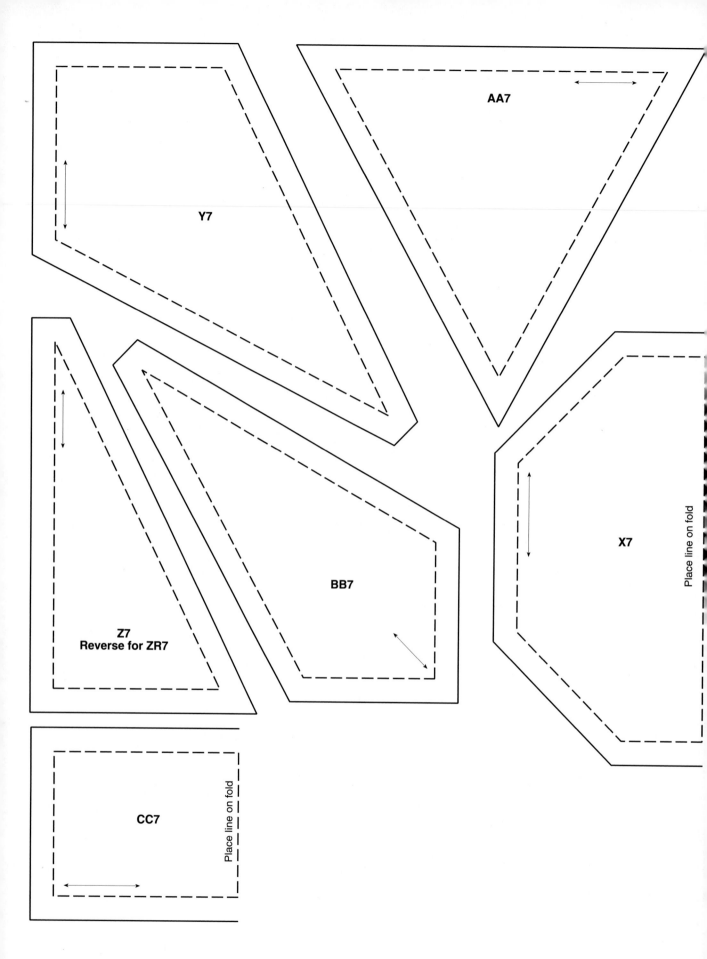

AA7

Y7

X7

Place line on fold

Z7
Reverse for ZR7

BB7

CC7

Place line on fold

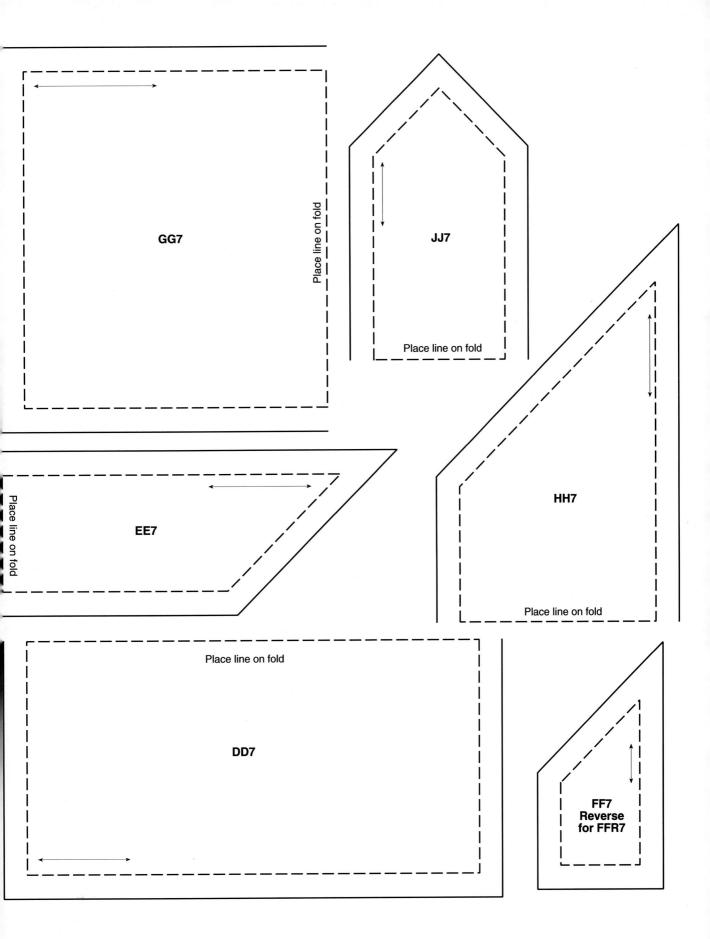

GG7

JJ7

Place line on fold

Place line on fold

EE7

HH7

Place line on fold

Place line on fold

Place line on fold

DD7

FF7
Reverse
for FFR7

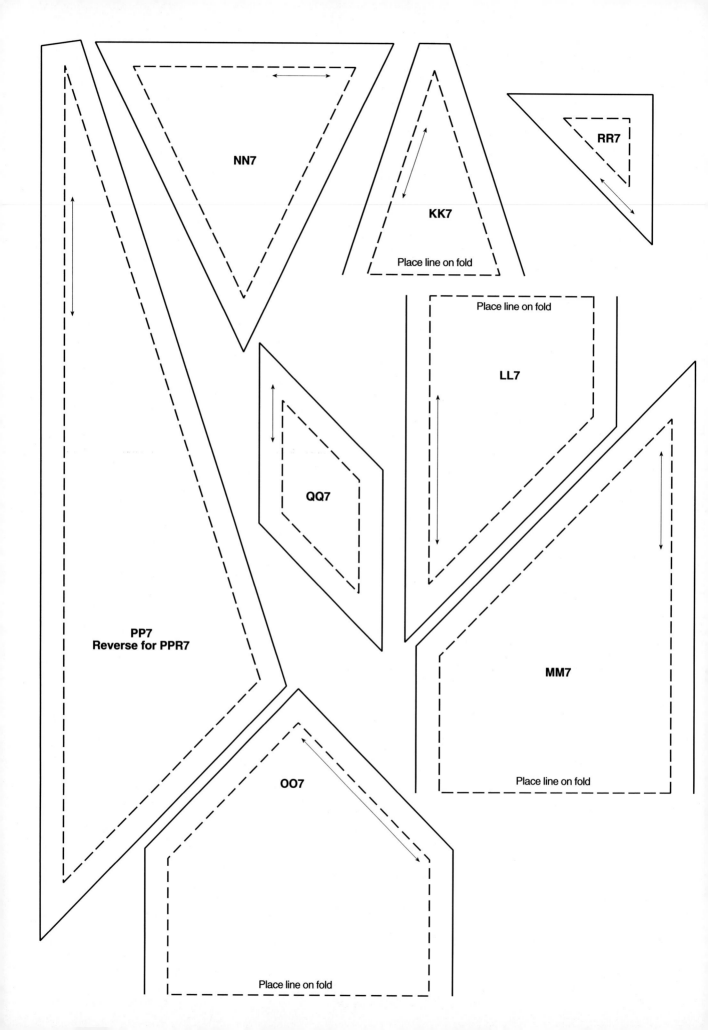

NN7

RR7

KK7

Place line on fold

Place line on fold

LL7

QQ7

PP7
Reverse for PPR7

MM7

OO7

Place line on fold

Place line on fold

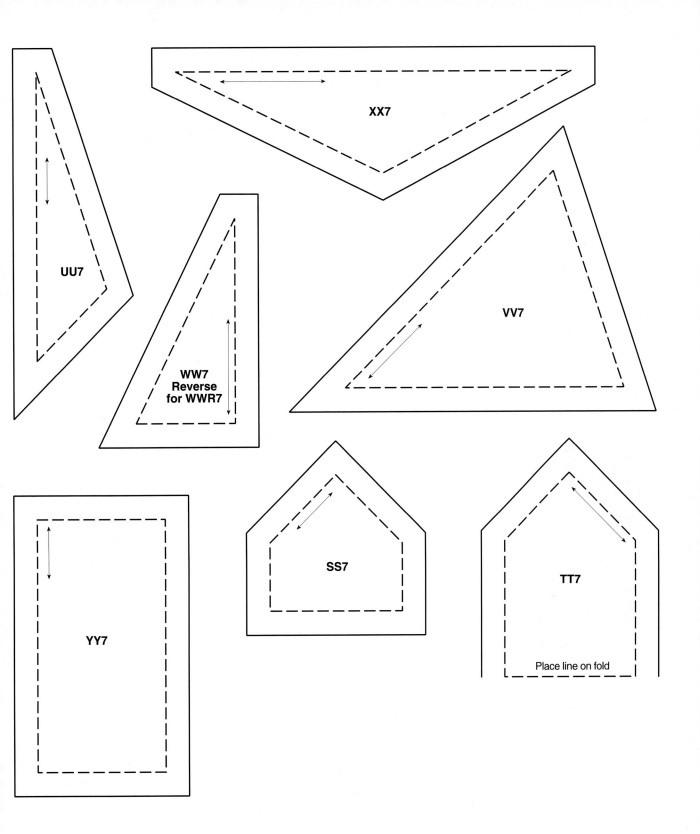

XX7

UU7

WW7
Reverse
for WWR7

VV7

YY7

SS7

TT7

Place line on fold

Blessed
and
Beloved

*The blocks in this
chapter are named
after Biblical or
inspirational people,
events or ideas. Quilts
from these blocks, as
with all quilts, will
inspire and bless you.
May you enjoy each
loving stitch you
make as you quilt this
beautiful sampler.*

Blessed and Beloved Sampler

By Ruth Swasey

Seventeen different blocks with inspirational names combine to make this large medallion-style sampler quilt.

PROJECT SPECIFICATIONS

Quilt Size: 104" x 104"

Block Size: 12" x 12"

Number of Blocks: 40

FABRIC & BATTING

- 1/2 yard dark green print
- 3/4 yard purple print
- 1 yard light green print
- 2 yards each lavender and light pink prints
- 2 1/2 yards each magenta and medium green prints
- 3 1/2 yards white print
- Backing 108" x 108"
- Batting 108" x 108"
- 12 yards self-made or purchased binding

SUPPLIES & TOOLS

- All-purpose thread to match fabrics
- Basic sewing tools and supplies, rotary cutter, mat and ruler

INSTRUCTIONS

1. Complete 40 blocks (17 different blocks) as desired referring to the Placement Diagram for positioning of colors within blocks. Blocks used in the sample are listed in Figure 1. *Note: You may choose any 17 blocks from this chapter or from other chapters in this book. Make 12 blocks each of two different blocks to use in the outer borders. The same block was used twice in the four-block center section.*

2. Square up blocks to 12 1/2" x 12 1/2".

3. Join four blocks to make quilt center.

4. Cut four strips each magenta and lavender prints 2" x 32". Join one strip of each color along length to make a pieced strip; repeat for four pieced strips.

5. Center and sew a pieced strip to each side of the pieced center, mitering corners. Trim excess at corners; press corner seams open; press seams toward strips.

6. Cut two strips each white, magenta, light green

COLOR KEY

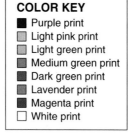

- ■ Purple print
- ▨ Light pink print
- ▨ Light green print
- ▨ Medium green print
- ▨ Dark green print
- ▨ Lavender print
- ▨ Magenta print
- □ White print

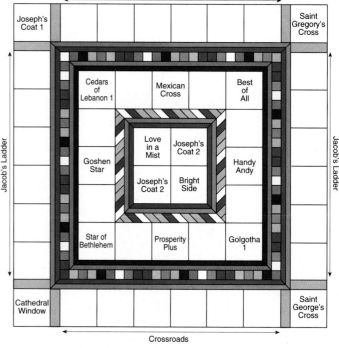

Figure 1
Use blocks shown or choose 17
of your favorites from this book.

and light pink prints 3 1/2" by fabric width. Join one strip each color in the order given with right sides together along length, staggering each strip 3" below top edge of previous strip to make a strip set as shown in Figure 2; repeat for two strip sets.

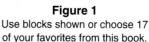

Figure 2
Stagger each strip 3" below
top edge of previous strip.

7. Cut each strip set into 2 5/8" segments at a 45-degree angle as shown in Figure 3. Join segments to make four 38"-long strips. Center and sew a strip to each side of the pieced center, mitering corners. Trim excess; press seams toward pieced strips. The

Figure 3
Cut each strip set into 2 5/8"
segments at a 45-degree
angle as shown.

pieced section should now measure 36 1/2" x 36 1/2".

Inspirational Blessings Sampler
Placement Diagram
104" x 104"

8. Cut eight 12 1/2" x 12 1/2" white print squares; Join two squares with one pieced block to make the top row; repeat for bottom row. Sew these rows to the pieced center; press seams away from rows.

9. Join three blocks and two squares white print to make a side row; repeat for two side rows. Sew a side row to each side of the pieced center; press seams away from rows.

10. Cut and piece four strips each purple and medium green prints 2" x 68". Join one strip each color

to make a pieced strip; repeat for four pieced strips.

11. Center and sew a pieced strip to each side of the pieced center, mitering corners. Trim excess at corners, press corner seams open; press seams toward strips.

12. Cut 92 squares using all fabrics 3 1/2" x 3 1/2". Join squares to make two strips with 22 squares and two strips with 24 squares. Sew a shorter strip to two opposite sides; press seams toward strips. Trim excess at ends, if necessary. Sew longer strips to the

Continued on page 198

The Cross Wall Quilt

By Pat Campbell

Make a wall quilt using The Cross block to hang during the Easter holidays.

Figure 1
Join 3 yellow print and
2 scrap 4 triangles.

Figure 2
Sew a scrap 5 triangle to
each end of each unit.

4. Join two yellow print and three scrap 4 triangles as shown in Figure 3; repeat for four units. Sew a previously pieced unit to one of these units as shown in Figure 4; repeat for four units.

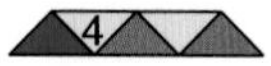

Figure 3
Join 2 yellow print and
3 scrap 4 triangles.

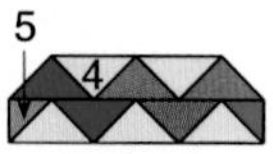

Figure 4
Sew a previously pieced
unit to 1 of these units.

5. Sew a yellow print 90 triangle to the short side of each unit to complete a corner unit as shown in Figure 5; repeat for four corner units.

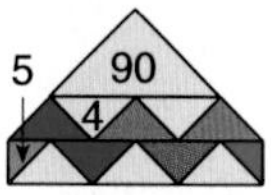

Figure 5
Sew a yellow print 90 triangle to
the short side of each unit to
complete a corner unit as shown.

6. Sew a corner unit to opposite sides of the pieced block; press seams toward corner units. Sew a scrap 5 triangle to each end of the remaining two corner units as shown in Figure 6; sew these units to the remaining sides of the pieced unit to complete the pieced top.

Continued on page 189

PROJECT SPECIFICATIONS
Project Size: Approximately 20" x 20"

Block Size: 12" x 12"

Number of Blocks: 1

FABRIC & BATTING
- 1/2 yard yellow print
- Scraps of assorted batiks, marbled, mottled or hand-dyed fabrics
- Backing 24" x 24"
- Batting 24" x 24"
- 2 5/8 yards self-made or purchased fabrics

SUPPLIES & TOOLS
- All-purpose thread to match fabrics
- Basic sewing tools and supplies

INSTRUCTIONS
1. Prepare one The Cross block referring to the Placement Diagram for placement of colors in the block. *Note: Yellow print is used as the background fabric; all other triangles are cut from scraps.*

2. To make block corners, join three yellow print and two scrap 4 triangles as shown in Figure 1; repeat for four units.

3. Sew a scrap 5 triangle to each end of each unit as shown in Figure 2.

The Cross Wall Quilt
Placement Diagram
Approximately 20" x 20"

Peaceful Hours Bib Apron

By Chris Malone

A pieced block makes the perfect bib front for a fancy apron.

PROJECT SPECIFICATIONS
Project Size: One size fits all
Block Size: 12" x 12"
Number of Blocks: 1

FABRIC & BATTING
- 1/4 yard each gold, red and green mottleds
- 1 3/4 yards floral print
- Batting 13" x 13 1/2"

SUPPLIES & TOOLS
- All-purpose thread to match fabrics
- Basic sewing tools and supplies

INSTRUCTIONS

1. Prepare one Peaceful Hours block referring to the Placement Diagram for placement of colors in the block.

2. Cut one 1" x 13 1/2" and two 1" x 12 1/2" strips green mottled. Sew the shorter strips to two opposite sides of the pieced block; sew the longer strip to one remaining side to make apron bib top. Press seams toward strips.

3. Cut two 3 1/2" x 22" strips floral print for ties. Fold one tie strip in half with right sides together

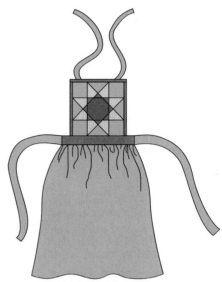

Peaceful Hours Bib Apron
Placement Diagram
One size fits all

along length; stitch along one long side and across one end. Clip corners; turn right side out and press. Repeat with second tie strip.

4. Pin a tie strip to the top edge of the pieced block 1 3/4" from each edge as shown in Figure 1.

5. Cut a 13" x 13 1/2" backing piece from floral print. Place right side up on top of the batting square. Place pieced block right sides together with backing square; pin through all layers. Stitch around the three bordered sides, leaving bottom edge open.

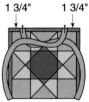

Figure 1
Pin a tie strip to the top edge of the pieced block 1 3/4" from each edge.

6. Turn right side out; press. Hand- or machine-quilt as desired to complete bib section; set aside.

7. Cut a 33" x 40" piece of floral print for apron skirt and two 6 1/2" x 30" strips for waist ties. Cut two 3" x 17 1/2" strips green mottled for waistband.

8. Press under 1/4" on one long edge of 33" x 40" floral print piece; press under 2" and stitch to make hem. Press 1/4" to the wrong side along both 33" sides of skirt; press under 1/4" again and stitch for apron sides.

9. Machine-stitch two lines of gathering stitches

Continued on page 189

Steps to the Temple Mat

By Carla Schwab

Make a table centerpiece in contrasting colors using one block.

PROJECT SPECIFICATIONS

Project Size: 21" x 21"

Block Size: 12" x 12"

Number of Blocks: 1

FABRIC & BATTING

- 1/4 yard each orange, gold, red and brown marbled fabrics
- 1/2 yard off-white marbled
- Backing 23" x 23"
- Batting 23" x 23"
- 2 1/2 yards self-made or purchased binding

SUPPLIES & TOOLS

- All-purpose thread to match fabrics
- Off-white quilting thread
- Basic sewing tools and supplies

INSTRUCTIONS

1. Prepare one Steps to the Temple block referring to the Placement Diagram for placement of colors in the block.

2. Cut two squares off-white marbled fabric 9 3/8" x 9 3/8"; cut each square on one diagonal to make

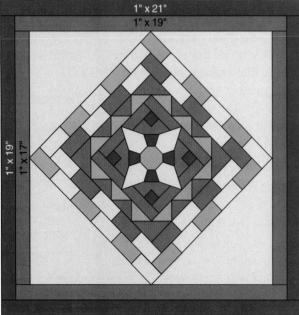

Steps to the Temple Mat
Placement Diagram
21" x 21"

corner triangles. Sew a corner triangle to each side of the pieced block.

3. Cut two strips each 1 1/2" x 17 1/2" and 1 1/2" x 19 1/2" brown marbled fabric. Sew the shorter strips to two opposite sides and remaining strips to the remaining sides; press seams toward strips.

4. Cut two strips each 1 1/2" x 19 1/2" and 1 1/2" x 21 1/2" red marbled fabric. Sew the shorter strips to two opposite sides and remaining strips to the remaining sides; press seams toward strips.

5. Sandwich batting between the prepared backing and pieced top; pin or baste layers together to hold. Quilt as desired by hand or machine. *Note: The sample shown was hand-quilted in the ditch of seams using off-white quilting thread.*

6. When quilting is complete, trim edges even; remove pins or basting. Bind edges with self-made or purchased binding to finish. ❖

Ruins of Jericho Pillow

By Connie Kauffman

One-block accent pillows can be used to highlight colors in a room.

PROJECT SPECIFICATIONS

Project Size: 12" x 12"
Block Size: 12" x 12"
Number of Blocks: 1

FABRIC & BATTING

- 1/8 yard cream-on-cream print
- 1/8 yard gold solid
- 1/8 yard dark cream print
- 1/8 yard green mottled
- 1/8 yard tan print
- 1/8 yard dark green print
- 2/3 yard green/brown print
- Lining 13" x 13"
- Batting 13" x 13"

SUPPLIES & TOOLS

- All-purpose thread to match fabrics
- 1 1/2 yards 1/4" cord
- Polyester fiberfill
- Basic sewing tools and supplies

INSTRUCTIONS

1. Prepare one Ruins of Jericho block referring to the Placement Diagram for placement of colors in the block.

2. Sandwich batting between the lining and pieced top; pin or baste layers together to hold. Quilt as desired by hand or machine.

3. When quilting is complete, trim edges even; remove pins or basting.

4. Cut a 13" x 13" backing piece and three 1 1/2"-wide bias strips from the green/brown print as shown in Figure 1.

5. Join the bias strips on the short ends to make one long strip as shown in Figure 2.

6. Fold the bias strip in

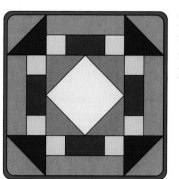

Ruins of Jericho Pillow
Placement Diagram
12" x 12"

Figure 1
Cut a 13" x 13" backing piece and three 1 1/2"-wide bias strips from the green/brown print as shown.

half with wrong sides together along length. Lay the cord inside the folded strip; stitch close to cord using a zipper foot to make piping as shown in Figure 3.

Figure 2
Join the bias strips on the short ends to make 1 long strip as shown.

Figure 3
Lay the cord inside the folded strip; stitch close to cord using a zipper foot to make piping.

7. Pin piping to quilted pillow top, overlapping beginning and end as shown in Figure 4; stitch.

Figure 4
Pin piping to quilted pillow top, overlapping beginning and end as shown.

8. Pin the 13" x 13" green/brown backing square to the quilted top with right sides together; stitch all around, leaving a 4" opening on one side. Clip corners; turn right side out. Stuff as desired with polyester fiberfill. Hand-stitch opening closed to finish. ❖

Cross & Crown Wall Quilt

By Marian Shenk

Pieced borders combine with a stripe border to enlarge one block to a wall-quilt size project.

Cross & Crown Wall Quilt
Placement Diagram
24" x 24"

PROJECT SPECIFICATIONS

Project Size: 24" x 24"

Block Size: 12" x 12"

Number of Blocks: 1

FABRIC & BATTING

- 1/8 yard mauve print
- 1/4 yard cream-on-cream print
- 1/4 yard blue-violet print
- 3/8 yard lavender print
- 3/4 yard border stripe
- Backing 28" x 28"
- Batting 28" x 28"
- 3 yards self-made or purchased binding

SUPPLIES & TOOLS

- All-purpose thread to match fabrics
- Off-white quilting thread
- Basic sewing tools and supplies

INSTRUCTIONS

1. Prepare one Cross & Crown block referring to the Placement Diagram for placement of colors in the block.

2. Prepare templates for A and B pieces; cut as directed on each piece. Cut four blue-violet and 12 cream-on-cream print common template 18 triangles and four mauve print common template 59 squares.

3. Sew a blue-violet print and a cream-on-cream print B and BR to A to make a side unit as shown in Figure 1; repeat for four side units.

Figure 1
Sew a blue-violet print and a cream-on-cream print B and BR to A to make a side unit.

4. Sew one blue-violet print and three cream-on-cream print 18 triangles to the sides of one mauve print 59 square to make a corner unit as shown in Figure 2; repeat for four corner units.

Figure 2
Sew 1 blue-violet print and 3 cream-on-cream print 18 triangles to the sides of 1 mauve print 59 square to make a corner unit.

5. Sew a side unit to two opposite sides of the pieced block; press seams toward side units. Sew a corner unit to each end of the remaining two side units as shown in Figure 3; press seams toward corner units. Sew these units to the remaining sides of the pieced block.

6. Cut four identical strips border stripe 3 1/2" x 26".

Figure 3
Sew a corner unit to each end of a side unit.

Center and sew the strips to each side of the pieced top, mitering corners. Trim excess at corner miters and press seam open; press seams toward border strips.

7. Sandwich batting between the prepared backing and pieced top; pin or baste layers together to hold. Quilt as desired by hand or machine. ***Note:*** *The sample shown was hand-quilted in the ditch of seams using off-white quilting thread.*

8. When quilting is complete, trim edges even; remove pins or basting. Bind edges with self-made or purchased binding to finish. ❖

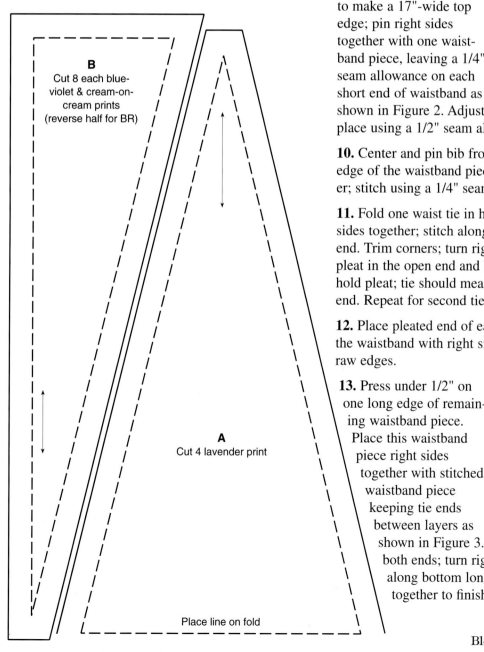

B
Cut 8 each blue-violet & cream-on-cream prints
(reverse half for BR)

A
Cut 4 lavender print

Place line on fold

The Cross Wall Quilt

Continued from page 184

Figure 6
Sew a scrap 5 triangle to each end of the remaining 2 corner units.

7. Sandwich batting between the prepared backing and pieced top; pin or baste layers together to hold. Quilt as desired by hand or machine.

8. When quilting is complete, trim edges even; remove pins or basting. Bind edges with self-made or purchased binding to finish. ❖

Peaceful Hours Bib Apron

Continued from page 185

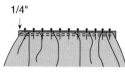

1/4"

Figure 2
Pin right sides together with 1 waistband piece, leaving a 1/4" seam allowance on each short end of waistband as shown.

along remaining long edge of skirt. Pull gathers to make a 17"-wide top edge; pin right sides together with one waistband piece, leaving a 1/4" seam allowance on each short end of waistband as shown in Figure 2. Adjust gathers to fit and stitch in place using a 1/2" seam allowance.

10. Center and pin bib front to the remaining long edge of the waistband piece with right sides together; stitch using a 1/4" seam allowance.

11. Fold one waist tie in half along length with right sides together; stitch along length and on one short end. Trim corners; turn right side out. Fold a 3/8" pleat in the open end and baste across raw edges to hold pleat; tie should measure 2 1/4" across this end. Repeat for second tie.

12. Place pleated end of each tie at the ends of the waistband with right sides together, matching raw edges.

13. Press under 1/2" on one long edge of remaining waistband piece. Place this waistband piece right sides together with stitched waistband piece keeping tie ends between layers as

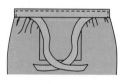

Figure 3
Place this waistband piece right sides together with stitched waistband piece keeping tie ends between layers as shown.

shown in Figure 3. Stitch along top and on both ends; turn right side out. Hand-stitch along bottom long edge to hold layers together to finish. ❖

Best of All

PIECING INSTRUCTIONS

1. Referring to the Piecing Diagram to piece one block, sew a lightest 5 to a dark 5 along the diagonal; repeat for eight units.

2. Join two units with one lightest and one medium 3 squares to complete a corner unit; repeat for four corner units.

3. Sew a lightest 5 to two adjacent sides of a medium 4; repeat for four units.

4. Sew a light 54 to two adjacent sides of a darkest 64; add a medium 5 to the two remaining sides. Repeat for four units.

5. Sew a 4-5 unit to a 5-54-64 unit to complete one side unit; repeat for four side units.

6. Arrange the pieced units in rows with the light 1 square referring to the Piecing Diagram. Join units in rows; join rows to complete one block.

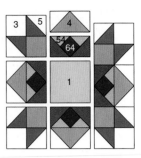

Best of All

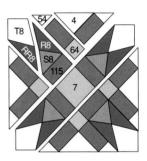

Templates needed:
1, 3, 4, 5, 54 & 64

Bright Side

PIECING INSTRUCTIONS

1. Referring to the Piecing Diagram to piece one block; sew a dark RR8 to one side of a lightest T8 and a dark R8 to one side of a medium S8; join the two pieced units and add a medium 115 to the S8 side to complete a corner unit. Repeat for four corner units.

2. Sew a lightest 54 to the end of a medium 115; repeat for two units. Sew a lightest 4 to one pieced unit. Sew a light 64 to the 115 end of the remaining pieced unit. Join the two units to complete a side unit. Repeat for four side units.

3. Sew a corner unit to two opposite sides of the light 7.

4. Sew a side unit to two opposite sides of the remaining two corner units to create two large corner units.

5. Sew a large corner unit to each long side of the center unit to complete one block.

Bright Side

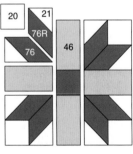

Templates needed:
4, 7, 54, 64, 115,
R8, RR8, S8 & T8

Butterfly at the Cross

PIECING INSTRUCTIONS

1. Referring to the Piecing Diagram to piece one block, sew a light 21 to a dark 76 and a dark 76R; join these units and set in a light 20 square to complete a corner unit.

2. Join two corner units with a medium 46; repeat.

3. Sew a dark 20 between two medium 46 pieces; sew between the two pieced units to complete one block.

Butterfly at the Cross

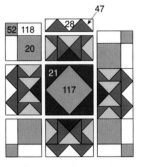

Templates needed:
20, 21, 46, 76 & 76R

Cathedral Window

PIECING INSTRUCTIONS

1. Referring to the Piecing Diagram to piece one block, sew a lightest 118 to a medium 20; sew a medium 52 to one end of a lightest 118 and sew to the pieced unit to complete a corner unit. Repeat for four corner units.

2. Join two dark 28 triangles with one lightest 28 triangle; add a lightest 47 to each end.

3. Sew a dark 47 to two adjacent sides of a light 28; repeat for two units. Sew a light 28 to a dark 28; sew a dark 28 to a darkest 28. Join the 28 units; add the 28-47 units to the sides and top to complete a side unit. Repeat for four side units.

4. Sew a darkest 21 to each side of a medium 117 to complete the center unit.

5. Arrange the pieced units in rows referring to the Piecing Diagram. Join units in rows; join rows to complete one block.

Cathedral Window

Templates needed:
20, 21, 28, 47, 52, 117 & 118

Cedars of Lebanon 1

PIECING INSTRUCTIONS

1. Referring to the Piecing Diagram to piece one block, sew a light 5 to two adjacent sides of a dark 3; sew a lightest 2 to the light side to complete one corner unit. Repeat for four corner units.

2. Sew a dark 5 to a light 5 along the diagonal; repeat for two units. Join these two units with two medium 3 squares to complete the center unit.

3. Arrange the pieced units in rows with medium 1 squares referring to the Piecing Diagram. Join units in rows; join rows to complete one block.

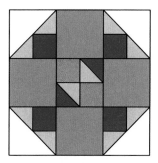

Cedars of Lebanon 1

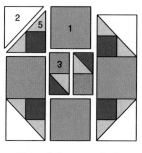

Templates needed:
1, 2, 3 & 5

Cedars of Lebanon 2

PIECING INSTRUCTIONS

1. Referring to the Piecing Diagram to piece one block, sew a light 5 to two adjacent sides of a dark 3; add a dark 2 to the 5 side to complete a corner unit. Repeat for four corner units.

2. Sew a dark 5 to opposite sides of the light B8 to complete the center unit.

3. Arrange the pieced units in rows with four medium 1 squares referring to the Piecing Diagram. Join units in rows; join rows to complete one block.

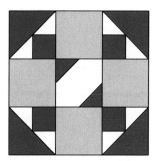

Cedars of Lebanon 2

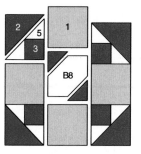

Templates needed:
1, 2, 3, 5 & B8

Crosses & Star

PIECING INSTRUCTIONS

1. Referring to the Piecing Diagram to piece one block, sew a dark V8 and a VR8 to two sides of a lightest A8; sew a lightest AA8 to two sides and a lightest 35 to the corner to complete one corner unit. Repeat for four corner units.

2. Join two corner units with a medium 46; repeat for two units.

3. Sew a light 20 between two medium 46 pieces to make a center row.

4. Join the two pieced units with the center row to complete one block.

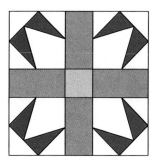

Crosses & Star

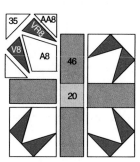

Templates needed:
20, 35, 46, A8, V8, VR8 & AA8

Crossroads

PIECING INSTRUCTIONS

1. Referring to the Piecing Diagram to piece one block, join four light 5 triangles with three dark 3 squares and two medium 2 triangles to make a corner unit; repeat for two corner units.

2. Join four light 5 triangles with three medium 3 squares and two lightest 2 triangles to make a corner unit; repeat for two corner units.

3. Join the pieced units referring to the Piecing Diagram to complete one block.

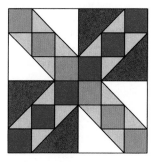

Crossroads

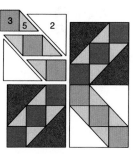

Templates needed:
2, 3 & 5

Cross Within a Cross

PIECING INSTRUCTIONS

1. Referring to the Piecing Diagram to piece one block, sew a dark 12 to two adjacent sides of a light 13 to complete a corner unit. Repeat for four corner units.

2. Sew a lightest 2 to opposite long sides of a medium L8; repeat for two units.

3. Sew a light 3 between two medium L8 pieces to make a center row; sew a 2-L unit to two opposite sides of the center row to complete the block center.

4. Sew a corner unit to each side of the block center to complete one block.

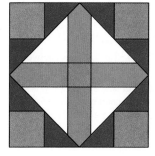

Cross Within a Cross

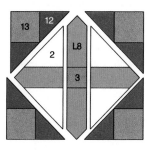

Templates needed:
2, 3, 12, 13 & L8

Crown of Thorns

PIECING INSTRUCTIONS

1. Referring to the Piecing Diagram to piece one block, sew a medium 12 to each side of the light 19 to complete the center unit.

2. Join one medium, three lightest, two dark and two darkest 16 triangles to complete a side unit; repeat for four side units.

3. Arrange the pieced units in rows with darkest 13 squares referring to the Piecing Diagram. Join units in rows; join rows to complete one block.

Crown of Thorns

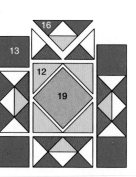

Templates needed:
12, 13, 16 & 19

Flowering Cross

PIECING INSTRUCTIONS

1. Referring to the Piecing Diagram to piece one block, join a light and medium 17 square; add a medium 23 to one side to complete one corner unit. Repeat for four corner units.

2. Sew a dark 23 to two opposite sides of a light 13 to complete a side unit; repeat for four side units.

3. Sew a light 16 to opposite sides of a dark 98; repeat for two units. Sew these units to opposite sides of a dark K8 to complete the center unit.

4. Arrange the pieced units in rows referring to the Piecing Diagram. Join the units in rows; join the rows to complete one block.

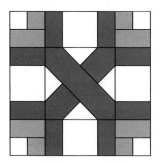

Flowering Cross

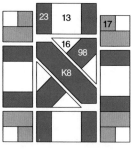

Templates needed:
13, 16, 17, 23, 98 & K8

Golden Wedding

PIECING INSTRUCTIONS

1. Referring to the Piecing Diagram to piece one block, sew a darkest 96 to each side of a light 59; set in four light 37 pieces to complete a quarter block. Repeat for two quarter blocks.

2. Sew a light 96 to each side of a medium 59; set in four dark 37 pieces to complete a quarter block. Repeat for two quarter blocks.

3. Join the pieced quarter blocks referring to the Piecing Diagram to complete one block.

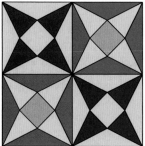

Golden Wedding

Templates needed:
37, 59 & 96

Golgotha 1

PIECING INSTRUCTIONS

1. Referring to the Piecing Diagram to piece one block, sew a darkest 54 between a light 30 and 30R; repeat for four units. Sew a unit to each side of a medium 1 square to complete the center unit.

2. Sew a darkest 54 between a dark 30 and 30R; sew to a light 6 to complete a side unit. Repeat for four side units. Sew one unit to each side of the center unit.

3. Sew a dark 30 to a dark 30R; repeat. Set in two lightest 54 triangles and a lightest 3 square to complete a corner units; repeat for four corner units.

4. Set in corner units referring to the Piecing Diagram to complete one block.

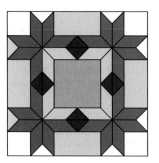

Golgotha 1

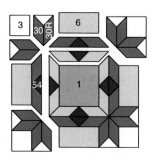

Templates needed:
1, 3, 6, 30, 30R & 54

Golgotha 2

PIECING INSTRUCTIONS

1. Referring to the Piecing Diagram to piece one block, sew a light 4 to each side of medium 119; repeat for two units.

2. Join a light 7 square with two medium 119 pieces; sew between the two previously pieced units to complete the block center.

3. Sew a dark 5 to each end of a medium 6; sew a light 54 to a dark 54 on the short sides. Sew a 54 unit to each end of the 5-6 unit; repeat to complete a side unit. Repeat for four side units. Sew a unit to opposite sides of the block center.

4. Sew a light 3 to each end of the remaining side units.

5. Sew a pieced unit to remaining sides of the pieced center unit to complete one block.

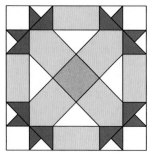

Golgotha 2

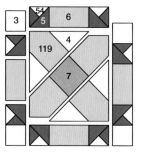

Templates needed:
3, 4, 5, 6, 7, 54 & 119

Goshen Star

PIECING INSTRUCTIONS

1. Referring to the Piecing Diagram to piece one block, sew a lightest 26 to a darkest 26 along the diagonal to complete one corner unit; repeat for four corner units.

2. Sew a lightest 18 to two adjacent angled sides of a dark C8 and a light 18 to the remaining angled sides to complete one side unit; repeat for four side units.

3. Arrange the pieced units in rows with a medium 13 square referring to the Piecing Diagram. Join units in rows; join rows to complete one block.

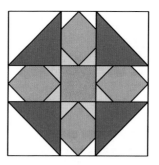

Goshen Star

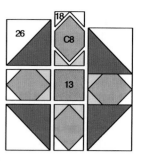

Templates needed:
13, 18, 26 & C8

Greek Cross

PIECING INSTRUCTIONS

1. Referring to the Piecing Diagram to piece one block, sew a lightest 2 to a light 2 along the diagonal to complete a corner unit; repeat for four corner units.

2. Sew a dark 6 to a lightest 6 to complete a side unit; repeat for four side units.

3. Arrange the pieced units in rows with the medium 1 square referring to the Piecing Diagram. Join units in rows; join rows to complete one block.

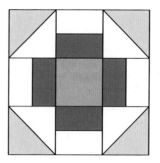

Greek Cross

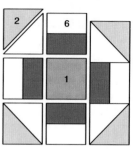

Templates needed:
1, 2 & 6

Handy Andy

PIECING INSTRUCTIONS

1. Referring to the Piecing Diagram to piece one block, sew a lightest 5 to each side of the light 7 square; sew a light 4 to each side of this pieced unit and a dark 2 to each side of the resulting unit to complete the block center.

2. Join two light 4 triangles with one medium 4 to make a side unit; repeat for four side units.

3. Sew a side unit to each side of the pieced center. Sew a darkest 2 to each side of the pieced unit to complete one block.

Handy Andy

Templates needed:
2, 4, 5 & 7

Jacob's Ladder

PIECING INSTRUCTIONS

1. Referring to the Piecing Diagram to piece one block, join two medium and two light 3 squares to make a Four-Patch corner unit; repeat for two corner units.

2. Join two light and two darkest 3 squares to make a Four-Patch unit; repeat for one center unit and two corner units.

3. Sew a dark 2 to a lightest 2 on the diagonal to make a side unit; repeat for four side units.

4. Arrange the pieced units in rows referring to the Piecing Diagram. Join units in rows; join rows to complete one block.

Jacob's Ladder

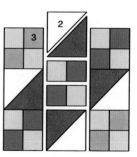

Templates needed:
2 & 3

Joseph's Coat 1

PIECING INSTRUCTIONS

1. Referring to the Piecing Diagram to piece one block, join one dark and three lightest 5 triangles; add a medium 2 to complete one corner unit. Repeat for four corner units.

2. Sew a lightest W8 and WR8 to adjacent sides of a medium P8; repeat for eight units. Join two units with a light Q8 to complete a side unit; repeat for four side units.

3. Arrange the pieced units in rows with a dark 1 square referring to the Piecing Diagram. Join the units in rows; join the rows to complete one block.

Joseph's Coat 1

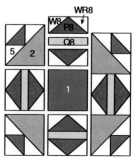

Templates needed:
1, 2, 5, P8, Q8, W8 & WR8

Joseph's Coat 2

PIECING INSTRUCTIONS

1. Referring to the Piecing Diagram to piece one block, sew a light BB8 to a dark BB8; repeat for four units. Join the units to complete the center unit.

2. Sew a lightest DD8 and DDR8 to a medium BB8 to make a corner unit; repeat for four corner units.

3. Sew a corner unit to each dark edge of the center unit.

4. Sew a darkest CC8 between each corner unit to complete one block.

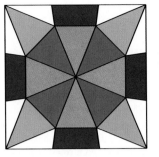

Joseph's Coat 2

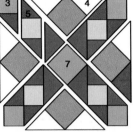

Templates needed:
BB8, CC8, DD8 & DDR8

Love in a Mist

PIECING INSTRUCTIONS

1. Referring to the Piecing Diagram to piece one block, sew a medium and dark 5 to a light 3; add a dark 4 to one side. Sew a medium 5 to a medium 3 and sew to the opposite side to complete one corner unit; repeat for four corner units.

2. Join two units with a medium 7 for a center unit.

3. Sew a lightest 4 to two adjacent sides of a light 7 to complete a side unit; repeat for four side units.

4. Sew a corner unit between two side units; repeat. Sew these units to opposite sides of the previously pieced center unit to complete one block.

Love in a Mist

Templates needed:
3, 4, 5 & 7

Mexican Cross

PIECING INSTRUCTIONS

1. Referring to the Piecing Diagram to piece one block, join two light and one lightest 64 to make a row; repeat for two rows. Join two lightest and one darkest 64 to make a row; join the rows to complete the Nine-Patch center unit.

2. Sew a dark 5 to the angled ends of each darkest G8 and GR8 pieces; sew one of each unit to opposite sides of a medium F8. Repeat for four units; sew a unit to opposite sides of the pieced center.

3. Sew a lightest 14 to opposite sides of the remaining 5-F-G units to complete a corner unit; repeat for two corner units.

4. Sew a corner unit to opposite sides of the center unit to complete one block.

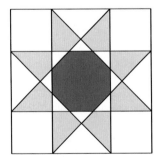

Mexican Cross

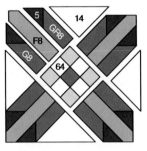

Templates needed:
5, 14, 64, F8, G8 & GR8

Peaceful Hours

PIECING INSTRUCTIONS

1. Referring to the Piecing Diagram to piece one block, sew a light 54 to a medium J8 and a light 49 to a medium JR8. Join the units to complete a side unit. Repeat for four side units.

2. Sew a light 18 to each side of the dark H8 to complete the center unit.

3. Arrange the pieced units in rows with four light 72 squares referring to the Piecing Diagram. Join units in rows; join rows to complete one block.

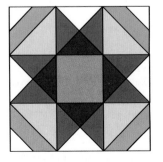

Peaceful Hours

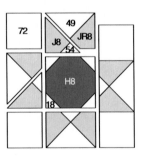

Templates needed:
18, 49, 54, 72, H8, J8 & JR8

Prosperity Plus

PIECING INSTRUCTIONS

1. Referring to the Piecing Diagram to piece one block, sew a lightest 5 to a medium 51 to a light 2 to complete one corner unit; repeat for four corner units.

2. Join one dark, one lightest and two darkest 4 triangles to complete one side unit; repeat for four side units.

3. Arrange the pieced units in rows with a light 1 square referring to the Piecing Diagram. Join units in rows; join rows to complete one block.

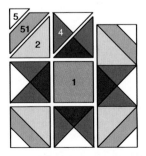

Prosperity Plus

Templates needed:
1, 2, 4, 5 & 51

Red & White Cross

PIECING INSTRUCTIONS

1. Referring to the Piecing Diagram to piece one block, sew a light 36 to a dark 36R; sew a light and dark 12 to sides of the pieced unit. Repeat for four units.

2. Sew a medium 12 to a light 12 along the diagonal; repeat for four units.

3. Set a 12 unit into each pieced unit to complete quarter units.

4. Join the quarter units to complete one block.

Red & White Cross

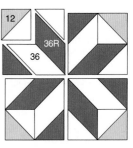

Templates needed:
12, 36 & 36R

Road to Paradise

PIECING INSTRUCTIONS

1. Referring to the Piecing Diagram to piece one block, sew a dark 2 to a light 2 along the diagonal to complete a corner unit; repeat for four corner units.

2. Sew a dark 10 and 10R to a light 9 to complete a side unit; repeat for four side units.

3. Sew a light 5 to each side of the dark 7 to complete the center unit.

4. Arrange the pieced units in rows referring to the Piecing Diagram. Join units in rows; join rows to complete one block.

Road to Paradise

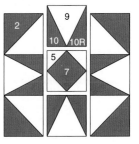

Templates needed:
2, 5, 7, 9, 10 & 10R

Ruins of Jericho

PIECING INSTRUCTIONS

1. Referring to the Piecing Diagram to piece one block, sew a light 12 to each side of the dark 19 to complete the center unit.

2. Sew a dark 17 to each end of a medium 23; sew a light 82 to the long side to complete a side unit. Repeat for four side units.

3. Sew a light 12 to a dark 12 along the diagonal to complete a corner unit; repeat for four corner units.

4. Arrange the pieced units in rows referring to the Piecing Diagram. Join units in rows; join rows to complete one block.

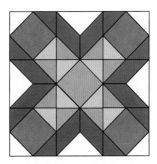

Ruins of Jericho

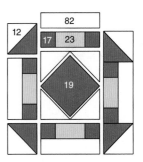

Templates needed:
12, 17, 19, 23 & 82

Saint George's Cross

PIECING INSTRUCTIONS

1. Referring to the Piecing Diagram to piece one block, sew one light, one lightest and two dark 5 triangles to the sides of a medium 7 to complete one corner unit; repeat for four corner units.

2. Sew a dark 38 and 38R to the short sides of a lightest 4 triangle; sew angled seam. Sew a medium 5 triangle to the 38 sides to complete a side unit; repeat for four side units.

3. Sew a light 5 to each side of a medium 7 to complete the center unit.

4. Arrange the pieced units in rows referring to the Piecing Diagram. Join units in rows; join rows to complete one block.

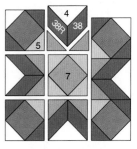

Saint George's Cross

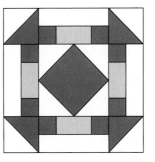

Templates needed:
4, 5, 7, 38 & 38R

Saint Gregory's Cross

PIECING INSTRUCTIONS

1. Referring to the Piecing Diagram to piece one block, sew three dark and one darkest 5 triangles to a medium 7 to complete one corner unit; repeat for four corner units.

2. Sew a medium 5 to two adjacent sides of a lightest 4; sew a light 5 to two adjacent sides of a dark 4. Join the two units to complete one side unit; repeat for four side units.

3. Arrange the pieced units with a medium 1 square in rows referring to the Piecing Diagram. Join units in rows; join rows to complete one block.

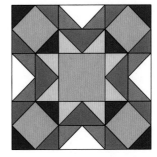

Saint Gregory's Cross

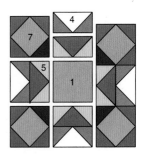

Templates needed:
1, 4, 5 & 7

Scottish Cross

PIECING INSTRUCTIONS

1. Referring to the Piecing Diagram to piece one block, sew a light 97 to a dark 97R on the short end; repeat for two units. Sew a dark 97 to a light 97R; repeat for two units.

2. Sew a light 90 to the short side of two pieced dark-97-light-97R units and a dark 90 to the remaining two units to complete quarter triangles.

3. Join two quarter triangles to complete half of the block; repeat for two halves. Join the halves to complete one block.

Scottish Cross

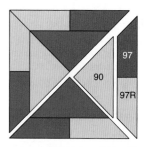

Templates needed:
90, 97 & 97R

Solomon's Star

PIECING INSTRUCTIONS

1. Referring to the Piecing Diagram to piece one block, sew a light 16 to a dark 16 along the diagonal; repeat for four units.

2. Join the four units to complete a pinwheel center; sew a medium 12 to each side of the pinwheel center to complete the center unit.

3. Sew a dark 12 to two adjacent sides of a light 14 triangle to complete a side unit; repeat for four side units.

4. Arrange the pieced units with light 13 squares in rows referring to the Piecing Diagram. Join units in rows; join rows to complete one block.

Solomon's Star

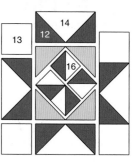

Templates needed:
12, 13, 14 & 16

Star of Bethlehem

PIECING INSTRUCTIONS

1. Referring to the Piecing Diagram to piece one block, sew a dark 40 to a light 40R; repeat for four units. Join the units to make a star center; set in light 16 and light 18 triangles to complete a octagon unit.

2. Sew a dark 40 and 40R to the sides of a medium 98; set in two lightest 18 triangles; add a medium 12 to make a corner unit. Repeat for four corner units.

3. Sew a lightest 16 to the two angled sides of a medium 55 to make a side unit; repeat for four side units.

4. Sew the side and corner units to the center octagon unit, sewing angled seams as pieces are added to complete one block.

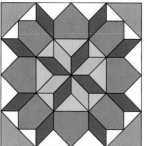

Star of Bethlehem

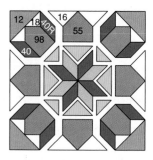

Templates needed:
12, 16, 18, 40, 40R, 55 & 98

Steps to Glory

PIECING INSTRUCTIONS

1. Referring to the Piecing Diagram to piece one block, sew a dark 17 to a light 17; add a dark 23 to make a corner unit. Repeat for two corner units.

2. Sew a lightest 17 to a medium 17; add a medium 23 to make a medium unit. Repeat for six medium units.

3. Join two dark and two light 17 squares to make a Four-Patch corner unit; repeat for two Four-Patch corner units.

4. Join two light and one each lightest and dark 17 squares to make a Four-Patch unit; repeat for four Four-Patch units.

5. Arrange the pieced units with two dark 13 squares in block quarters referring to the Piecing Diagram. Join units in block quarters; join quarters to complete one block.

Steps to Glory

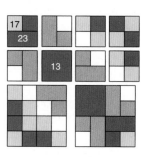

Templates needed:
13, 17 & 23

Steps to the Altar

PIECING INSTRUCTIONS

1. Referring to the Piecing Diagram to piece one block, sew a light 2 to a dark 2 along the diagonal to make a corner unit; repeat for two corner units.

2. Sew a light 2 to a medium 2 along the diagonal to complete a side unit; repeat for four side units.

3. Join two light and two dark 3 squares to make a Four-Patch unit; repeat for three Four-Patch units.

4. Arrange the pieced units referring to the Piecing Diagram. Join units in rows; join rows to complete one block.

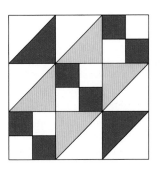

Steps to the Altar

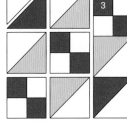

Templates needed:
2 & 3

Steps to the Temple

PIECING INSTRUCTIONS

1. Referring to the Piecing Diagram to piece one block, sew a darkest Z8 to two opposite sides of the light U8. Sew a darkest Y8 to the remaining sides to complete the center unit.

2. Join two dark and three medium 54 triangles to make a unit; repeat for four units. Sew a 54 unit to each side of the center unit; add a dark 5 to each medium corner.

3. Join two light and two medium 32 pieces; repeat. Sew a unit to opposite sides of the pieced center. Join two medium and three light 32 pieces; repeat. Sew a unit to remaining sides of the pieced center.

4. Join two darkest and three lightest 32 pieces; sew to one side of pieced center. Join two lightest and three darkest 32 pieces; sew to opposite side of center. Join three each darkest and lightest 32 pieces; repeat. Sew a unit to remaining sides of the pieced center.

5. Prepare dark 94, light N8, dark O8 and medium X8 pieces for appliqué. Appliqué to center of block referring to the Piecing Diagram for positioning of pieces to complete one block.

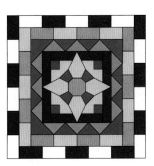

Steps to the Temple

Templates needed:
5, 32, 54, 94, N8,
O8, U8, X8, Y8 & Z8

The Cross

PIECING INSTRUCTIONS

1. Referring to the Piecing Diagram to piece one block, sew a light 4 to a colored 4 and add a colored 2; repeat. Join the 2-4 units.

2. Sew a colored 4 to two adjacent sides of a light 4; add a light 5 to each end. Sew the 4-5 strip to the 2-4 strip; add a light E8 to complete a block half.

3. Sew a light 4 to a colored 4 on short sides. Add a light 5 to the remaining short side of the colored 4.

4. Sew the 4-5 strip to one long side of the remaining light E8. Add a light 2 to the short side of E8.

5. Sew a light 2 to a colored 2; add a colored 2 and 4 to the colored 2 sides. Sew a light 5 to the 4 side of the pieced unit.

6. Sew the pieced unit to the E8 unit to complete a second block half. Join the block halves to complete one block.

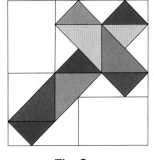

The Cross

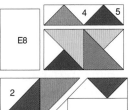

Templates needed:
2, 4, 5 & E8

The Star of Bethlehem

PIECING INSTRUCTIONS

1. Referring to the Piecing Diagram to piece one block, sew a light 33 to each side of a medium 13 square, sewing angled seams to complete the center units.

2. Sew a dark 12 to two adjacent sides of a lightest 14 to complete a side unit; repeat for four side units.

3. Arrange the pieced units in rows with four lightest 13 squares referring to the Piecing Diagram. Join units in rows; join rows to complete one block.

The Star of Bethlehem

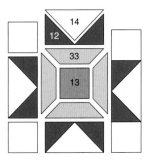

Templates needed:
12, 13, 14 & 33

Walls of Jericho

PIECING INSTRUCTIONS

1. Referring to the Piecing Diagram to piece one block, sew a light 35 to a dark D8 to a lightest 62 to complete a block quarter; repeat for four block quarters.

2. Join two block quarters with a medium 71; repeat.

3. Join two medium 71 pieces with a dark 24 square to complete the center row.

4. Join the two block quarters with the center row to complete one block.

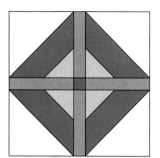

Walls of Jericho

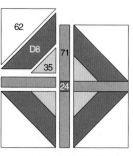

Templates needed:
24, 35, 62, 71 & D8

Wedding Ring

PIECING INSTRUCTIONS

1. Referring to the Piecing Diagram to piece one block, join one light, two medium and two lightest 20 squares to make the center row.

2. Sew a lightest 76 and 76R to the angled ends of a medium M8; repeat for two units. Sew a lightest M8 to each unit and sew these units to opposite sides of the center row.

3. Sew a dark 22 triangle to each corner of the pieced unit to complete one block.

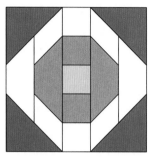

Wedding Ring

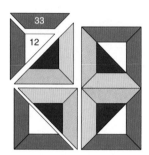

Templates needed:
20, 22, 76, 76R & M8

White Cross

PIECING INSTRUCTIONS

1. Referring to the Piecing Diagram to piece one block, sew a dark 33 to two adjacent sides of a light 12.

2. Sew a medium 33 to two adjacent sides of a darkest 12.

3. Join two opposite units to complete a block quarter; repeat for four block quarters.

4. Join the block quarters to complete one block.

White Cross

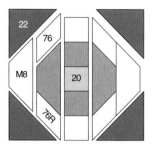

Templates needed:
12 & 33

Inspirational Blessings Sampler

Continued from page 183

remaining sides; press seams toward strips. Trim excess at ends, if necessary. The center should now measure 72 1/2" x 72 1/2".

13. Cut and piece four strips each magenta and lavender prints 2 1/2" x 82". Join one strip each color to make a pieced strip; repeat for four pieced strips.

14. Center and sew a pieced strip to each side of the pieced center, mitering corners. Trim excess at corners, press corner seams open; press seams toward strips.

15. Cut eight strips light green print 4 1/2" x 12 1/2" for strip ends.

16. Join six identical blocks with two strip ends to make a side strip as shown in Figure 4; repeat for two side strips. Sew these block rows to opposite sides of

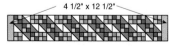

4 1/2" x 12 1/2"

Figure 4
Join 6 identical blocks with 2 strip ends to make a side strip.

the pieced center referring to the Placement Diagram for positioning of strips; press seams toward strips.

17. Join six identical blocks with two strip ends to make a top strip as shown in Figure 5; repeat for bottom strip. Add a block to each end of each strip to make block rows. Sew these block rows to top and bottom of the pieced center referring to the Placement Diagram for positioning of strips; press seams toward strips.

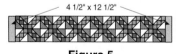

4 1/2" x 12 1/2"

Figure 5
Join 6 identical blocks with 2 strip ends to make top and bottom strips.

18. Sandwich batting between the completed top and prepared backing piece; pin or baste layers together to hold.

19. Quilt as desired by hand or machine. ***Note:*** *The sample shown was machine-quilted in a meandering flower pattern using pink thread.*

20. When quilting is complete, trim edges even; remove pins or basting.

21. Bind edges with self-made or purchased binding to finish. ❖

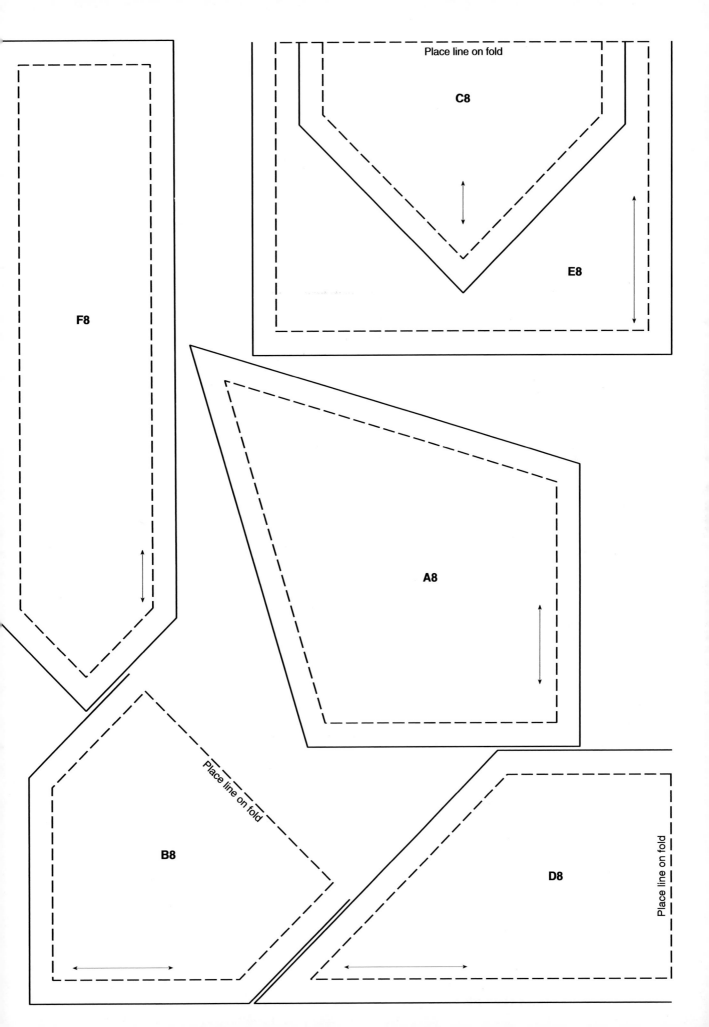

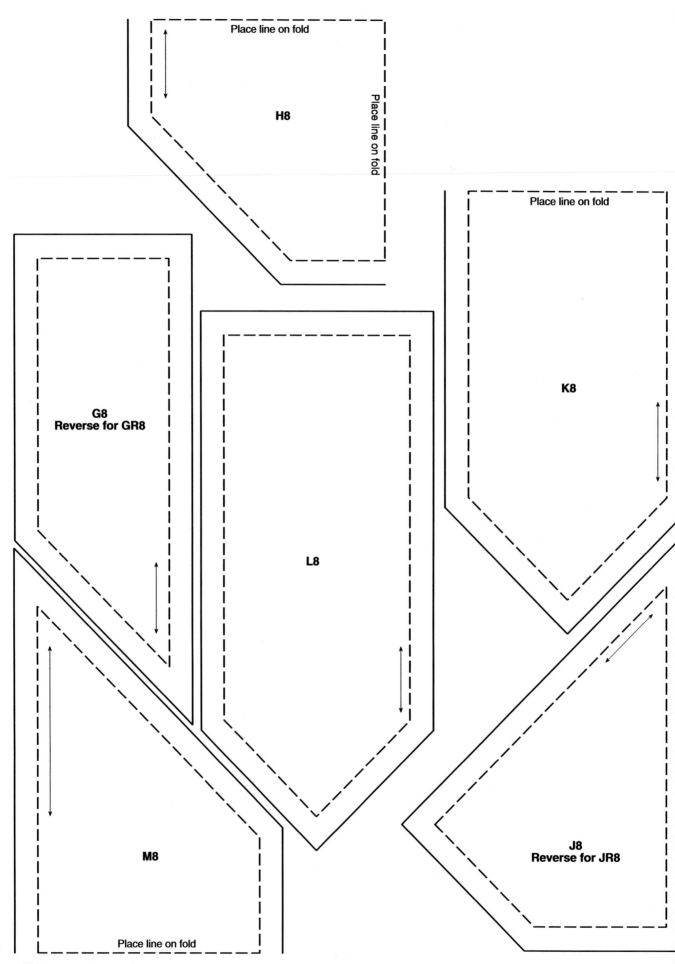

Place line on fold

H8

Place line on fold

Place line on fold

K8

G8
Reverse for GR8

L8

M8

J8
Reverse for JR8

Place line on fold

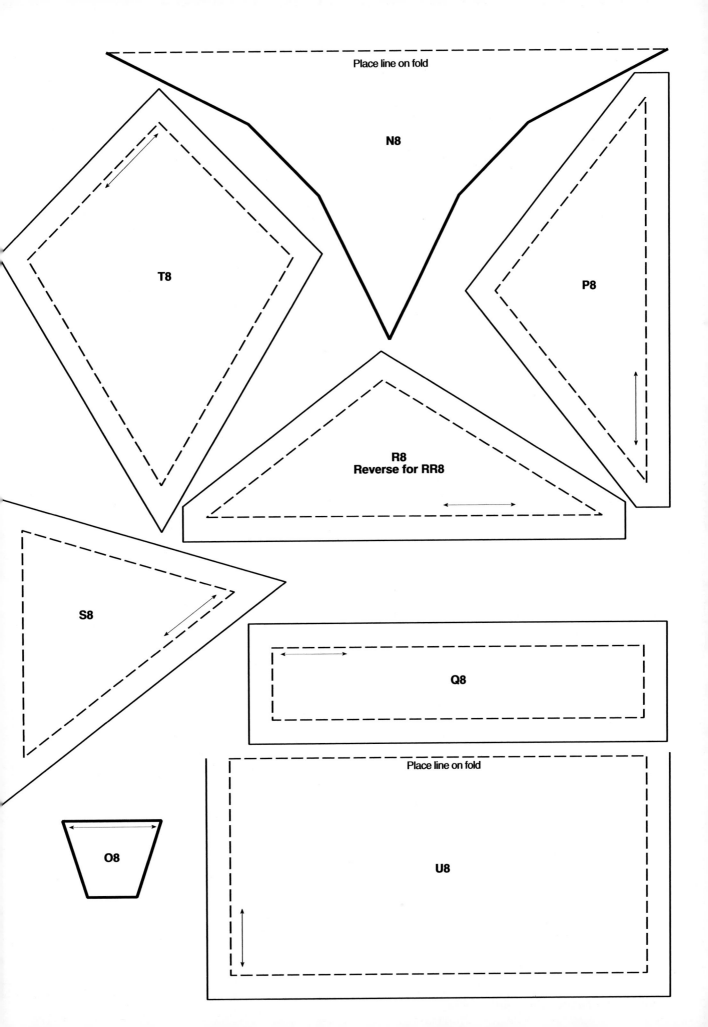

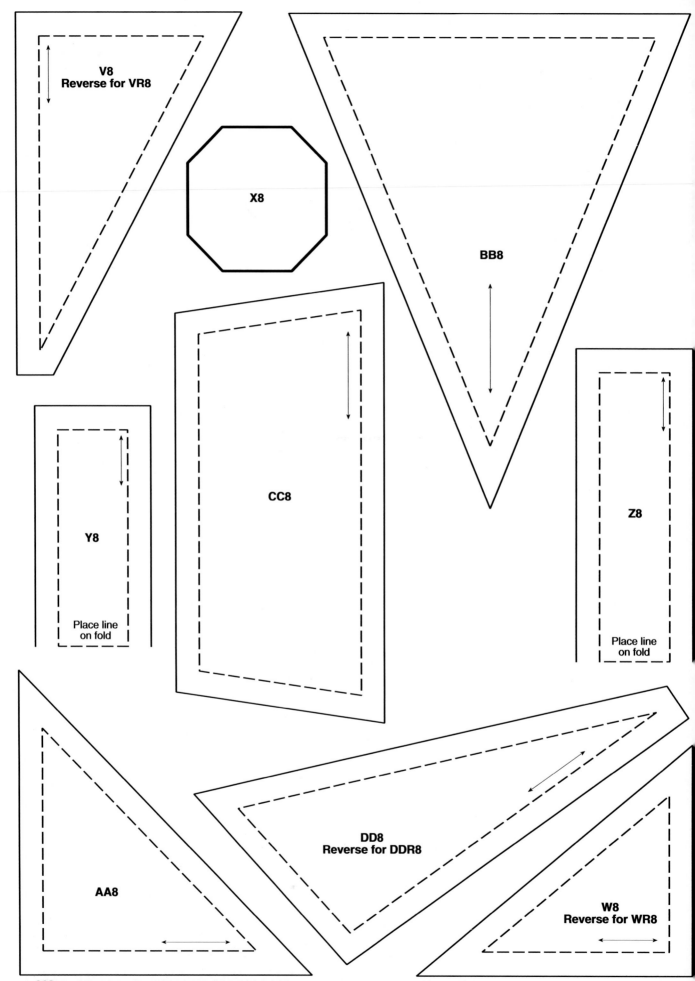

V8
Reverse for VR8

X8

BB8

CC8

Y8

Place line
on fold

Z8

Place line
on fold

AA8

DD8
Reverse for DDR8

W8
Reverse for WR8

Common Templates

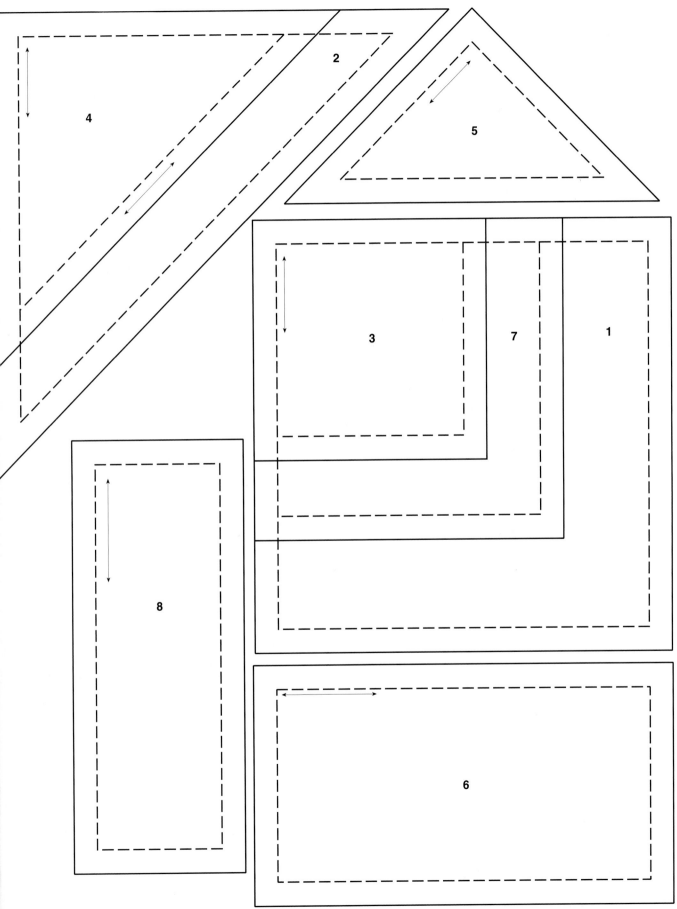

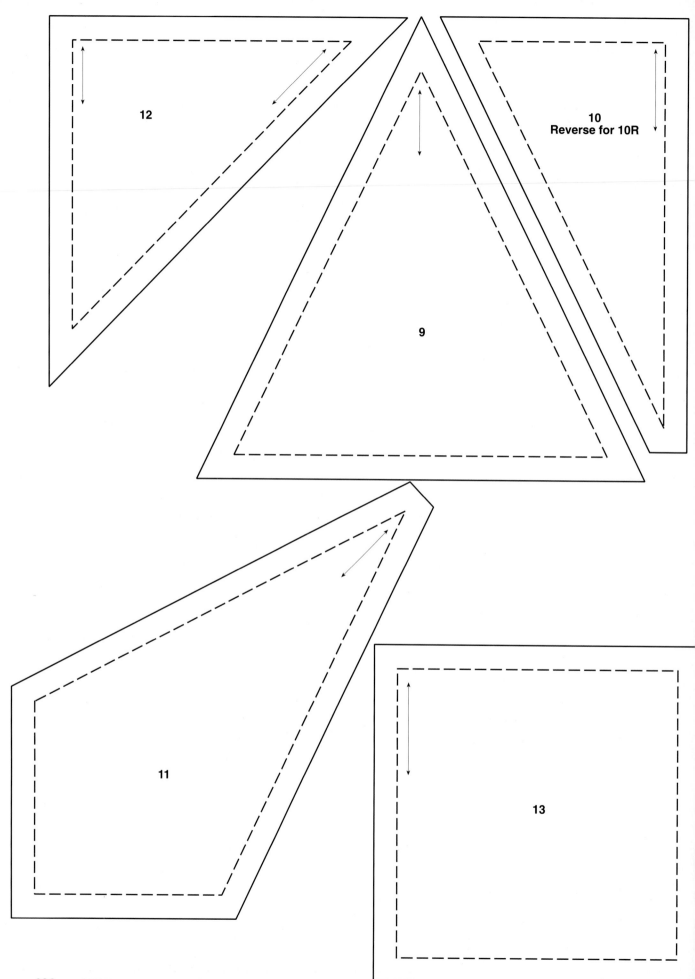

12

10
Reverse for 10R

9

11

13

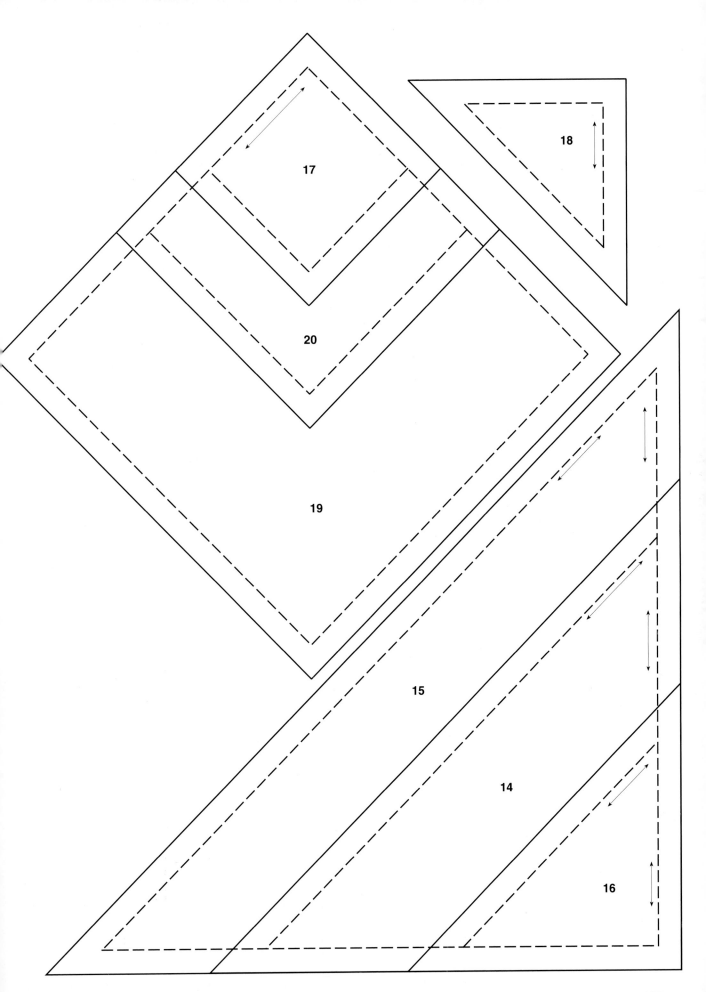

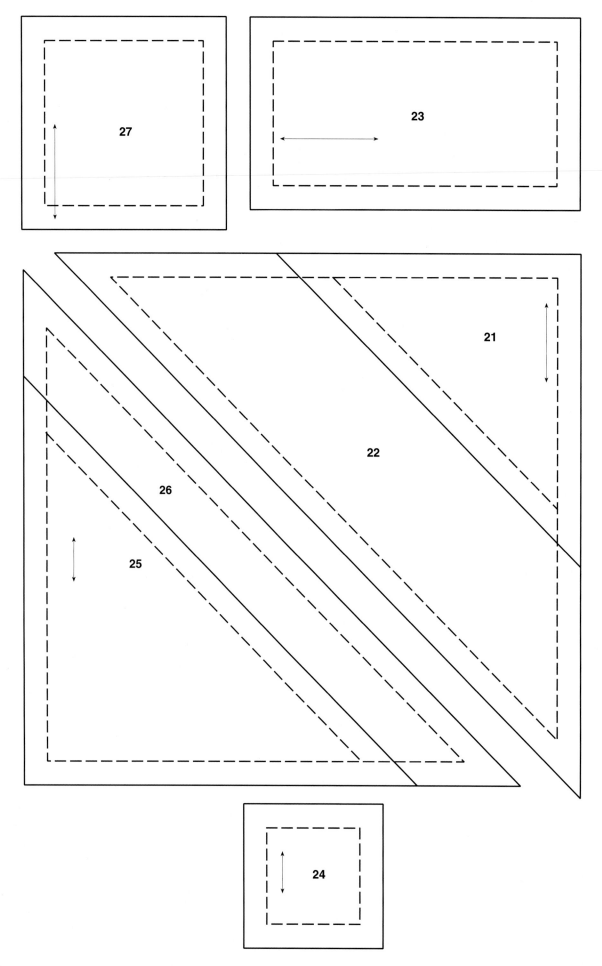

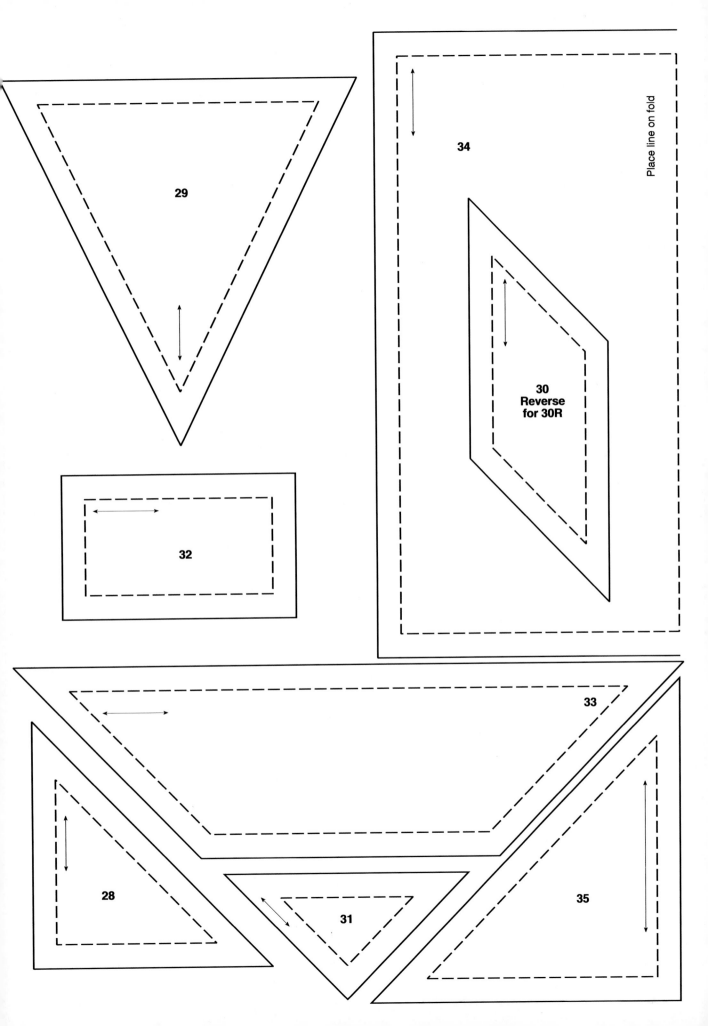

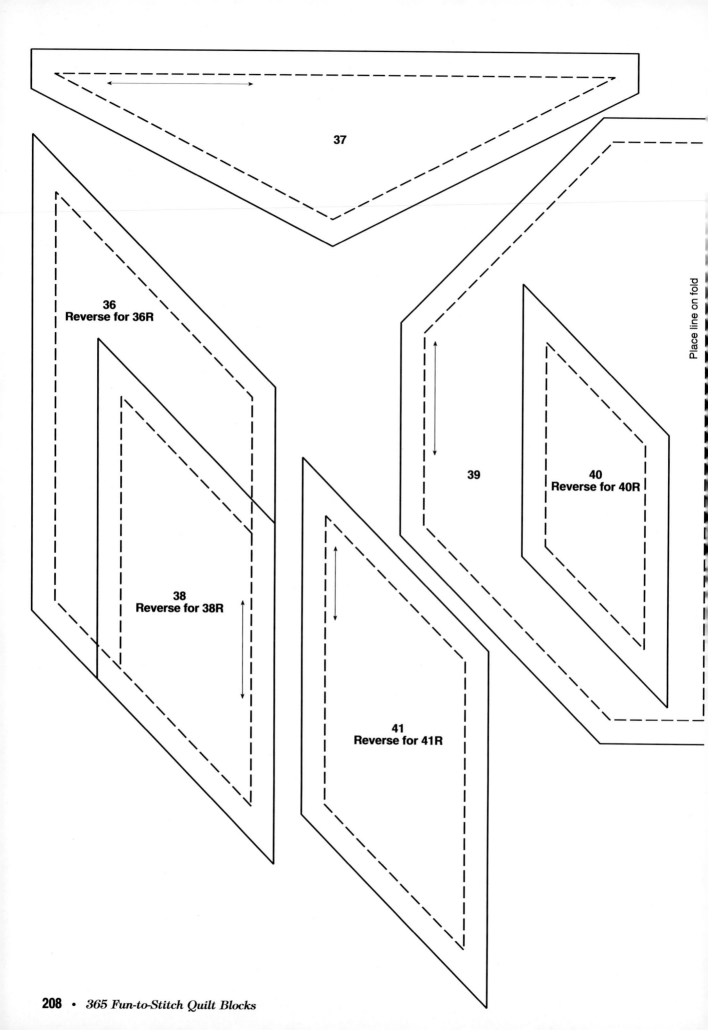

37

36
Reverse for 36R

39

40
Reverse for 40R

Place line on fold

38
Reverse for 38R

41
Reverse for 41R

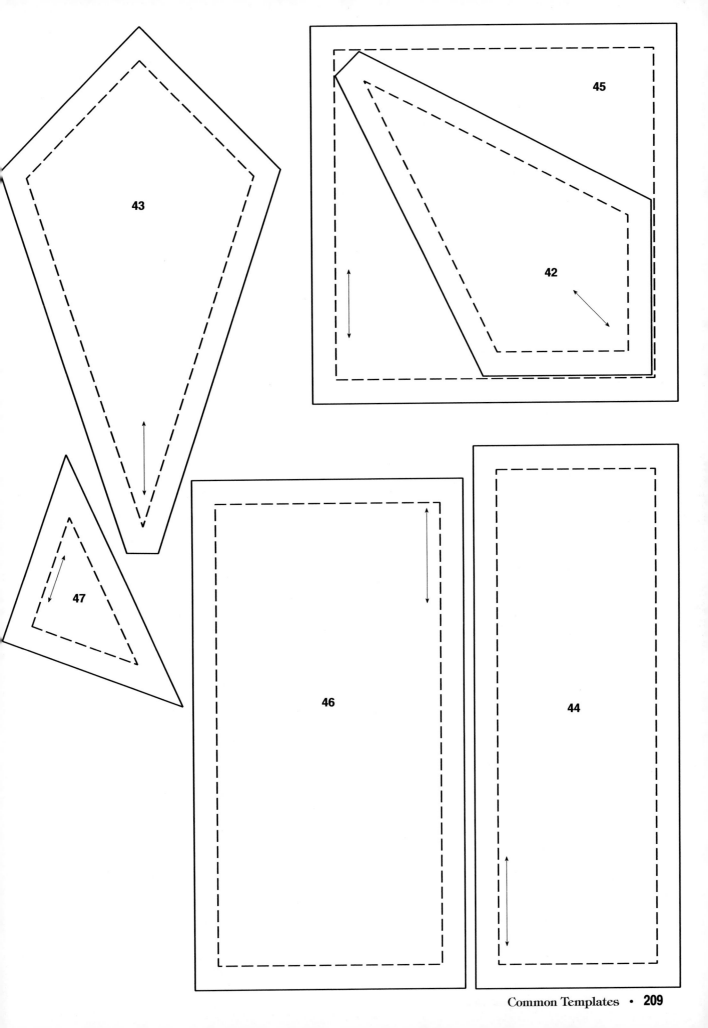

43

45

42

47

46

44

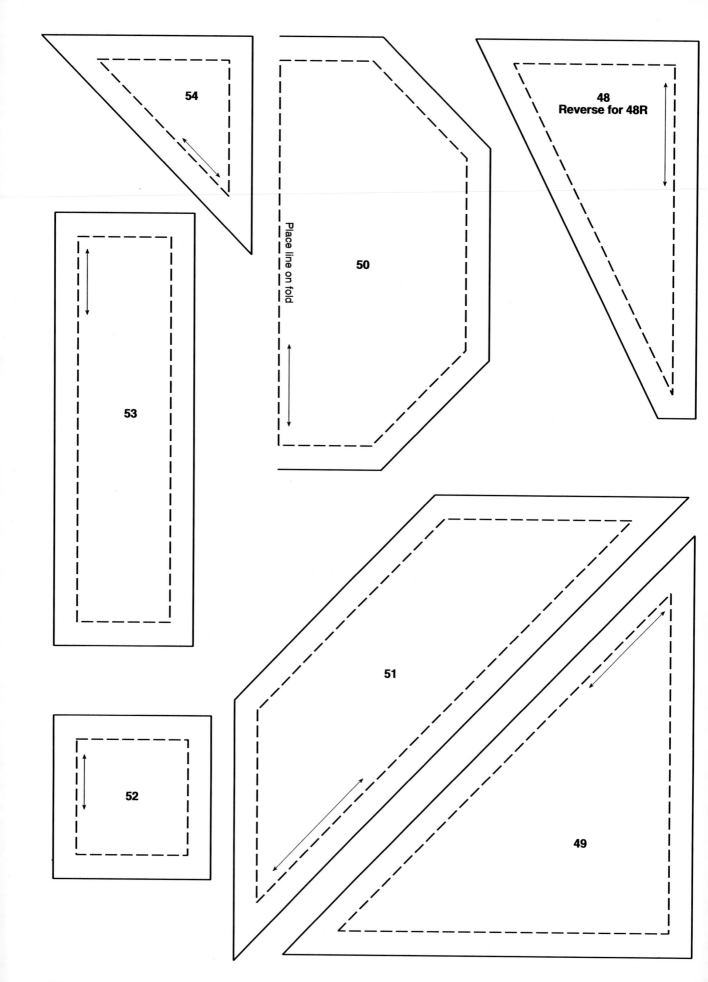

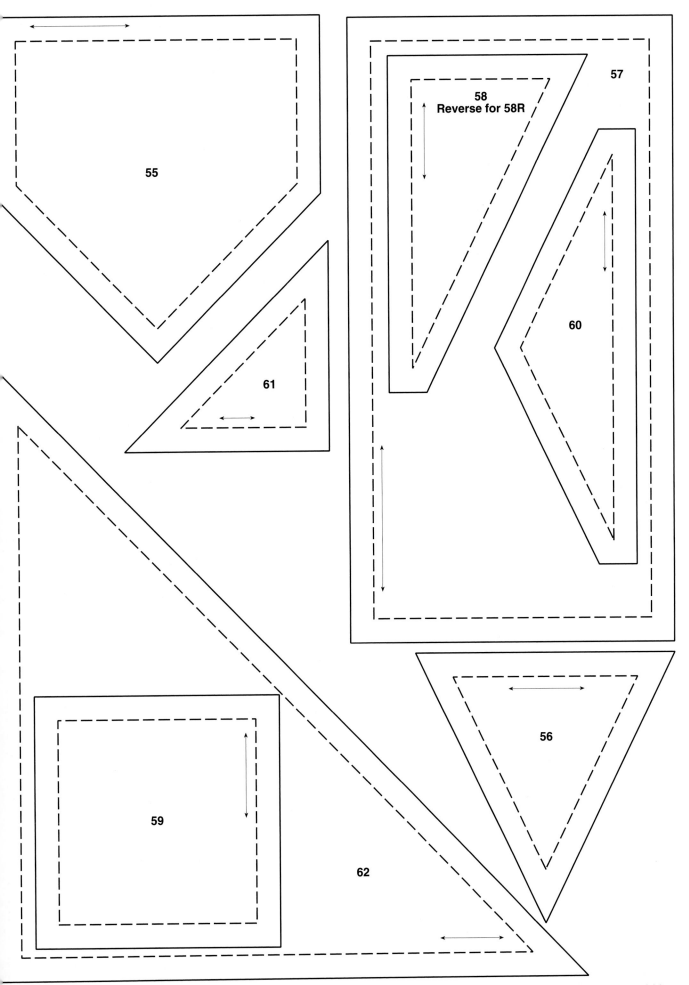

55

57

58
Reverse for 58R

60

61

56

59

62

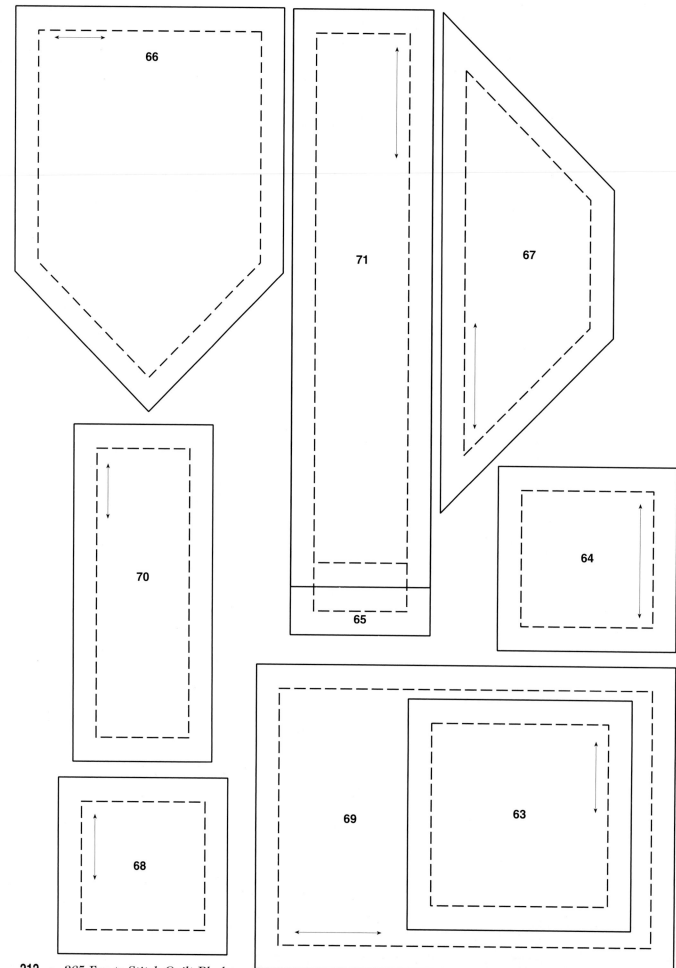

66

71

67

70

65

64

68

69

63

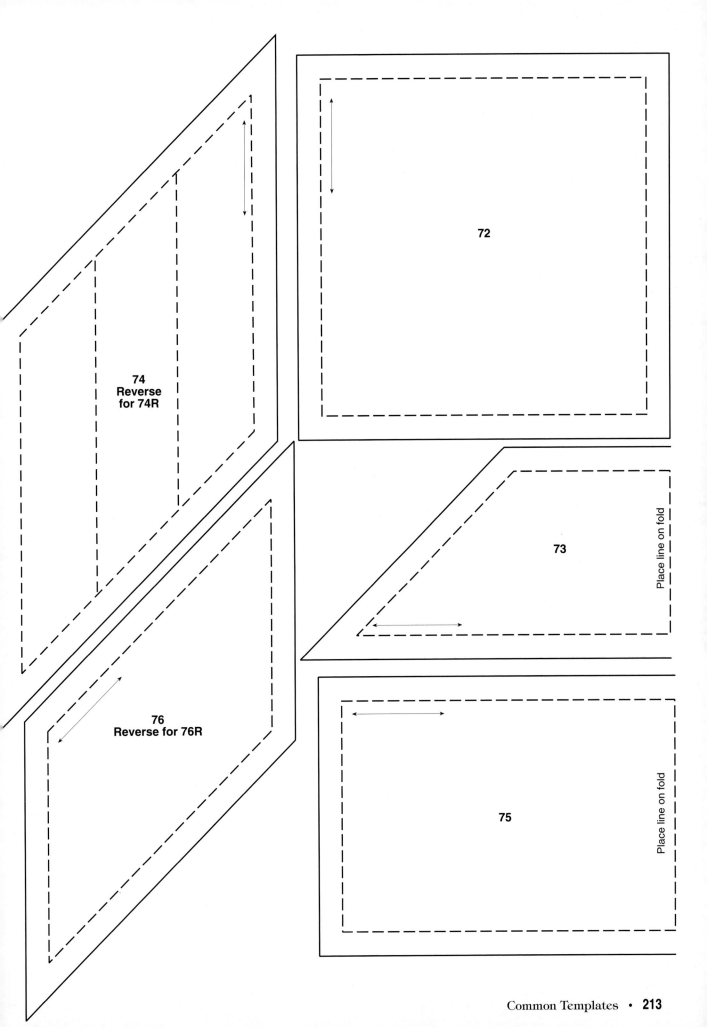

74
Reverse
for 74R

72

73

Place line on fold

76
Reverse for 76R

75

Place line on fold

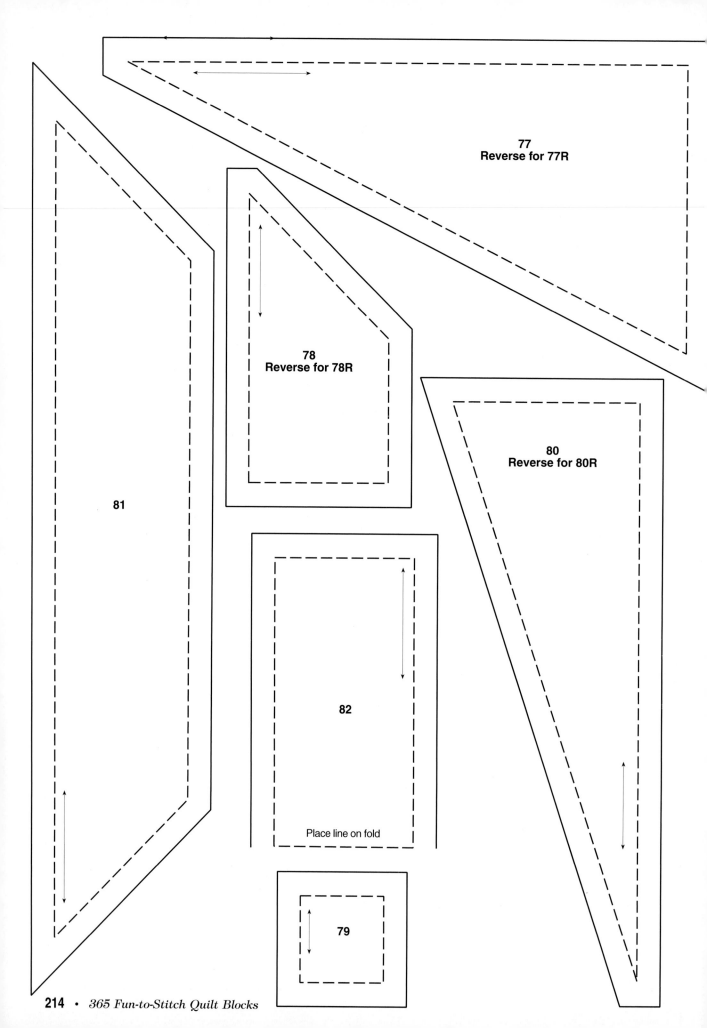

77
Reverse for 77R

78
Reverse for 78R

80
Reverse for 80R

81

82

Place line on fold

79

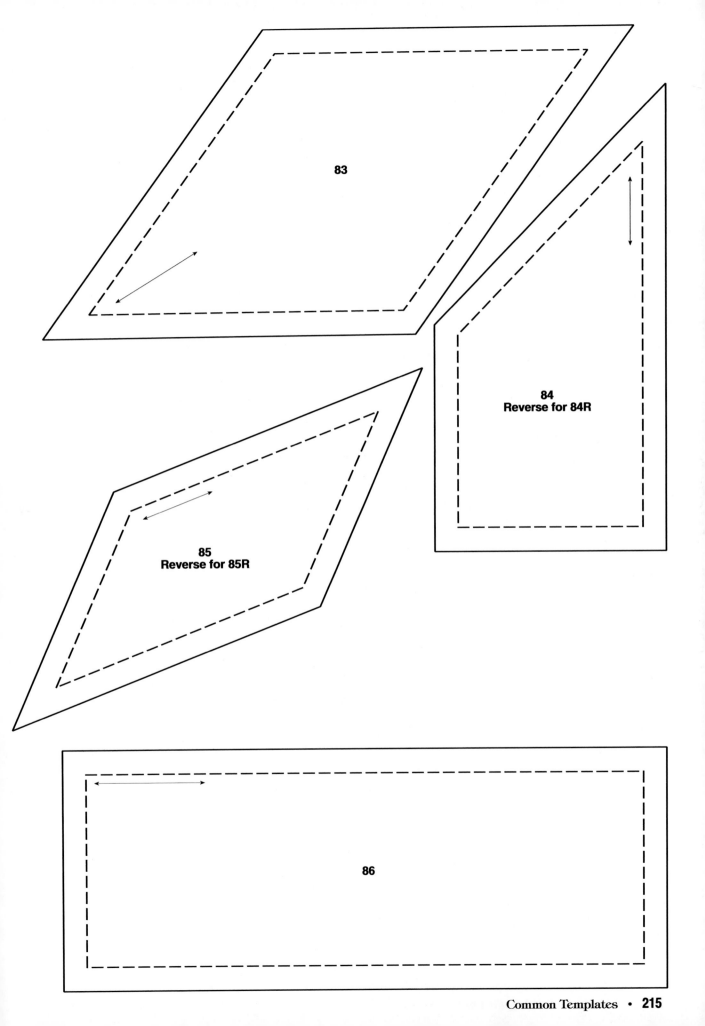

83

84
Reverse for 84R

85
Reverse for 85R

86

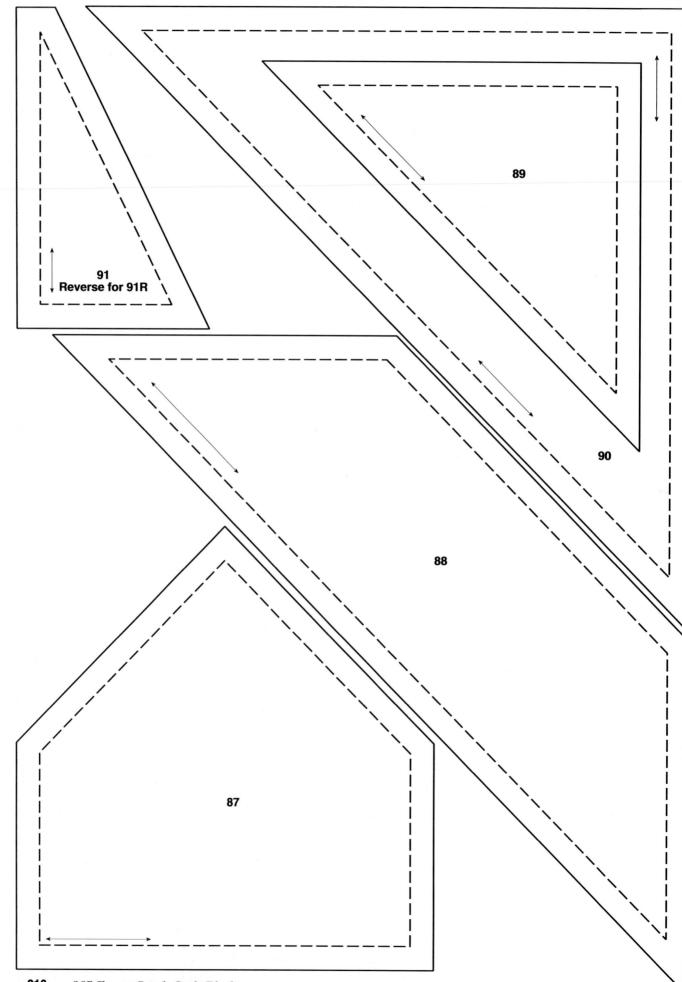

89

91
Reverse for 91R

90

88

87

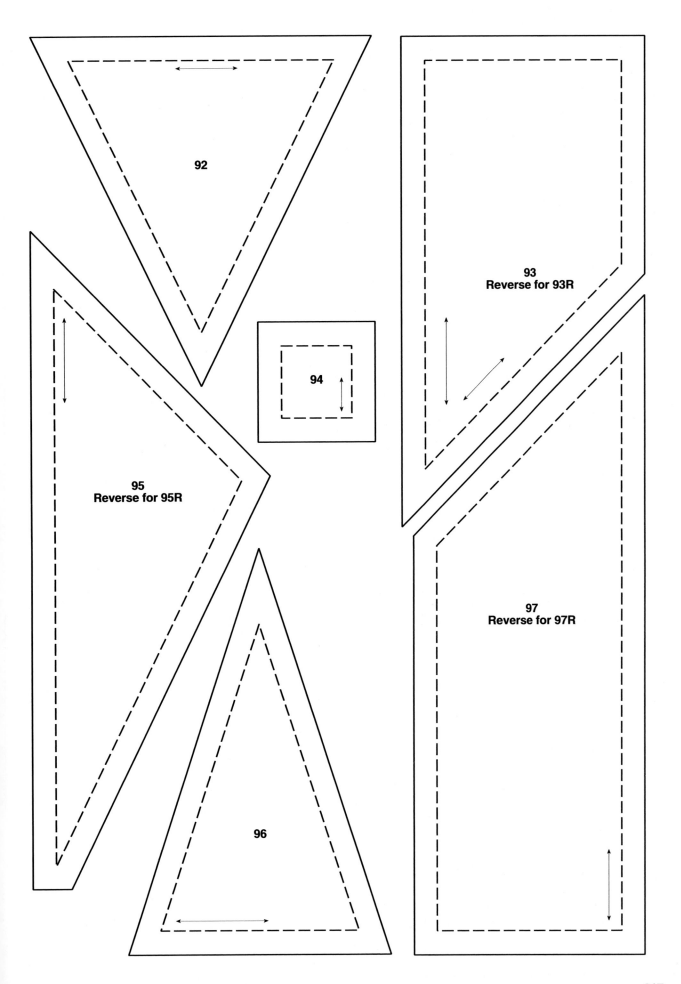

92

93
Reverse for 93R

94

95
Reverse for 95R

96

97
Reverse for 97R

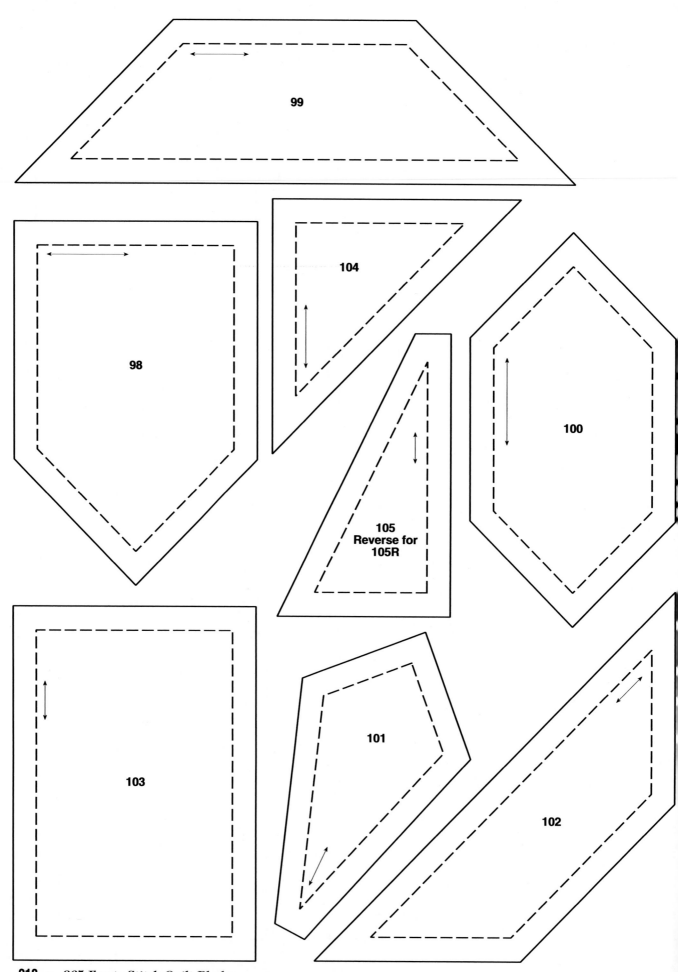

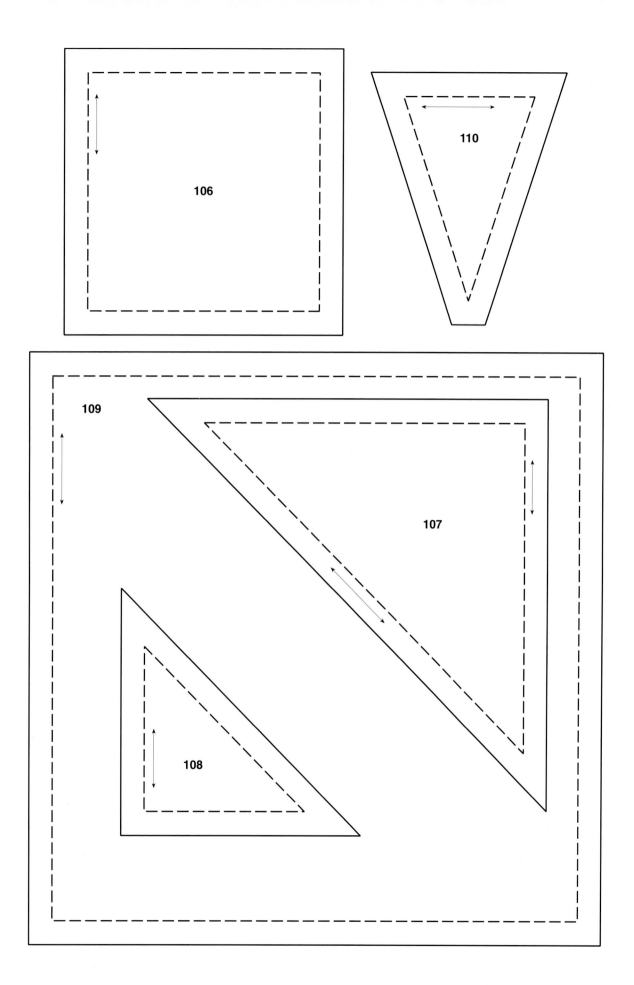

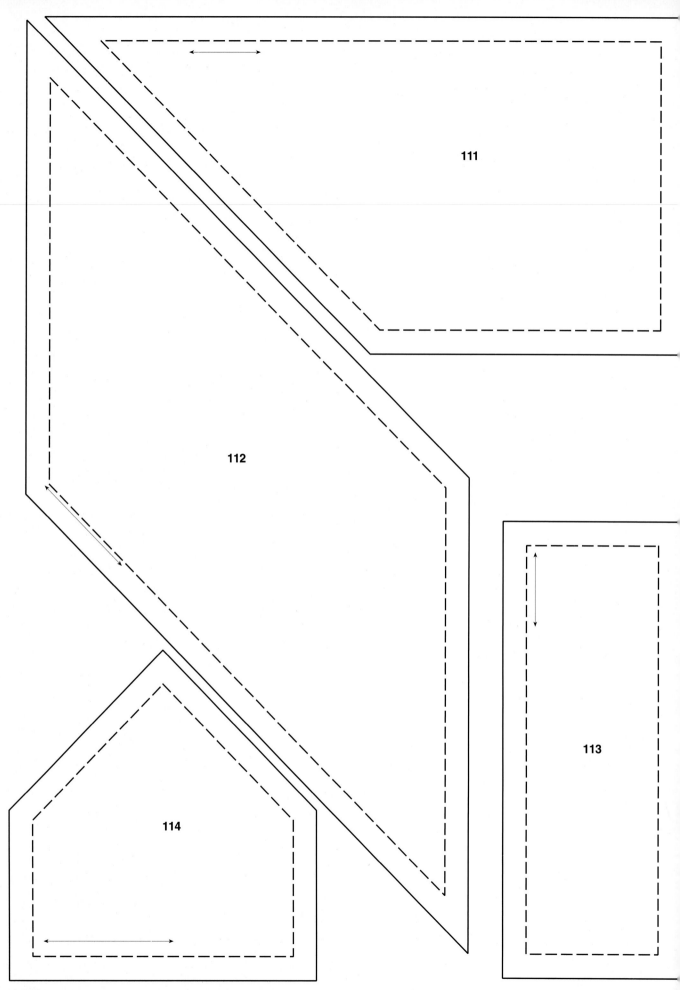

111

112

113

114

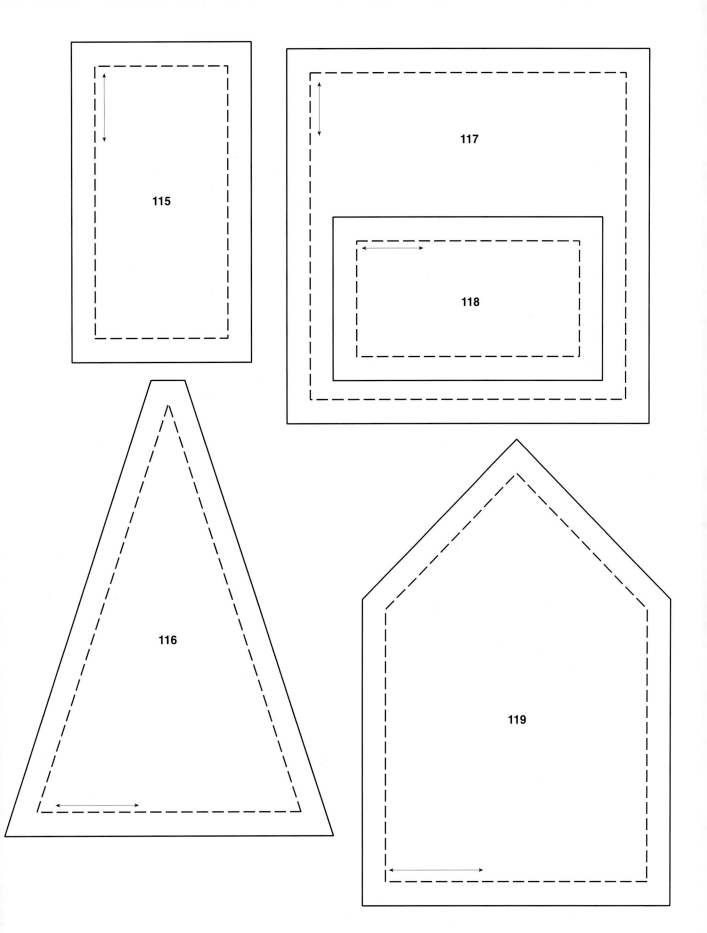

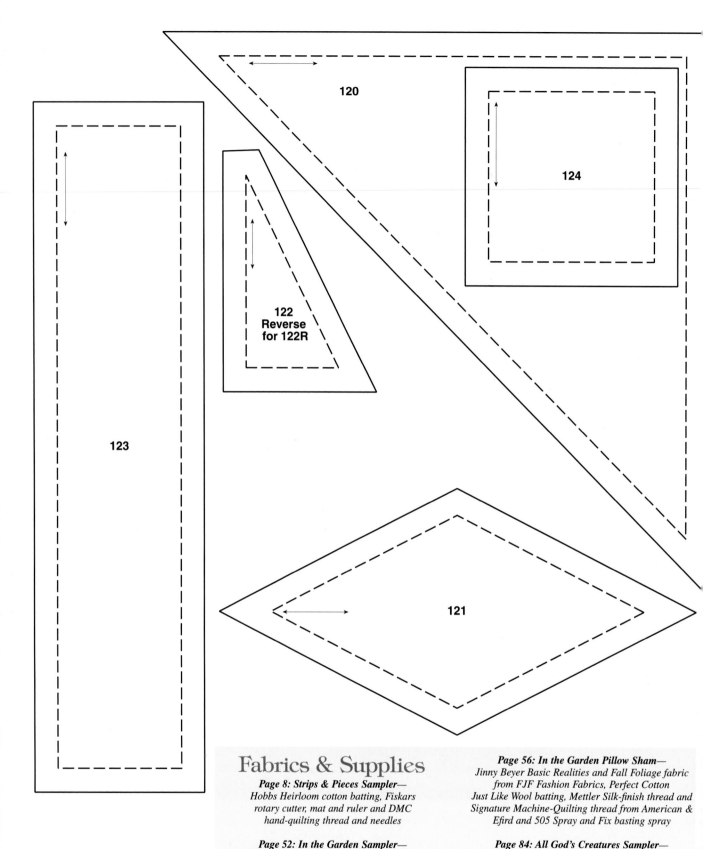

120

124

122
Reverse
for 122R

123

121

Fabrics & Supplies

Page 8: Strips & Pieces Sampler—
Hobbs Heirloom cotton batting, Fiskars
rotary cutter, mat and ruler and DMC
hand-quilting thread and needles

Page 52: In the Garden Sampler—
Jinny Beyer Basic Realities and Fall Foliage fabrics
from RJR Fashion Fabrics, Perfect Cotton Just
Like Wool batting and Mettler silk-finish thread
from American & Efird. Pieced by Emma Jean
Cook and professionally machine-quilted
by Dianne Hodgkins.

Page 91: Wild Goose Chase Cover—
Fiskars rotary cutter, mat and ruler

Page 56: In the Garden Pillow Sham—
Jinny Beyer Basic Realities and Fall Foliage fabric
from FJF Fashion Fabrics, Perfect Cotton
Just Like Wool batting, Mettler Silk-finish thread and
Signature Machine-Quilting thread from American &
Efird and 505 Spray and Fix basting spray

Page 84: All God's Creatures Sampler—
Honor Diversity and Rainforest fabric
collections from Cotton Classics

Page 113: Autumn Leaf Vest—
5/8"-wide HeatnBond Lite and 1/4"-wide Quilter's
Edge Lite from Therm O Web

Page 136: King's Star Basket Cover—
Fabri-Tac permanent adhesive from Beacon

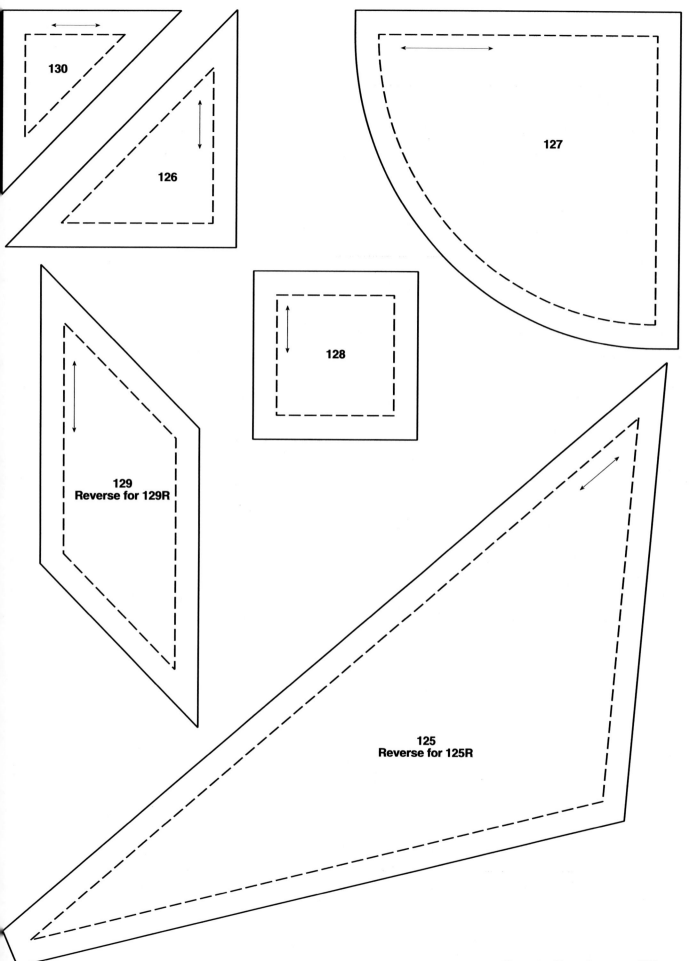

130

126

127

128

129
Reverse for 129R

125
Reverse for 125R

Index of Blocks

Special Thanks

We would like to thank the talented quilt designers whose work is featured in this collection.

Kathy Brown
Melon Patch Runner, 33

Pat Campbell
The Cross Wall Quilt, 184

Barbara Clayton
Double Tulip Pillow, 60
Pigeon Toes Place Mat, 90
St. Louis Tote Bag, 156
Pride of Italy Centerpiece, 160

Holly Daniels
Nature's Glory Sampler, 108
Around the World Sampler, 154

Sue Harvey
In the Garden Sampler, 52
In the Garden Pillow Sham, 56

Connie Kauffman
Toad Puddle Candle Mat, 13
Album Block Cushion, 32
Path in the Woods Pillow, 115
Morning or Evening
Star Mat, 139
Broken Windows Monitor
Cover, 159
Ruins of Jericho Pillow, 187

Chris Malone
Sheepfold Place Mat, 14
The Comfort Quilt Block
Table Runner, 15
Stars of Stripes Chair Pad, 137
King's Star Basket Cover, 136
Texas Cactus Basket
Pillow, 157
Chinese Lanterns
Tea Cozy, 158
Peaceful Hours Bib Apron, 185

Patsy Moreland
Cats & Mice Vest, 87
Bluebell Basket Topper, 114
Dogwood Blossoms
Valance, 112

Connie Rand
All God's Creatures
Sampler, 84

Judith Sandstrom
Strips & Pieces Sampler, 8
Wild Goose Chase Sampler, 91
Autumn Leaf Vest, 113
Blue Heaven Hot Mat, 111

Carla Schwab
Nez Pearce Purse, 56
Steps to the Temple Mat, 186

Marian Shenk
Flower Basket Pillow, 34
Snail's Trail Picnic Cloth, 88
Cross & Crown Wall Quilt, 188

Ruth Swasey
The Good Old Days
Sampler, 30
Blessed and Beloved
Sampler, 182

Julie Weaver
Roman Square Pillow, 12
Tall Ships Wall Quilt, 36
Rosebud Table Mat, 63
Maple Leaf Trivet, 57
Dad's Flannel Pillow, 89
Mexican Star Basket, 138

Johanna Wilson
Beneath the Stars Sampler, 134